Globalization and East Asia
Opportunities and Challenges

Khosrow Fatemi, PhD
Editor

NEW YORK AND LONDON

First published 2006 by International Business Press®

Published 2013 by Routledge
605 Third Avenue, New York, NY 10017
4 Park Square, Milton Park, Abingdon, Oxon OX14 4RN

Routledge is an imprint of the Taylor & Francis Group, an informa business

Cover design by Lora Wiggins.

Library of Congress Cataloging-in-Publication Data

International Trade and Finance Association. Conference (12th : 2002 : Bangkok, Thailand)
Globalization and East Asia : opportunities and challenges / Khosrow Fatemi, editor.
p. cm.
Rev. papers selected from the 12th Conference of the International Trade and Finance Association, held in Bangkok, Thailand, May 29-June 2, 2002.
Includes bibliographical references and index.
1. East Asia—Economic conditions—Congresses. 2. East Asia—Economic policy—Congresses. 3. Globalization—Economic aspects—East Asia—Congresses. 4. East Asia—Foreign economic relations. I. Fatemi, Khosrow. II. Title.

HC460.5.I583 2002
337.5—dc22

2005029313

ISBN 13: 978-0-789-02743-6 (hbk)
ISBN 13: 978-0-789-02744-3 (pbk)

CONTENTS

PART II: COMPARATIVE STUDIES

ABOUT THE EDITOR

Khosrow Fatemi, PhD, is president of Eastern Oregon University located in La Grande, Oregon. He has taught international classes and has been a guest lecturer in several countries around the world.

Dr. Fatemi has published several books, including *Contemporary Developments in International Business* (with Didier Jourdan); *International Public Policy and Regionalism at the Turn of the Century; The New World Order: Internationalism, Regionalism, and the Multinational Corporations; International Trade in the 21st Century; North American Free Trade Agreement: Opportunities and Challenges; The North American Free Trade Agreement* (co-edited with Dominick Salvatore); *Foreign Exchange Issues, Capital Markets, and International Banking in the 1990s* (co-edited with Dominick Salvatore); *Selected Readings in International Trade; The Maquiladora Industry: Economic Solution or Problem?; International Trade: Existing Problems and Prospective Solutions; International Trade and Finance: A North American Perspective;* and *U.S.-Mexican Economic Relations: Prospects and Problems.*

His articles have been published in the *International Journal of Finance, Journal of Borderland Studies, Issues in International Business, The Middle East Journal, International Management Development Journal,* and *The Wall Street Journal.*

Dr. Fatemi has presented more than 100 papers at national and international conferences dealing with international trade, the North American Free Trade Agreement, U.S.-Mexico issues, and international education.

Dr. Fatemi is the founding editor of the *Global Economic Quarterly* and *The International Trade Journal*. He is a founding member and serves as executive vice president for the International Trade and Finance Association.

Globalization and East Asia: Opportunities and Challenges

doi:10.1300/5463_a

Dr. Fatemi also serves on the editorial or review boards of *Journal of Teaching in International Business, International Business Review,* the *Border Business Journal, SAM Advanced Management Journal, International Journal of Finance,* and *Latin American Business Journal.* He is active in such professional organizations as the International Management Development Association and the International Trade and Finance Association.

CONTRIBUTORS

Manuel Angeles has a master of arts in economics degree from the New School University in New York. He is a full professor of economics and senior researcher at the Universidad Autonoma de Baja California Sur, Mexico, where he teaches macroeconomics and growth theory; graduate level courses include international trade and natural resource and environmental economics. His current research interests focus on the impact of globalization on small countries and regions. He has published two books on economic dynamics and linear theory. Professor Angeles is also head of Budget Department in the UABCS.

Parviz Asheghian earned his PhD at Georgia State University, and is a professor of economics at California State University, San Bernardino. He teaches international economics, economic development, and economic theory. His major research interests are in the areas of international economics/finance, multinational corporations, and economic development. He is the co-author of a textbook on international business, a textbook on the external environment of global business, and a textbook on the internal environment of global business. He has written a textbook on multinational corporations, and a textbook on economic development. He has also published more than two dozen articles in academic journals such as *Journal of International Business Studies, Quarterly Journal of Business and Economics, Quarterly Review of Economics and Business, Managing International Development, Journal of Economic Development, Development Policy Review,* and the *Asian Pacific Journal of Business Economics and Business.* Dr. Asheghian has served on the editorial boards of several scholarly journals, including the *International Trade and Finance Journal, Journal of Third World Development,* and *Journal of Business and Economic Perspectives.* In addition to his writings and research,

Globalization and East Asia: Opportunities and Challenges

doi:10.1300/5463_b

Dr. Asheghian has consulted with businesses and taught executive training programs in the United States.

Nicholas Billington is head of the Victoria Graduate School of Business at Victoria University in Australia. He is also the chair of postgraduate studies and research associate of the Centre for Strategic Economic Studies. His research interests cover the fields of financial modeling, mathematics, and operations research. He has a PhD in information science and mathematics from La Trobe University, and had vast industrial experience in corporate planning and operations research working for Shell Australia before joining the University. Dr. Billington undertakes professional consultancies in financial modeling ranging from the investigation and evaluation of performance of superannuation funds to industry analysis of the impact of the goods and services tax on the new motor vehicle retail market. On occasion he is invited to present guest seminars to graduate schools of other Australian institutions in his area of expertise. Before taking up his position as head of the Victoria Graduate School of Business, Dr. Billington was employed by the university as research manager and senior lecturer in business information systems.

Chandana Chakraborty is an associate professor in the Department of Economics and Finance at Montclair State University in New Jersey.

Vincent Dropsy is professor of international economics at California State University, Fullerton. He obtained his PhD in international economics from the University of Southern California in 1989, after he received two graduate degrees in economics and statistics in Paris, France. Since then, his research interest has revolved around the foreign exchange markets. In particular, he has investigated the role of heterogeneous exchange rate expectations, nonlinearities, structural breaks in explaining exchange rate misalignment and instability. His research has also focused on currency crises, such as the 1994-1995 Mexican Peso crisis and the 1997-1998 Asian crisis. In addition, he has examined other economic issues related to international equity markets, external indebtness, and international trade. He has presented his research at numerous international conferences and published his findings in a wide range of reputable academic journals and books.

H. Peter Gray graduated from Cambridge University after the Second World War. He worked for a small firm in London before migrating to Toronto to open a factory. He moved to San Francisco in 1957 and applied for admission to the graduate program in economics at the University of California, Berkeley. He became a Brookings fellow in 1961-1962 and received his PhD in 1963. Since then he has held professorial positions at Wayne State University, Rutgers University, and Rensselaer Polytechnic Institute. He has been president of the Eastern Economic Association and the International Trade and Finance Association. Since his retirement from full-time teaching in 1990 he has been giving seminars and serving on dissertation committees in the doctoral program in international business at the Rutgers University Faculty of Management.

To-Ming Ho is an associate professor in the City University of Hong Kong's Department of Economics and Finance. He has a PhD in economics from the University of Southampton in the United Kingdom, an MSc in econometrics and mathematical economics from the London School of Economics and Political Science, and a first-class honors degree in economics from the University of Warwick. Dr. Ho has also worked in industry as the assistant economic analyst for China Light and Power in their Economic and Corporate Planning Section. He is a frequent speaker at events in Hong Kong, the United States, and Europe, and has had works published on Hong Kong's international trade and finance.

Sardar M. N. Islam, PhD, LLB, manages the Sustainable Growth Program at the Center for Strategic Economic Studies, Victoria University, and is associated with the Financial Modeling Program and the Law and Economics Program. He has taught for more than 15 years at different universities in various countries and has also senior-level experience in economic planning and economic development administration. His areas of teaching and research interests are finance, mathematical economics, welfare economics, financial econometrics, computerized economic modeling, development and growth economics, project planning and appraisal, environmental and resource economics, health economics, economics of climate change, and mathematical interpretation of history of economic thought. He has published nine books and more than 110 technical papers in the areas mentioned. His research has gained international reputation. He currently supervises nine doctorate students.

Antonina Ivanova is a full professor of economics and senior researcher at Universidad Autonoma de Baja California Sur (UABCS), Mexico. Her main teaching activities center on international trade, international finance, and economic integration. At the graduate level, she lectures on trade and environment issues, as well as regional economic blocs. She received her master in science degree from the University for International Economics in Sofia, Bulgaria, and her doctoral degree from Universidad Nacional Autonoma de Mexico. She is author of three books and over 40 scholarly papers. Her latest co-authored book deals with trade flows and sustainable development in Baja California Sur. In addition, Dr. Ivanova is director of research and graduate studies in the UABCS.

Kennita Kind, PhD, is an assistant professor in the Department of Textiles and Consumer Sciences in the College of Human Sciences at Florida State University (FSU). Dr. Kind received a PhD in consumer economics in 1999 and an MS in merchandising in 1995, both from the University of Georgia. While completing her dissertation, Dr. Kind received the 1999 International Trade and Finance Association's Best Student Paper Award in Casablanca, Morocco, for her research using intraindustry trade theory to analyze U.S. trade flows in the textiles and apparel industry. Dr. Kind teaches residential science classes at FSU.

Yunhua Liu, assistant professor of economics at Nanyang Technological University, Singapore, received his PhD in economics from Ohio State University. His research interests include economic development in China, international trade of Southeast Asia and urban economics. His articles have appeared in journals as *Economic Development and Cultural Change, Quarterly Review of Economics and Finance, China Economic Review, ASEAN Economic Bulletin,* and the *Journal of Chinese Political Science*. Dr. Liu teaches principles of economics, urban economics, and international economics for undergraduate and PhD students.

Robin H. Luo is a lecturer in economics and finance in the Faculty of Business at Auckland University of Technology in New Zealand. He is a PhD candidate in economics at Nanyang Technological University, Singapore. His research interests include international economics, open economy macroeconomics, china economy, and Internet economics.

Rajesh Mohnot earned his PhD in finance from Jai Narain Vyas (JNV) University, India. Before he started working as a senior lecturer in the College of Business Management, University Tenaga National, Malaysia, in October 2000, Dr. Rajesh Mohnot worked as assistant professor in SNPJ College, an affiliate of JNV University, for nine years. He has taught a variety of subjects including economics, accounting, management, finance, and statistics. He has co-authored one book on accountancy and has several publications in national and international journals. He has presented academic research papers at international conferences in India, Malaysia, Thailand, and Singapore, and has chaired technical sessions at international conferences. His current research interest is in capital markets and international finance. In addition to his academic work, Dr. Rajesh has rendered financial consultancy to various corporations.

Terutomo Ozawa is a professor of economics at Colorado State University, and a research associate at the Center on Japanese Economy and Business, Columbia Business School. He was president of the International Trade and Finance Association in 2003.

Joseph Pelzman received his PhD in economics from Boston College. After 20 years as an economics faculty member, Professor Pelzman entered the George Washington University (GWU) Law School and completed his JD in 1998. He is admitted to practice in the State of Maryland. Professor Pelzman has been a faculty member at GWU since 1980. He has also taught international economics and economies in transition at Harvard University, Boston College, the Hebrew University of Jerusalem, and to U.S. diplomats at the Foreign Service Institute. Professor Pelzman also teaches law and economics at the GWU Law School, and on a visiting basis at the Radzymer School of Law in Herzlia, Israel, and the Catholic University Law School in Washington, DC. Professor Pelzman currently teaches undergraduate and graduate courses in international trade theory and policy as well as international trade law and economics. He has published articles in numerous academic journals including the *American Economics Review, European Economic Review, South-*

ern Economic Review, Journal of Political Economy, Economic Development and Cultural Change, Integracion Latinoamericana, and *Weltwirtschafliches Archiv,* and has been a contributor to more than 20 books.

Dennis J. Pollard, PhD, Claremont Graduate University, has spent more than 36 years in parallel careers in both the world of business and the academic and research landscape. In terms of business, he has held corporate management and marketing positions with Hunt Foods and Industries, Mattel Inc., and E.&J. Gallo Winery. A series of entrepreneurial ventures led to creation of his trade marketing and development firm, P.S.C. International, which worked with such U.S. corporations as Mattel, Pick 'n Save, and Tonka Toys, and the following countries' governments: Thailand, Indonesia, the Philippines, Taiwan, Hong Kong, and China. In the academic area, Dr. Pollard has recently joined his alma mater graduate and undergraduate California State University, Fullerton, as a member of the faculty in the Department of Economics. He teaches courses in Pacific Rim economies, international economics, and economics in transition, and helps on occasion with seminar in strategic management. His areas of research interest are Asia-Pacific cultural impacts on economic performance, Asian diffusion of innovation, evaluation of strategic direction in Asia. He has recently published and co-authored three peer-reviewed articles on Asia.

Joanna K. Poznanaska is a professor of international business at Seattle Pacific University. She holds an MA from the University of Warsaw, a PhD from the Technical University of Warsaw, and has completed postgraduate studies at Cornell University.

Glenville Rawlins is a professor of economics at Montclair State University in New Jersey. He teaches various graduate and undergraduate courses in development economics and international economics and finance. Dr. Rawlins holds a PhD in economics from New York University, an MA in economics from Howard University, and a BA in modern languages and economics from the University of the West Indies.

Kathleen Rees is an associate professor of textiles, apparel, and merchandising in the School of Human Ecology at Louisiana State University. She holds a PhD in Human Ecology from the University of

Tennessee, Knoxville. Her research interests focus on international trade and trade policy, with specific emphasis on textiles, apparel, and retailing. Dr. Rees has been a participant and research presenter at regional, national, and international conferences of academic and professional societies. She has published articles, book chapters, and papers in proceedings of national and international organizations, including the International Trade and Finance Association and the International Textiles and Apparel Association.

Wan Fadzilah Wan Yusoff is a senior lecture at the College of Business Management, University Tenaga National, where she teaches accounting. She is pursuing her PhD in technology management, and has contributed five papers to journals and conferences. Her current research areas are behavioral accounting, intellectual capital, and knowledge management.

Sethapong Watanapalachaikul is a research assistant at Victoria University in Australia. His field of teaching is finance and econometrics. He is completing his PhD in business administration at Victoria University. The title of his thesis is "Financial Econometrics of a Developing Economy: A Study of the Thai Stock Market."

M. Raquib Zaman is the Charles A. Dana professor of finance and international business at Ithaca College. His publications are in the areas of international business and finance, foreign direct investment and economic development, securities markets, transitional economies, Islamic banking and finance, and a number of other related fields.

Preface

The economies of East Asian countries have undergone major changes over the past few decades. The phenomenal growth experienced by a number of countries in East Asia is unparalleled and without historical precedent. The region's economic development is often cited as an example of a model that could—and should—be followed by others, and yet decades after it began, the East Asian economic miracle has not been replicated anywhere else.

The main objective of this book is to examine different aspects of the economic performance of East Asian countries during the past three decades with the expectation that understanding the intricacies of the region will make it more likely and more practical for the experience to be duplicated elsewhere. The studies presented in this volume were first presented at the 12th International Conference of the International Trade and Finance Association held from May 29 to June 1, 2002, in Bangkok, Thailand. Of the more than 100 papers presented at the meeting, 19 were selected and the authors were asked to update and revise their papers for inclusion in this book.

PART I: INTRODUCTION

In Chapter 1, M. Raquib Zaman provides a state-of-the-art introduction on globalization in East Asia. He notes that at the advent of the twenty-first century, "some of the LDCs, notably East Asian economies, joined the ranks of the new industrialized countries (NICs)." This short chapter demonstrates the distinctive characteristics of the policy measures that the East Asian Countries (EACs) adopted successfully to generate sustainable economic growth in their countries over the past four decades.

Chapter 2 by H. Peter Gray builds on the Zaman introduction by identifying some of the characteristics of economic growth and de-

Globalization and East Asia: Opportunities and Challenges

doi:10.1300/5463_c

velopment in East Asia. He shows in general terms how that experience has or will benefit countries that follow in the footsteps of the East Asian nations.

PART II: COMPARATIVE STUDIES

Part II includes a collection of comparative studies of different countries and/or industries. In Chapter 3, Professor Terutomo Ozawa provides a study of East Asian countries during the past 50 years. He maintains that despite the financial crises of 1997-1998, the "region as a whole has recorded unprecedentedly rapid growth since of the end of World War II . . . [and] in fact, the crisis-afflicted economies have already rebounded quickly (except Japan which has been mired in an economic slump over more than a decade ever since the bursting of the asset bubble of 1987-90.)" Professor Ozawa further argues that "one dominant explanation for the region's super-growth in the past four decades is that the region adopted outward-oriented, export-propelled industrialization (EPI) strategies."

In Chapter 4 Parviz Asheghian evaluates the relative efficiency and leveraging of assets of eight matched-pair U.S. and four dragon (FD) industries. He uses the Wilcox matched-pairs signed-rank test to assess five hypotheses comparing several financial ratios for the United States and the four dragon economies of Asia. He concludes that the absence of statistically significant differences between the United States and the four dragon industries suggests that the U.S. and FD industries are similar to each other with respect to the efficiencies of their operations.

Vincent Dropsy and Dennis Pollard examine the impact of structural differences in Asian countries of their comparative economic performance in Chapter 5. They argue that despite the fact that the Asian nations outperformed other countries for decades in terms of economic growth, the Asian crisis of 1997-1998 revealed structural weaknesses in some of these Asian nations and their economies. To substantiate their argument, the authors compare the individual differences in macroeconomic policies, economic resources, and political structure of Asian countries and estimate the effects of these differences on standards of living and economic growth. They use an empirical study to point out that not only traditional economic factors, but also trade openness, financial liberalization, smaller governments, and stronger legal structures tend to significantly improve standards of living and/or economic growth. Dropsy and Pollard conclude that the severity of the Asian crisis was virtually unpredictable and unwarranted, and that data suggest that a return to precrisis growth levels is unlikely.

In Chapter 6, a bilateral, sector-specific study of trade, Kennita Kind presents an exploratory analysis of trade flows between the United States and Thailand in the home furnishing industry. She uses selected trade classification categories from the home furnishing industry to examine the bilateral trade between the two countries. Her research leads her to conclude that trade flows between the two countries are very imbalanced, with the United States importing more home furnishings products from Thailand than it exports. In addition, the data indicate that the United States will continue to be one of the leading markets for Thai exports of home furnishings.

In Chapter 7 Antonina Ivanova and Manuel Angeles discuss the process of environmental cooperation among Asia-Pacific Economic Cooperation (APEC) countries, and the progress made in recent years. Their central argument is that regional economic integration must be complemented by the creation of regional frameworks for environmental management. Consequently, they argue that APEC countries must cooperate to create conditions which provide incentives for sustainable resources and ecosystem use. In this way, trade and environmental policies can mutually reinforce each other. The authors conclude by proposing some guidelines and strategies to achieve APEC's environmental goals.

In Chapter 8, Glenville Rawlins and Chandana Chakraborty analyze the changes in the composition and direction of financial resource flows to the five largest foreign direct investment (FDI) recipients in East Asia during the 1990s. They also study the varied pattern of these flows by exploring the macroeconomic environment of the recipient countries and evaluate the significance of macro policy tools in attracting resource flows with a brief empirical analysis of the link between the exchange rate, trade, and FDI. The authors maintain that net resource flows in the 1990s were dominated by private flows, and not by official flows. They further argue that although FDI showed a fairly steady growth rate for the region, portfolio flows exhibited relative volatility over their study period. Finally, Rawlins and Chakraborty maintain that the East Asian financial crisis resulted in a slight decrease in net flows but in a marked shift in the composition of flows from portfolio to FDI.

PART III: INTERNATIONAL FINANCE

Part III contains a compilation of several country- and/or sector-specific studies. The first chapter provides an analysis of the Malaysian financial markets and the implication of the Asian financial crisis on these markets. In Chapter 9 Rajesh Mohnot and Wan Fadzilah Wan Yusoff argue that a diversified and competitive financial market system is crucial for long-term economic growth and development, and that the future of the financial markets lies in financial players who are able to support the domestic economy and are efficient, competitive, sound, and stable enough to facilitate the economic transformation process. The authors further argue that well-functioning markets can result in several positive outcomes, such as the financing of more and better projects, better management in the interest of investors, increased innovation, and more.

Chapters 10 and 11 analyze China's economic transition and exchange rate policies of the last several years. In Chapter 10, Joanna K. Poznanska traces the impact of globalization on economic transition in China. She maintains that with the collapse of communism and the subsequent building of markets by the former communist economies, the worldwide process of globalization greatly accelerated. But globalization itself has also left some important marks on the process of forming market institutions in these economies. She uses China's efforts in replacing the previous state-run system with the market-driven one to illustrate her point. She postulates that while reforming its institutions, China has showed the fastest growth rate ever reported in modern times. All relevant indicators suggest that China has used its reform process to become an open economy, but it has done this in a very gradual and selective way. While China's tariffs are relatively low for a semi-industrialized economy, it keeps in place some unconventional barriers to make sure that opening serves as a stimulant and not a detriment.

Poznanska then examines the transition of a Chinese economy that cannot be considered complete without opening itself to the outside world. For more than a decade China has been liberalizing its trade and by now its economy is already quite open by world standards, or at least by comparison with other industrializing countries in the region. China, with a well-composed state, has chosen a relatively cautious approach to foreign exchange with a clear intention of using liberalization to stimulate domestic production and export the main elements of the pattern of reform in China.

In Chapter 11, Robin Luo and Yunhua Liu estimate the long-run equilibrium path for the real exchange rate in China using three different approaches: Purchasing Power Parity (PPP), Shadow Price of Foreign Exchange (SPFE), and Fundamental Equilibrium Exchange Rate (FEER). They concluded that (1) the PPP approach is not an appropriate method to estimate the equilibrium real exchange rate of the Chinese yuan; (2) when SPFE was used, the real exchange rate was overvalued throughout the whole sample period (1980 to 2001) except the period before 1983; and (3) when the equilibrium real exchange rate was measured by the FEER approach, overvaluation and undervaluation appeared alternately. They test the relationship between trade balance and the two types of misalignment through unrestricted vector autoregression systems. Their results show that China's trade balance has been affected very little by the misalignment of the yuan.

In Chapter 12, To-Ming Ho uses the dual-production-theory approach to model the industry as a competitive firm in the world economy. The Hong Kong household electrical appliances industry assembles electrical appliances using imported electrical parts and components, and exports more than ninety percent of its output to overseas countries. The author uses a variable profit function, a dual representation of technology, with labor, imported capital, parts and components, appearing as production inputs, and total quantity of appliances produced appearing as output. He then assumes a flexible functional form for the function in order to estimate various price (trade) elasticities using the seemingly unrelated regressions estimation method. Ho concludes that the resultant elasticity estimates shed an important light on the complementarity of inputs/imports, the effects of export prices on input/import demands, and the effects of input/import prices on export supplies, all of which could be important for policy makers in newly industrialized countries attempting to export industrial products.

In Chapter 13 Sethapong Watanapalachaikul, Sardar M.N. Islam, and Nicholas Billington provide an overview of financial characteristics of a sector-specific industry in the developing countries using the telecommunications sector in Thailand to illustrate their points. Their analysis focuses on the valuation of the Thai telecommunications stocks and concludes by proposing a valuation model that supports the existence of a significant, long-run relationship between stock prices and macroeconomic factors affecting telecommunications stocks listed on the Stock Exchange of Thailand. The results show the existence of high unsystematic risk elements and that the Thai telecommunications sector is substantially exposed to idiosyncratic factors rather than systematic factors.

PART IV: INDUSTRY-SPECIFIC AND FUTURE RESEARCH

Joseph Pelzman provides a review of the Vietnamese textile and apparel industry in Chapter 14. He traces the development of bilateral trade negotiations in textiles and apparel between the United States and Vietnam. He points out that the transition of Vietnam to a market economy has been supported by the United States in large part by its bilateral agreement, which reduced U.S. tariffs to their most-favored-nation levels in exchange for legal and institutional reforms in Vietnam. Despite these positive measures, the prospect of a textile and apparel agreement still looms, and it is unclear whether such an agreement will come to fruition in the near future. He maintains that even if such an agreement is reached, capacity constraints in the Vietnamese textiles and apparel industry will bar it from becoming a major player in the U.S. market or becoming a threat to the domestic producers in the United States. He concludes that it is clear from the current environment that continued discussion of a bilateral agreement does nothing more than add unwarranted uncertainty to investor confidence in Vietnam. The latter is inconsistent with the aim and sprit of the U.S.-Vietnam bilateral trade agreement.

Chapter 15 by Kathleen Rees examines the status of U.S. apparel imports. She points out that export production of apparel destined for key international markets has been a survival strategy used by many countries in recent years, and that the major component of this strategy is the U.S. market. In fact, the U.S. market is one of the world's largest markets for both developing countries seeking entry to international trade and means of economic development and developed countries desiring to maintain mature textile and apparel sectors.

Rees' study builds on the seminal analysis of market penetration and shift in market shares for primary apparel categories by Daris and Sul and subsequent research by Xiao and Rees. She uses the Markov process to examine changes in market shares held by seven world regions for twelve categories of apparel. She concludes that over the time period covered by her study, market share will shift from OECD countries to developing regions, and that shares for various categories will move between and among different regions. She maintains that her research will contribute to enhanced understanding of the restructuring of the global apparel industry and examination of export strategies undertaken by Asian and other developing countries as they attempt to maintain competitive positions within the global economy.

Part IV concludes with an epilogue by M. Raquib Zaman. Here he discusses the future of globalization and resulting research interests on the East Asia region. He proposes future research on interest whether will exist in forming an East Asian Union, and how poverty issues, an aging population, and scarity of labor will effect globalization and economic development.

Acknowledgments

I would like to express my sincere appreciation to the authors of the studies presented in this book. Their cooperation, their willingness to revise their studies, and their diligence in meeting deadlines are trademarks of their professionalism. It was indeed a pleasure working with such a group of professional colleagues in completing this book. I am also grateful to Rangsan Saengsook, the rector of Ramkhamhaeng University of Thailand and his colleagues for their hard work in successfully organizing the conference. My special thanks go to Sue Nichols, special projects director at the Imperial Valley Campus of San Diego State University, for her hard work and dedication to this project. Finally a special note of appreciation to my distinguished colleague Erdener Kaynak, for his invaluable assistance in bringing this project to fruition.

doi:10.1300/5463_d

PART I: INTRODUCTION

Chapter 1

East Asian Economic Performance in Retrospect

M. Raquib Zaman

INTRODUCTION

Since the 1950s economists and development experts have been trying to decipher what factors, actions, and/or policies, are behind spectacular performance in economic development by some countries, and lack of progress by others. The less developed countries (LDCs) were, as a whole, more or less at a similar stage of economic growth in the 1950s and 1960s. Yet at the advent of the twenty-first century, some of the LDCs, notably East Asian economies, joined the ranks of the newly industrialized countries (NICs), whereas others have made little progress in economic development.

It is interesting to note that over the past four decades the East Asian countries, as well as some of the Latin American countries, pursued similar policies of import substitution and export promotion at various stages of their economic growth with varied results. The idea that economic development can be facilitated by promoting import substitution and protecting the nascent domestic industries through facilitating fiscal and monetary policies was so prevalent among the development experts and policymakers that at one time or another this was tried out by Taiwan (Eckes, 1993; Chu, 1994; Birdsall et al., 1995; Ranis, 1995), Korea (Alam, 1989; Aggarwal and Agmon, 1990; Dollar, 1990; Birdsall et al., 1995; Ranis, 1995), Singapore, Malaysia, and the Latin American countries (Aggarwal and Agmon, 1990; Turner, 1992; Nelson, 1994). Since import substitution policies did not achieve the results hoped for, the LDCs had to find an alternative strategy. The

Globalization and East Asia: Opportunities and Challenges

doi:10.1300/5463_01

East Asian countries (EACs) decided to follow the Japanese model of export-led economic growth.

The Japanese model of economic growth called for targeting industries with export potential for preferential access to capital and for protecting them from competition in the domestic market (Wolf, 1998). This model worked for the EACs until the 1997-1998 financial crises, when the shortcomings of the strategy became quite apparent (Zaman, 1998a, 2000).

This short chapter tries to demonstrate the distinctive characteristics of the policy measures that the EACs adopted successfully to generate sustainable economic growth in their countries since the 1960s. It explains why it will be difficult to replicate the performance record of the EACs by the LDCs of today, given the present skepticism about globalization and trade liberalization, and because some of the special circumstances and institutions that played crucial roles in economic transformation of the EACs are no longer available to the newcomers. Added to these are the emergence of the information technology revolution, which enables countries to access information and know-how at a rapid pace, and the rise of a tech-savvy workforce in a number of relatively better-off LDCs that can attract foreign multinational corporations (MNCs) to relocate production and service facilities in their midst.

THE EAST ASIAN "MIRACLE"

The term *East Asian Miracle* was popularized by a World Bank (1993) policy research report of the same title to dramatize the progress the EACs had made in economic growth and development in a mere three decades. Taiwan was the first country among the EACs to follow the Japanese economic model for growth. It embarked on economic development by imposing land reforms that boosted investment in agriculture, raised productivity, and ultimately released human resources for deployment in a manufacturing sector that was geared toward exports. Simultaneously, the nation invested heavily in education, first focusing on primary education, then promoting vocational training and skills, and following up with graduate-level science and technology fields. It also pursued policies and undertook measures to reduce fertility. The presence of a strong government, albeit not democratic, and clarity in economic policies, along with trade liberalization, proved to be the other important factors that propelled the country to achieve spectacular economic growth (Ranis, 1995; Birdsall et al., 1995).

Taiwan was followed by South Korea, and then the other EACs, all pursuing essentially a similar path of economic development. The public policies in these countries were geared toward adapting to the changing needs of time and to weathering external economic shocks. In their drive toward modernization, the EACs followed policies of import substitution, trade liberalization, and export promotion at appropriate times (Krueger, 1997), unlike many LDCs in Asia, Africa, and Latin America.

The role of business organizations, that is, business networks, in advancing economic growth in the EACs has not received the recognition it deserves. It can be argued that the networks, such as the *keiretsus* in Japan, *chaebols* in Korea, *guanxi* in China, Chinese *huran gongsi* and *jituan gongsi,* the overseas Chinese networks in Indonesia, Singapore, Malaysia, and Thailand, and the overseas Indian networks in southeast Asia, were the driving force behind entrepreneurial risk-taking that propelled economic growth in the region (Richter, 1999; Weidenbaum and Hughes, 1996). These business networks "have played an important role in spurring, maintaining, and enhancing entrepreneurial activities" (Zahra et al., 1999, p. 55). The absence of such networks possibly has made a difference in the pace of economic development in the non-EAC regions.

In 1960 Argentina, Chile, and Mexico had higher per capita GNP than Hong Kong, South Korea, Taiwan, and Singapore (except Mexico). Yet by 2001 these EACs far out stripped their Latin American counterparts. China, Indonesia, Malaysia, and Thailand first embarked on trade liberalization policies in the 1980s. Yet Malaysia has already surpassed Brazil in terms of economic growth. If we examine the purchasing power parity (PPP) data, we find that EACs as a whole has been developing at a faster rate than the other selected countries.

Perhaps better indicators of economic development are given by the rates of growth in total productivity and in fixed capital stock. South Korea and Taiwan generated higher rates of growth of output per worker, during practically all the three time periods of 1960-1973, 1973-1984, and 1984-1994, than the Latin American, South Asian, and OECD countries. Only during the period of 1960-1973 was the performance of Latin American workers somewhat respectable. Not only did South Korea and Taiwan attain positive and higher growth rates in total factor productivity, but they achieved these through higher rates of utilization of physical capital and education per worker. Even South Asia had higher rates of growth in total productivity in 1973-1984 and 1984-1994 than both the Latin American and OECD countries. In the 1950s and 1960s some of the Latin American countries had better performance records than the EACs.

The reasons for the hapless performance of the Latin American economies beginning in the 1970s have been discussed widely (see, for example, Sachs, 1990; Turner, 1992; Solanet, 1994), and were summarized by Zaman (1998b) as follows:

(1) pursuance of inward-oriented trade policies that encouraged production of poor quality import substitution goods, with;
(2) a heavy reliance on foreign debt;
(3) over-regulation of trade and investment policies;
(4) lack of discipline in monetary and fiscal policies that resulted in high levels of inflation; and
(5) lack of adequate political and social reforms.

It is only in the 1980s that some of the countries embarked on economic reforms.

An exception is Venezuela, which is in the same doldrums as the oil-exporting Middle Eastern countries. It seems

> that resource-poor countries grew two to three times faster than the resource-rich countries between 1960 and 1990. . . . The resource-rich countries began to lag only after the 1970s . . . after oil wealth started to pour in. (*The Economist,* May 24, 2003, p. 78)

According to *The Economist,* this can be explained by two factors. First, "an oil bonanza causes a sudden rush of foreign earnings," which drives up the value of the nation's currency. This in turn leads to the second factor, which is decreased competitiveness of domestically produced goods at home and abroad. Eventually, growth suffers as agriculture and domestic manufacturing fade.

Over a period of four decades, beginning with 1950-1960, the EACs generated higher rates of growth in capital stock than did several countries of Latin America, South Asia, and the OECD. This was possible because of the development measures and policies (described earlier) that the EACs followed in a timely fashion. Growth in capital stock was facilitated by the rush of foreign direct investments, FDI, in the region. Looking at the FDI inward stock of selected countries since 1980 at five-year intervals, China, Hong Kong, and Singapore experienced massive build ups of FDI inward stock in a mere two decades, compared to Argentina, Chile, and India. China's performance is unprecedented. From a mere $6.25 billion worth of FDI stock in 1980, it ballooned to more than $447 billion by 2002. Tiny Hong Kong's FDI inward stock had been larger than that of China until 2001. Hong Kong has been the gateway to the Chinese market for decades. It served as the transshipment center for Chinese trade with the West when it was a British colony. The mainland has now come of age, as far as FDI is concerned. The city-state of Singapore thrived by pursuing trade liberalization policies that attracted a massive inflow of FDI, first in import substitution industries, followed by export oriented activities, and finally financial services industries. It has also been a transshipment center for ship-to-ship transfers of legal and illegal products.

An examination of the data on merchandise exports and imports (see Table 1.1) further corroborates the fact that the EACs made better progress in industrialization than the other regions. It should be noted that the percentage share of manufacturing exports of South Asia, though it looks similar to that of EACs, is not that significant once we look at the total exports from the regions. Total exports of EACs in 1990 and 2002 were $156 billion and $606 billion, respectively. The comparable figures for South Asia were $28 billion and $71 billion; and that of Latin America and the Caribbean were $143 billion and $348 billion (World Bank, 2002, Table 4.5).

Perhaps data on the shares of the regions in world exports of manufactures, and value-added manufacturing would shed further light on the superior performance of the EACs over other regions. Most of the shares of the world exports of manufactures that the developed countries lost between 1980 and 1997 were picked up by the EACs. When comes to the share in world value-added manufacturing we again find that the lion's share of the developing countries' gain came from the EACs. Latin America actually lost some ground between 1980 and 1997.

TABLE 1.1. Structure of merchandise exports and imports of EACs and selected regions (percentage of totals).

	Food		Agricultural raw materials		Fuels		Ores and metal		Manufacturing	
Countries/region	1990	2002	1990	2002	1990	2002	1990	2002	1990	2002
Exports										
East Asia & Pacific	15	7	6	2	14	8	3	2	59	79
Latin America & Caribbean	26	22	4	3	24	17	12	8	34	48
South Asia	16	13	5	1	2	4	4	3	71	77
Imports										
East Asia & Pacific	7	6	4	3	6	9	3	4	77	76
Latin America & Caribbean	11	9	3	2	13	9	3	2	69	78
South Asia	9	8	4	3	23	30	6	4	54	54

Source: World Bank, 2004, Tables 4.5 and 4.6.

Note: Total exports and imports of South Asia are miniscule compared to the other two regions.

THE FINANCIAL CRISES OF 1997 AND 1998 AND THE AFTERMATH

The crisis in the financial markets in Asia was ushered in by the collapse of the Thai currency, the baht, in July 1997. The contagion spread rapidly through East and Southeast Asia and the global financial markets. Table 1.2 presents data on the percentage change in the real gross domestic product (GDP) of EACs and selected countries between 1996 and 2003. The 1996 data show the position of the countries before the advent of the crisis. The growth rates slowed down in 1997 in Korea, China, Indonesia, Malaysia, and the Philippines, and became negative for Thailand. By 1998 all the economies of the region felt the contagion, and except for Taiwan, China, and Singapore, all experienced negative growth in their real GDPs.

TABLE 1.2. Percentage change in real GDP of selected countries.

Region/country	1996	1997	1998	1999	2000	2001	2002	2003
EACs								
Korea	7.1	5.5	–5.5	10.9	8.8	3.0	6.1	3.1
Taiwan	5.7	6.9	4.9	5.4	6.0	–1.9	3.5	3.2
Hong Kong	4.9	5.3	–5.1	3.1	10.5	0.1	2.3	3.3
Singapore	6.9	7.8	1.5	5.9	9.9	–2.1	2.2	1.1
China	9.7	8.8	7.8	7.1	8.0	7.3	8.0	9.1
Indonesia	8.0	5.0	–13.7	0.8	4.8	3.3	3.7	4.1
Malaysia	8.6	7.8	–6.8	5.8	8.5	0.4	4.2	5.2
Philippines	5.7	5.1	–0.5	3.3	3.9	3.4	4.6	4.5
Thailand	5.5	–0.4	–8.0	4.2	4.3	1.8	5.2	6.7
Latin America								
Argentina	4.2	8.4	4.2	–3.4	–0.5	–4.4	–11.0	8.7
Brazil	2.8	3.0	0.2	0.8	4.2	1.4	1.5	–0.2
Chile	7.2	6.6	3.3	–1.1	5.4	2.8	2.0	3.3
Mexico	5.2	7.0	4.9	3.8	6.9	–0.3	0.9	1.3
Developed Economies								
United States	2.8	3.8	3.9	4.2	4.1	0.3	2.4	3.1
Japan	3.9	0.9	–2.8	0.8	1.7	0.4	0.3	2.7
Germany	1.4	2.2	2.8	1.6	3.0	0.6	0.2	–0.1
France	1.5	2.4	3.1	3.2	3.2	2.0	1.2	0.2
United Kingdom	2.2	3.3	2.1	2.3	3.0	2.0	1.6	2.3

Source: International Monetary Fund, 1998-2003.

The EACs were on the road to recovery beginning in 1999, with some slow down in 2001 as a result of the technology bubble burst and the terrorism crisis in the United States. Argentina's financial and political crises manifested themselves in the declines in its economy since 1999.

It is instructive to dwell on the causes of the Asian financial market's collapse in 1997-1998. The World Bank, in a sequel to *The East Asian Miracle,* published *East Asia: The Road to Recovery* (1998) to explain what went wrong with "the Asian miracle." It is as follows:

> Rapid growth, urbanization, and industrialization were spawning new and difficult development problems prior to the crisis. These were building in three dimensions. First, rapid growth, in the absence of sophisticated financial and capital markets and with a large government presence, left the corporate financial sectors unusually reliant on financing long-term investments with short-term debt capital. . . . Second, economic growth was undermining the traditional protection mechanisms for the unemployed, the sick, and the elderly. East Asia relied on high personal savings and family ties to provide security for its elderly. It came to rely on growth itself to provide an even more buoyant labor market. The forces of growth, with their demands for an increasingly mobile labor force, migration, and wider scope for personal consumption, were putting strains on traditional ways of solving social problems. In the transition countries of China and Vietnam, the old commune and state enterprise system of welfare was under analogous strains with the spread of markets. In the wealthiest countries, lifetime employment guarantees in the corporate sector were proving increasingly out of tune with the modern economy's needs for rapid change and flexibility. Third, a weakness of a different kind resulted from the exploitation of natural resources, particularly forests. Southeast Asian growth was fueled, in part, by over-logging, intensive exploitation of fisheries, and wasteful agricultural practices . . . some estimates are that Malaysia's growth in gross domestic product (GDP) would have been approximately 20 percent less if adequate allowance had been made for resource depletion. (pp. 3-4)

Some blame the collapse of the financial market on the pursuit of the Japanese model, which created an unsustainable momentum of economic growth (Wolf, 1998), whereas others attribute it to the floating exchange rates and speculative capital flows (Kuttner, 1998; *The Economist,* 1998); some feel that the trade liberalization urged by the IMF was premature (Sachs, 1998); yet others blame it on the IMF prescription for keeping domestic interest rates high (Fischer, 1998), which encouraged speculative flow of private capital from abroad, where interest rates were much lower, to finance speculative real estate buildup (Barro, 1998) in the absence of an adequate regulatory system to monitor domestic credit expansion (The World Bank, 1998; Caprio and Honohan, 1999; Goldstein, 1998; McLeod and Garnaut, 1998; Mishkin, 1999).

The weakness in the banking sector, especially the lack of transparency, indiscriminate network-based lending without due considerations for risk, has slowly been checked by the EACs. However, a lot more needs to be done. Judging from the steady economic performance of the regional economies in recent years, it appears that lessons have been learned from the follies that led to the collapse of the financial markets in 1997-1998.

LESSONS FROM THE EAC MODEL OF ECONOMIC DEVELOPMENT

The stellar economic performance of the EACs since the 1960s, with, of course, some bumps along the way, raises an interesting question—can an aspirant LDC replicate the model for its own economic growth. The answer is an unqualified no. What worked in the earlier decades cannot work now. Not only have times changed, but also the global economic environment.

The EACs embarked on economic development at a time when the Cold War was in full swing, and the world was divided into economic blocks where the superpowers were vying for zones of influence. The EACs, excluding China, were in alliance with the market economies led by the United States. For this they were rewarded with special considerations, such as investments, and access to their vast markets. These special preferences were extended to China when it opted for the market economy in the late 1970s.

Since the mid-1980s more and more countries have liberalized their trade and opened their economies to the MNCs of the world. The competition for FDI from the advanced economies has become so intense that the MNCs not only can pick and choose, but also they can choose at will to relocate or take their business elsewhere. At an initial stage of economic development, an LDC cannot absorb such shocks of sudden entry or departure of foreign MNCs.

Only a country with sound infrastructures and a trained human resource pool and/or a vast supply of easily developable natural resources can expect to attract investment resources that can lift it to a stage of sustainable economic development at this time in history. The MNCs of the advanced economies are already engaged in outsourcing of their manufacturing production and service functions to such countries. This may create islands of economic prosperity within a country without benefiting all the sectors of the economy. The recent Indian experiment is a testimony to this malady.

For some time now there has been an increased awareness about the pitfalls of globalization, and the accesses of the foreign MNCs in terms of exploitation of labor and natural resources in the poor countries. The closures of production and service facilities in the advanced economies and the relocation of these facilities to foreign locations in an effort to reduce costs has created an unemployed labor force that has become increasingly resentful of MNCs and the idea of globalization, and they have joined forces with the environmentalists and anarchists to stop the trend. A growing movement exists in the relatively affluent countries, such as the EACs, to mind the environment and reduce the depletion of natural resources. An inadequate supply of fresh water may become a limiting factor for economic development.

Whether globalization has gone far enough (Bradford and Lawrence, 2004), or whether more is to be gained from further liberalization, the direction of future courses will depend on the political will of the major economic powers. The movement toward sustainable economic development will gain momentum, and it is up to the world's intellectuals to convince all parties that shared economic growth is beneficial to the world as a whole.

REFERENCES

Aggarwal, R. and Agmon, T. (1990). The international success of developing country firms: Role of government directed comparative advantage. *Management International Review,* Vol. 30, No. 2, 163-180.

Alam, M.S. (1989). The South Korean "Miracle": Examining the mix of government and markets. *Journal of Developing Areas,* Vol. 23, No. 2, 223-257.

Barro, R.J. (1998). The IMF does not put out fires, it starts them. *Business Week,* December 7, 18.

Birdsall, N., Ross, D., and Sabot, R. (1995). Inequality and growth reconsidered: Lessons from East Asia. *World Bank Economic Review,* Vol. 9, No. 3, 477-508.

Bradford, S.C. and Lawrence, R.Z. (2004). *Has Globalization Gone Far Enough? The Costs of Fragmented International Markets.* Washington, DC: Institute for International Economics.

Capiro, G. and Honohan, P. (1999). Restoring banking stability: Beyond supervised capital requirements. *The Journal of Economic Perspectives,* Vol. 13, No. 4, 43-64.

Chu, W.W. (1994). Import substitution and export-led growth: A study of Taiwan's petrochemical industry. *World Development,* Vol. 22, No. 5, 781-794.

Dollar, D. (1990). Patterns of productivity growth in South Korean manufacturing industries, 1963-1979. *Journal of Development Economics,* Vol. 33, No. 2, 309-327.

Eckes, A.E. (1993). International trade paradox. *Vital Speeches,* Vol. 59, No. 23, 734-736.

The Economist (2003). The devil's excrement: Is oil wealth a blessing or a curse? May 22, 78.

The Economist (1998). Time to turn off the tap? September 12, 83-85.

Fischer, S. (1998). Reforming world finance: Lessons from a crisis. *The Economist,* October 3, 23-27.

Goldstein, M. (1998). *The Asian Financial Crisis: Causes, Cures, and Systemic Implications.* Washington, DC: Institute of International Economics.

International Monetary Fund (1998-2004). *World Economic Outlook,* April/May Issues.

Krueger, A.O. (1997). Trade policy and economic development: How we learn. *The American Economic Review,* Vol. 87, No. 1, 1-22.

Kuttner, R. (1998). What sank Asia? Money sloshing around the world. *Business Week,* July 27, 16.

McLeod, R.H. and Garnaut, R. (Eds.) (1998). *East Asia in Crisis: From Being a Miracle to Needing One?* London: Routledge.

Mishkin, F.S. (1999). Global financial instability: Framework, events, issues. *The Journal of Economics Perspectives,* Vol. 13, No. 4, 3-20.

Nelson, R. (1994). Ignore the hot air. *World Trade,* Vol. 7, No. 6, 18-20.

Noland, M. and Pack, H. (2003). *Industrial Policy in an Era of Globalization: Lessons from Asia.* Washington, DC: Institute for International Economics.

Ranis, G. (1995). Another look at the East Asian miracle. *World Bank Economic Review,* Vol. 9, No. 3, 509-534.

Richter, F.-J. (Ed.) (1999). *Business Networks in Asia: Promises, Doubts, and Perspectives.* Westport, CT: Quorum Books.

Sachs, J. (Ed.) (1990). *Developing Country Debt and Economic Performance,* Vol. 2. Chicago: University of Chicago Press.

Sachs, J. (1998). Global Capitalism: Making it work. *The Economist,* September 12, 23-25.

Solanet, M.A. (1994). Privatization: The long road to success in Argentina. *Business Forum,* Vol. 19, No. 1-2, 28-31.

Turner, R. (1992). Brazil: Industry—An end to protectionism. *Institutional Investor,* Vol. 26, No. 8, 516-517.

United Nations Conference on Trade and Development (2002). *Trade and Development Report 2002: Developing Countries in World Trade.* New York: United Nations.

United Nations Conference on Trade and Development (2003). *World Investment Report 2003: FDI Policies for Development—National and International Perspectives.* New York: United Nations.

Weidenbaum, M. and Hughes, S. (1996). *The Bamboo Network: How Expatriate Chinese Entrepreneurs Are Creating a New Economic Superpower in Asia.* New York: The Free Press.

Wolf, C., Jr. (1998). What caused Asia's crash? Too much government control. *The Wall Street Journal,* February 4, A22.

World Almanac Books (2004). *The World Almanac and Book of Facts 2004.* New York: World Almanac Books.

World Bank (1993). *The East Asian Miracle: Economic Growth and Public Policy.* New York: Oxford University Press.

World Bank (1998). *East Asia: The Road to Recovery.* Washington, DC: World Bank.

World Bank (2002). *World Development Indicators 2002.* Washington, DC: World Bank.

World Bank (2003). *World Development Report 2003.* Washington, DC: World Bank and the Oxford University Press.

World Bank (2004). *World Development Indicators 2004.* Washington, DC: World Bank.

Zahra, S., George, G., and Jarvis, D.M. (1999). Networks and entrepreneurship in Southeast Asia: The role of social capital and membership commitment. In Richter, F.-J. (Ed.) *Business Networks in Asia: Promises, Doubts, and Perspectives.* Westport, CT: Quorum Books.

Zaman, M.R. (1998a). The causes and consequences of the 1997 crisis in the financial markets of East Asia. *Journal of Global Business,* Vol. 10, No. 17, 37-44.

Zaman, M.R. (1998b). Impact of trade and investment policies on economic transformation in East Asia, the Middle East, and Latin America. In Dunning, J.H. (Ed.) *Globalization, Trade, and Foreign Direct Investment.* Oxford: Elsevier Science, Ltd.

Zaman, M.R. (2000). Restoring Asian economies after the financial markets collapse of 1997-1998. *Global Economy Quarterly,* Vol. 1, No. 2, 179-190.

Chapter 2

East Asia: The Growth Center of the Late Twentieth Century

H. Peter Gray

INTRODUCTION

The chapters in this book focus on economic developments and institutions in East Asian countries. Appropriately, they originally were presented in Bangkok, the capital city of one of the second wave of newly industrializing nations of the region, at the international conference of the International Trade and Finance Association hosted by Ramkhamhaeng University from May 29 to June 1, 2002.

No region was more dynamic, more subject to stress, and made greater economic and social progress in the last quarter of the twentieth century than East Asia. It is true that the progress has been scarred with serious "growing pains" and financial instability. East Asian progress was preceded by two serious wars, one in Korea in the early 1950s, and one in Vietnam in the late 1950s to the mid-1970s. Some countries, such as Indonesia and Malaysia, are only beginning in the twenty-first century to follow in the flight path of the first and second echelons of the wild-geese flying formation. The progress came at a heavy price but that has always been true about the process of economic development. The result has been that many of the countries of East Asia have provided, and continue to provide, a laboratory with many ongoing and interrelated economic "experiments" on how development takes place. Their achievements also provide the basis of a rich economic literature, which is enhanced by this book. The lessons learned in East Asian countries have relevance now to countries in other parts of the world, including the transition economies of East-

Globalization and East Asia: Opportunities and Challenges

doi:10.1300/5463_02

ern Europe, and they are also proving beneficial in bringing about some revision of earlier and mistaken policies of the supranational institutions.*

This brief introduction seeks to identify some of the characteristics of economic growth and development in East Asia and to show, in general terms, how experience here has been or will be of benefit to countries that follow. A short introductory essay is no place for a general treatise, so this chapter will focus on three special aspects of East Asian progress: the financial dangers of "borrowed growth" (Ozawa, 2001); the benefits from open industrialization in a macroregion (Altomonte et al., 2000; Ozawa, 2003); and the need for a well-developed socioeconomic infrastructure when development policies require close involvement with more sophisticated systems.

BORROWED GROWTH

"Borrowed growth" takes place when a country (at any level of development) enhances its rate of capital formation by harnessing foreign savings through a current account deficit. Traditionally, the idea was compatible with national income and product accounting that evolved from the Keynesian model: that deficits on the current account necessarily reflected additional capital formation (if public-sector revenues were balanced). Harnessing foreign savings was a valuable developmental strategy because the transfer of savings was equaled by the increase in the value of capital formation and the incoming foreign exchange was spent on types of capital, which could not be produced in the developing country. (Technologically advanced machine tools are the traditional example of the induced imports but the funds could be spent on any type of capital.) The capital formation was financed by long-term loans floated in the capital markets in industrial countries, from supranational institutions, or directly from foreign governments. These transfers financed specific projects deemed intramarginal by the lenders. Provided that the projects yielded a return sufficient to fund the cost of the borrowed capital, and that they generated sufficient net foreign exchange to avoid an

*Such as the role of the International Monetary Fund in the July 1997 financial crisis in Bangkok (Shelburne, 2005), and through contagion in Indonesia, Malaysia, and the Philippines. For a good description of "contagion" see Crockett (1997).

unmanageable deficit on outstanding international loans, this was a successful strategy. It played a substantial role in the United States in the nineteenth and early twentieth centuries.

This formula for capital formation has been reinforced in the second half of the twentieth century by the sudden growth of multinational enterprise and foreign direct investment (FDI). Multinational enterprises (MNEs) transfer funds to countries whose endowments mesh well with the special attributes of the investing enterprise. In terms of the eclectic paradigm (Dunning, 2000), the ownership advantages of the firm had to correspond with the locational advantages of the host country. The MNEs conduct an assessment of the advantages of locating affiliates in the host country, and the criteria of the selection and decision processes are dominated by private-sector criteria for economic efficiency (profit) as distinct from the broader set of criteria used by supranational institutions. Subject to a qualification given later, FDI fits in well with the earlier conduits of international transfer of savings.

This straightforward picture has been tainted by recent experience, most obviously the collapse of the Thai baht in July 1997. Here a new phenomenon must be introduced to the detriment of the positive assessment of borrowed growth presented earlier. Emerging nations have been encouraged by the supranational institutions (and the U.S. Department of the Treasury) to create local stock and bond markets. The implications of such institutions were not analyzed carefully before they became operational, partly because their basis was ideological and disregarded the history of instability in even the most sophisticated financial markets (Galbraith, 2002). Foreign investments in financial markets are denominated in the currency of the country, which contains the market. Assets in these markets can be easily encashed, though not with any requisite assurances about price, and the proceeds converted to a foreign currency, likely the functional currency of the beneficiary owner (usually that of the country of residence). Reliance on the transfer of foreign savings to growth-oriented projects in a developing country through the conduit of a stock exchange or a bond market is fraught with danger. Since foreign-owned assets can be quickly sold and the proceeds converted to a foreign currency, the national economy is borrowing on short term to finance projects whose payoffs will be long term. In Thailand, immediately before July 1977, the huge inflow of foreign funds can be attributed to the fixed rate of exchange between the baht and the U.S. dollar. When that link showed signs of imminent rupture, funds were encashed and converted out of the baht. In this way, the Thai economy was thrown into deep recession and three other countries were seriously damaged by flight from their financial currencies.

If borrowed growth is to be a successful strategy, the developing country must ensure that the liabilities be long term and that any maturity mismatch be the immediate focus of attention by the host's treasury and central bank. Inward FDI obeys these strictures because most assets owned by foreign MNEs are physical assets, which cannot be sold without long lead times and high transaction costs. The possible exception is the working capital of MNEs. Working capital is highly fungible and its currency of denomination can be changed quickly. Moreover, MNEs maintain financial staffs whose duty is to make sure that all assets are protected against depreciation of their currency of denomination (and vice versa).

Nations using foreign savings to fund worthwhile investment projects, the essence of "borrowed growth," must recognize that need for the use of funds that cannot be withdrawn from the host nation when financial markets are perceived to be fragile. This does not preclude allowing trading in financial assets within the host country or restricting the amount of easily encashable capital owned by nonresidents (Chiu, 2000).

THE BENEFITS OF OPEN INDUSTRIALIZATION IN A MACROREGION

Provided that financial instability is avoided through vigilance by central banks and treasuries, open industrialization has been proven by countries in East Asia to be a good strategy. In considering the benefits that derive from presence in a macroregion, it is necessary, following Ozawa (2003), to distinguish between de jure and de facto macroregions. The former are created by negotiation: they are geographically restricted and usually comprise nations with limited divergence in per capita GDP. In contrast, de facto macroregions comprise national economies, which are geographically and culturally proximate, but with varying levels of per capita GDP. It is in de facto macroregions, such as East Asia, that the potential for reaping the benefits of the flying-geese model reach their peak. The stimuli that are available to laggard nations derive from the greater ease of transfer of stimuli that results from geographic and cultural proximity, and from the close economic interaction that will exist. A fundamental feature of the flying-geese model is that the transfer of stimuli contributes to the elevation of the level of development in the poorer economies, and that within the macroregion, a country can be simultaneously a recipient and a source of external stimuli. Usually, the geographic and cultural proximity allows FDI to take place more easily because the economies will interact on several levels (including sending gifted students from poorer countries to universities in countries that are richer and more advanced technologically).

A de facto macroregion offers a greater degree and a greater dimensionality of integration so that it is a special subunit of the world, which will benefit from the efficiency of intercommunication of ideas and knowledge among the member nations. This is a special and more intense version of what is known more broadly as globalization. Johnson (2002), in an Olympian overview of the benefits of globalization (and, by inference, "macroregionalization"), emphasizes the transfer of knowledge as one of the great benefits that derive from closer relations with other countries. While the transfer of technical knowledge is well recognized as a beneficial phenomenon in the literature on FDI, Johnson, a distinguished agricultural economist, also notes that the transfer of knowledge that relates to people, animals, and plants has generated amazing benefits to the global population, and this knowledge has been developed mostly within the past 150 years. The results are better health, better nutrition, and longer life expectancy worldwide. This insight underlies the formation of the Society for the Intercommunication of New Ideas (Guitton, 1992).

THE IMPORTANCE OF SOCIAL ORGANIZATION

If nations of different levels of affluence and sophistication are to interact, it is necessary that both nations, particularly the less-developed nation of an interacting pair, understand the problems that may derive from the interaction. This is not easily done if only because detailed knowledge of arrangements abroad is not usually available in the less developed nation of an interacting pair. Necessarily, the greater the gap in economic accomplishment, the less likely the socioeconomic infrastructure will be adequate to preclude the misadventures of interaction.

One example of this was the lack of sophistication of the actors in financial markets in Thailand in 1997. The opening of the Thai financial system to the global financial system allowed foreign investors to take positions in Thai securities, but these investors were equipped with much better knowledge of "how things worked" and of the availability of international risk-hedging services than either the participants in Thai markets or the regulators and overseers of the sector.

A second kind of interaction that can generate severe social costs in the less developed country of an interacting pair can involve the introduction of a technology in a less developed country that does not have the infrastructure, socioeconomic or technological, to cope with it. Such disasters can derive from either international trade or foreign direct investment. An obvious example of a disaster derived from international trade is the sale of infant formula by Nestlé in third world countries: the transplanted consumer technology led to disaster (Beauchamp, 1983; Cateora, 1987). A spectacular example of a disaster deriving from transplanted technology in South Asia involved the creation of poison gas by a subsidiary of Union Carbide and the death of approximately 2,000 people in Bhopal, India, 1984. No one can be precisely sure of the root cause of that tragedy or of its social cost. It is self-evident that safety measures in the plant in Bhopal were inadequate. Until that time, Union Carbide India Ltd. had been a model foreign affiliate. Neither the government of India nor the multinational corporation emerged blameless. The process in the plant involved the use of chemicals with the potential to create a poisonous gas. Some reports suggested that the workers in the plant were underinformed in that they had no idea of the severity of the consequences of generating the gases in question. Others suggest that the regulatory oversight by the Indian government was inadequate. The existence of an imported technology must be handled with care by all three parties concerned: workers, management, and government. One analysis (Gladwin and Walter, 1985) suggests that management was trained in the United States where the regulatory climate existed to preclude such accidents. The parties involved simply failed to realize the magnitude of the differences between the two regimes.

In an excellent diagnostic treatment of the appropriate social responsibility of a multinational corporation (MNC) toward its nonindustrialized host country, Walter (1975, p. 148) identified the mutual interest of the MNC and the host government. They are

> partners in a non-zero (positive) sum game in which both can gain in a mutually advantageous working relationship. Periodic conflict is inevitable, just as it is between business and society at the national level. It is often acerbic and politically visible. But conciliation is usually both possible and fundamentally in the interest of both sides.

This degree of sophistication in negotiation requires a level of social organization that may not yet have been attained by the developing country. This will (or perhaps should) limit the kinds of technology that may beneficially be imported. It also requires clear understanding of the division of responsibilities between the host-country government and the parent corporation.

CONCLUSION

The experience gained in East Asia may one day be transferred profitably to other *potential* macroregions: Latin America, North Africa, and sub-Saharan Africa spring quickly to mind. The transference of analysis and understanding will need to be qualified by cultural, geographic, and political differences. The author has some doubts that substantial changes in culture and political systems can be achieved in the immediate future, so it may well be that East Asia, reinforced by the larger macroregion that comprises the Asia-Pacific Economic Community, will continue to advance both absolutely and relatively to Latin America and other potential macroregions, and in this way point home the theory of modern economic development to laggard regions.

REFERENCES

Altomonte, C., Bolwijn, R., and H.P. Gray (2000). "Open industrialization as a development strategy: The example of East Asia," in Fatemi, K. (Ed.), *The New World Order: Internationalism, Regionalism, and the Multinational Corporations.* Amsterdam: Pergammon, pp. 109-123.

Beauchamp, T. (1983). "Marketing infant formula," *Case Studies in Business, Society, and Ethics.* Englewood Cliffs, NJ: Prentice Hall, 221-233.

Cateora, P.R. (1987). *International Marketing* (6th ed.). Homewood, Illinois: Richard D. Irwin, 676-682.

Chiu, P.C.H. (2000). "Taiwan's experience in dealing with the Asian financial crisis and examination of the role of short-term flows in the emerging market economy," *Review of Pacific Basin Financial Markets and Policies 5,* June, 557-564.

Crockett, A. (1997). "Why is financial stability a goal of public policy?" *Federal Reserve Bank of Kansas City,* Fourth Quarter, 1997, 5-20.

Dilyard, J.R. and Gray, H.P. (2000). "Increasing the contribution of FDI and foreign portfolio investment to sustainable development: Recent domestic and international policy measures," in Holst, J. (Ed.), *Finance for Sustainable Development: Testing New Policy Approaches.* New York: United Nations.

Dunning, J.H. (2000). "The eclectic paradigm as an envelope for economic and business theories of MNE activity," *International Business Review 9,* 163-190.

Galbraith, J.K. (2002). "The Brazilian swindle and the larger international monetary problem," *Levy Institute Policy Note 2002/2.* Annandale-on-Hudson, NY: The Jerome Levy Economics Institute of Bard College.

Gladwin, T. and Walter, I. (1985). "Bhopal and the multinational," *The Wall Street Journal,* January 16.

Guitton, H. (1992). "The International Society for the Intercommunication of New Ideas," *International Journal of New Ideas 1,* Number 1, 12-14.

Johnson, D.G. (2002). "Globalization: What it is and who benefits," *Journal of Asian Economics 13,* Fall, 427-439.

Ozawa, T. (2001). "Borrowed growth, current account deficit-based development finance," in Fatemi, K. (Ed.), *International Public Policy and Regionalism at the Turn of the Century.* New York: Pergammon, pp. 95-113.

Ozawa, T. (2003). "Towards a theory of hegemon-led macro-clustering," in Gray, H.P. (Ed.), *Extending the Eclectic Paradigm in International Business: Essays in Honor of John Dunning,* Cheltenham, UK Edward Elgar Publishing.

United Nations Conference on Trade and Development (2000). *World Investment Report 2000.* Geneva: United Nations.

Walter, I. (1975). "A guide to social responsibility of the multinational enterprise," in Backman, J. (Ed.), *Social Responsibility and Accountability.* New York: New York University Press, pp. 146-185.

PART II: COMPARATIVE STUDIES

Chapter 3

Comparative Advantage Recycling and Clustered Growth: The Flying-Geese Paradigm of Tandem Catch-Up on the Pacific Rim

Terutomo Ozawa

INTRODUCTION

Even though the Asian financial crises of 1997-1998 considerably dampened our enthusiasm about, and interest in, East Asian growth, that region as a whole has recorded unprecedented rapid growth since the end of World War II. The World Bank (1993) called the growth "the East Asian Miracle." In fact, the crisis-afflicted economies have already rebounded quickly (except Japan, which has been mired in an economic slump for more than a decade ever since the bursting of the asset bubble of 1987-1990). One dominant explanation for the region's supergrowth is that the region adopted outward-oriented, export-propelled industrialization (EPI) strategies—instead of the import-substituting industrialization (ISI) approach that was once intensively pursued by Latin America until the late 1980s. (An exception was Chile, which switched from ISI to EPI in 1976 and began to grow rapidly.) The general consensus derived from these two regions' contrasting performances is that EPI is growth promoting, whereas ISI is growth stunting.

In empirical studies, a strong statistical correlation is found to exist between the rate of growth of exports and that of real gross domestic product (GDP) (ADB, 1999). This relationship is similarly observable between "openness" (measured by a trade-GDP ratio on the

Globalization and East Asia: Opportunities and Challenges

doi:10.1300/5463_03

basis of purchasing power parity [PPP] conversion) and per capita income (World Bank, 2001). More recently, international flows of foreign direct investment (FDI) have been increasingly singled out as another key explanatory variable (another intervening channel) in connection with East Asia's rapid growth. In fact, East Asian economies have attracted the lion's share of total FDI to developing countries, and consequently come to possess higher inward FDI stocks than other developing regions.

Furthermore, multivariate analyses of growth have demonstrated that trade and FDI have been central to rapid growth in East Asia (Harrison, 1996). Using data for 11 economies in East Asia and Latin America, Zhang (2001, p. 175) found that "although FDI is expected to boost host economic growth, it is shown that the extent to which FDI is growth-enhancing appears to depend on country-specific characteristics" (such as liberalized trade regime, improved education and human capital conditions, export-oriented FDI, and macroeconomic stability). These characteristics represent the institutional setups of the host economies.

FDI is thus strongly identified as an important explanatory factor, but it is still uncertain why and through what mechanisms inward FDI stimulates growth, whenever it coincides with some favorable country-specific institutional characteristics. The ordinary, casual explanation is that FDI accompanies the transfer of superior technology and management skills, access to overseas markets, and access to world money and capital markets. However, this firm-level (microeconomic) explanation alone does not elucidate the dynamic macrostructural linkages between FDI, trade, and growth, especially for a regionally clustered growth as witnessed in East Asia. Why have trade, FDI and rapid growth been regionally clustered so intensively in that particular region more than in any other developing region? In other words, the East Asian Miracle needs to be conceptualized as a *regional economic agglomeration* specifically endemic to East Asia, and its causes need to be explored.

In this connection it should be noted that much study has been made recently of subnational (intra-country) regional clusters or "microregions" (Piore and Sabel, 1984; Porter, 1990; Krugman, 1991; Markusen, 1996; Nachum, 1999; Dunning, 2000) in the wake of sudden rediscovery and interest in "geography" as a key factor in growth. Surprisingly, however, little has been said and understood of the phenomenon of a supranational (cross-border) growth cluster as another form of economic agglomeration.

The leitmotif of this chapter is that trade and FDI are the major conduits of learning and that a set of institutions and policies can maximize the benefits of trade and FDI in the course of catch-up growth. However, it is impossible to explain East Asian growth agglomeration without considering the special role played by the United States as the leader (hegemon) of the Pax Americana, and Japan's role as a critical, industrial-upgrading intermediary and a capacity augmenter via comparative advantage recycling. Japan's role has been particularly crucial in clustering growth in that particular part of the world, and the newly industrializing economies (NIEs) (Hong Kong, Singapore, South Korea, and Taiwan) have in turn stepped in and begun to duplicate the Japanese experience in catch-up growth and industrial dissemination across borders, thereby further reinforcing the regionally clustered growth. The entire episode/analysis can be augmented in terms of the so-called "flying-geese" paradigm of tandem catch-up.

HEGEMON-LED MACROCLUSTERING AND THE FLYING-GEESE PARADIGM

So, what is the global environment in which trade and FDI serve as engines of growth in East Asia? In the first place, the role of the United States as the hegemon of market capitalism needs to be recognized. The World Bank (1993) study looked at only the individual economies' internal policies and institutions, and did not refer to the favorable global economic environment created by the Pax Americana, the very external environment that made the individual Asian economies' outward-oriented policies and institutions effective in their catch-up efforts—especially for Japan and the NIEs during the postwar golden age of capitalism of 1950-1971, but also for others in general up to the present.

In a nutshell, the Pax Americana constitutes an economic system of what may be called "hegemon-led macroclustering," which is an extended outcome of Pax Britannica–led macroclustering (Ozawa, 2003a,b). Macroclustering is a phenomenon in which a hegemon economy propagates growth stimuli to its closely aligned cohort of countries that are at lower stages of development and structural upgrading. The growth stimuli include the dissemination of technology, knowledge, skills, market information, demand (via access to the hegemon's home markets), and above all, growth-inducing institutional arrangements of open-market capitalism through the medium of trade, FDI, and other forms of international business activity. This contributes to the higher levels of productivity and efficiency, hence rapid growth, in the follower countries. The low-echelon countries can "free ride" and thrive on these stimuli. In other words, "economies of hierarchical concatenation" exist in which the follower countries can reap from the forces of hegemon-led macroclustering, so long as they are capable of formulating and executing suitable public policies in a judicious manner.

The East Asian growth has basically been a region-wide type of economic agglomeration or a type of regionalized endogenous growth in which cross-border knowledge transfers and agglomeration (learning and knowledge generation) via trade and FDI are fundamentally market-driven (profit-motivated and guided), although individual countries, especially those that are lower echelon, are usually involved in market-enhancing, dirigiste catch-up strategies. To put it simply, a hierarchy of countries led by a lead country matters—and matters a lot for regional economic growth in general, and for individual countries' economic development in particular.

This perspective dovetailis nicely with the so-called "flying-geese" (FG) model of tandem catch-up. Although this metaphor originated with Kaname Akamatsu's seminal work (inter alia, 1935, 1962), it has been elaborated on and expanded in terms of the critical role of FDI most persistently and extensively in Kojima (2000, 2003, 2004), Kojima and Ozawa (1984, 1985), and Ozawa (1992, 2000, 2005). Others such as Yamazawa (1990) and Shinohara (1996) have also contributed, stressing mostly its related patterns of trade.

In his original form, Akamatsu envisioned a world economy in which latecomers ("follower geese") can industrialize by capitalizing on the gaps of knowledge and income vis-à-vis more advanced countries ("lead geese") through a dynamic process of infant-industry protection and maturation (imports → local production under protection → exports). His analyses were thus presented from the perspective of a catching-up country (notably Japan), and all the elaborated versions, too, are so far based on this "narrow" perspective. Yet the FG paradigm can be interpreted in such expanded a way that the model of hegemon-led macroclustering itself falls under the FG paradigm: the United Kingdom was the very "first goose" that led the Industrial Revolution, whereas Europe and the United States were once the eagerly emulating "follower geese" under the Pax Britannica regime of macroclustering during the 1846-1914 period; the United States then became the new "lead goose," as it has established the Pax Americana regime from 1941 to present.

EVOLUTIONARY PATTERNS OF TRADE AND INVESTMENT

The patterns of trade and investment relationships between the West (the United States and Europe) on one hand and East Asian countries on the other have evolved swiftly and dramatically since the end of World War II. This evolutionary unfolding process needs to be sketched out chronologically in order to understand the nature of the region's experiences with FDI and trade as growth catalysts.

Phase I (Roughly 1950s and Late 1960s)

This period was basically the postwar golden age of capitalism (1950-1971) when exchange rate stability was maintained under the Bretton Woods regime and capital controls were permitted—and even encouraged (Rodrik, 2000). Japan started its successful catch-up growth by restricting imports, inward FDI, and short-term capital flows in order to build up national (i.e., not foreign-owned and -controlled) domestic industries without much dependence on borrowings from overseas. Advanced Western technologies were purchased avidly and primarily through licensing agreements (that is, in an unbundled fashion) (Ozawa, 1974), and such dirigisme was tolerated by the United States in the wake of the Cold War. Japan imported raw materials/natural resources mostly from other Asian countries, processed them into manufactures, and exported them to the West. Japan thus followed the workshop-of-the-world model pioneered previously by resource-exigent Britain. The West provided Japan with hard-currency markets, while the rest of Asia supplied raw materials. Proto-NIEs (Singapore, Hong Kong, Taiwan, South Korea) had been engaged primarily in inward-focused import-substitution until the mid-1960s.

Throughout the 1950s Japan was preoccupied with the recovery of its own economy. It was only after its continuous economic expansion in the early 1960s that it began to look seriously to the rest of Asia as an additional market, supplementary to Western markets, for exports and as a source of supply for industrial raw materials. Moreover, it was not until the late 1950s that Japan began to settle the problem of reparations and to restore normal relations with other Asian countries. From 1954 to 1958, over $1 billion of grant reparations and other forms of economic cooperation worth about $700 million were negotiated, and the 1960s saw increasing flows of reparations and economic aid supplementing such payments from Japan (Caldwell, 1972). Japan used these flows as an effective conduit for reestablishing commercial relations with its Asian neighbors. Since both reparations and economic aid were tied to the purchase of Japanese industrial products, new markets were opened for exports. The reparations agreements often included as an integral part commercial loans and direct investment, an arrangement that encouraged the direct involvement of Japanese industry in key local projects.

Throughout this period, however, Japan experienced deficits in its balance of payments whenever its economy had an economic expansion/boom, and had to apply monetary brakes to cope with the payment problem. It was only in 1968 that Japan's balance of payments finally began to register surpluses as a long-term trend.

Phase II (From mid-1960s to 1980s)

Japan's catch-up development continued to proceed rapidly during this period. In the latter half of the 1960s, labor shortages of young factory workers began to appear, causing wages to rise quickly and to weaken the country's labor-intensive manufacturing industries, such as textiles and apparel, toys, and sundries. For the first time in the postwar period, Japanese manufacturers, especially small ones, began to transplant low-wage-dependent, light industry activities onto Japan's neighboring countries where low-cost labor was still in abundance. This coincided with the adoption of outward-looking strategies by other Asian countries, and Japan's foreign direct investment was welcomed in its neighboring countries—first in the NIEs and soon afterwards in the Association of Southeast Asian Nations (ASEAN)-4: Thailand, Malaysia, Indonesia, and the Philippines. Consequently, the phenomenon of "comparative advantage recycling" (Ozawa, 1993; UNCTAD, 1995) was set in motion, and the region began to register rapid growth. That is to say comparative advantages in labor-intensive manufactures started to be recycled/relayed from Japan, first to the NIEs and then to the ASEAN-4 (and most recently to China).

In this connection, the EPI strategy adopted by East Asia's rapidly growing countries proved to be supported heavily by imports of capital goods and key industrial supplies—to such an extent that the strategy was actually an "import- and export-led growth" paradigm (Klien, 1990; Dutta, 2000)—instead of being merely "export led." Trade and FDI, both outward and inward, in the Pacific Rim region thus became crucial catalysts for regionally clustered growth. Communist China remained "contained" by the Free World and "secluded" until 1987 when it adopted an open-door policy to reorient its economy toward the outside world for the first time.

Phase III (From 1990s Onward)

The information technology (IT) revolution first occurred most successfully in the United States and spread quickly across the globe, particularly during the latter half of the 1990s. Practically all the East Asian economies (Japan, the NIEs, and the ASEAN-4) became major suppliers of IT-related electronics goods for the U.S. market. With an amazing speed, China, which initially concentrated on labor-intensive light industry manufactures (such as apparel and shoes), moved into the low-to-mid-end segments of electronics hardware and software. The geographical pattern of comparative advantage recycling spread quickly to China not only from Japan and the NIEs but also from the ASEAN-4, which have not yet graduated fully from the stage of labor-driven industrialization.

China's emergence as a high-growth economy is now considered both an opportunity for further regional agglomeration and a competitive threat (or prod) to its neighboring economies in particular—but equally for the world as a whole. Fears of industrial hollowing-out are expressed in the NIEs and Japan in particular—and even in the ASEAN-4.

THEORY OF COMPARATIVE ADVANTAGE RECYCLING

East Asia is credited for an effective use of EPI policy, along with other complementary policies, to get the fundamentals right by way of

1. carefully limited and market-compatible government activism,
2. strong export orientation,
3. high levels of domestic savings,
4. accumulation of human and physical capital,
5. good macroeconomic management,
6. acquisition of technology through openness to direct foreign investment and licensing,
7. flexible labor markets, and
8. shared growth. (World Bank, 1993)

However, these public policies adopted by the region's countries proved effective *because* of the willingness of the West, especially the United States, to disseminate growth stimuli overseas by way of providing technology, management, and capital through overseas investments and absorbing manufactured goods in their import markets. In this respect, the United States has been the major provider of *demand* (markets) for East Asia, with the latter enjoying huge trade surpluses.

Market Sharing and Recycling in the U.S. Import Market

One aspect of U.S. trade relations with East Asia is illustrated in Figure 3.1. Although Japan was the first country to capture the U.S. markets for labor-intensive goods (SITC categories 65, 66, 81, 82, 83, 84, 85), initially 25 percent in 1962, the Japanese share declined steadily to only 2 percent in 1997. In the meantime, the NIEs' share rose from 1.5 percent in 1962 to a high of 40 percent in 1983, and then quickly fell to 10 percent in 1997. ASEAN-4's share rose slowly, but was soon taken over by China, which captured 25 percent in 1997, the same share enjoyed by Japan in the early 1960s. This clearly demonstrates how Japan's share in the U.S. market for labor-intensive imports has been passed along down the East Asian hierarchy of economies, first to the NIEs, then to ASEAN-4, and most recently to China—hence, the phenomenon of comparative advantage recycling. Similar patterns of comparative advantage also started to be observ-

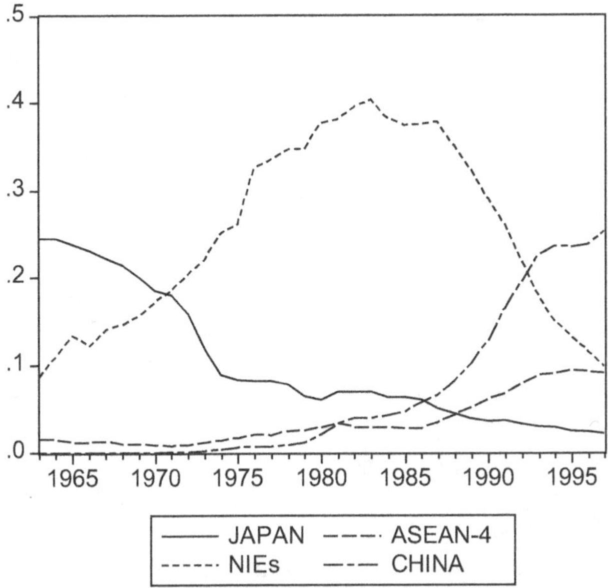

FIGURE 3.1. Comparative advantage recycling in the U.S. import market for labor-intensive goods. *Source:* Adapted from Cutler, Berri, and Ozawa, 2003.

able in more capital-intensive goods, such as iron and steel, metal manufactures, and electric machinery (Berri and Ozawa, 1997).

Japan As an Industrial (Comparative Advantage) Recycler

Why does such an effective market recycling exist among the East Asian countries? This reflects a quickly changing pattern of comparative advantage that is associated with its corresponding changes in the industrial structure of the Asian countries involved. Japan was the first to initiate this rapid process of industrial upgrading. It quickly climbed the ladder of industry, first from labor-intensive Heckscher-Ohlin industries (e.g., textiles) from 1950 to the mid-1960s, and scale-driven, nondifferentiated Smithian industries (steel) from the late 1950s to the early 1970s, to assembly-based differentiated Smithian industries (automobiles and the early generation of electronics) from the late 1960s onward, to R&D-based Schumpeterian industries (computers and microchips) from the mid-1980s to the present, and finally to IT-based McLuhan industries (the Internet) from the mid-1990s onward—all along the path of industrial upgrading already trodden and demonstrated by the United States. These five tiers of growth have been each led by some leading industry as the main engine of development. The chronological demarcation lines between the stages are necessarily blurry and overlapping as one stage phases into the next. Indeed, these five leading growth sectors have been created under, and gone through by, the Pax Britannica (primarily the first two sectors) during the first Golden Age of Capitalism (1870-1913) and under the Pax Americana (mostly the last three sectors) during the second Golden Age of Capitalism (1950-1971) and the emergence of the IT-driven New Economy (early 1990s-present) (Ozawa, 2003a).

This stages model of industrial upgrading (IU) is a reformulated version (Ozawa, 1992, 2001a, b) of the FG theory. The IP model is basically a "leading growth sector" theory, à la Schumpeter (1934), in which a sequence of growth is punctuated by stages that have a certain industrial sector as the main locomotive of structural transformation. The Japanese economy has gone through the five stages swiftly during the course of its catch-up growth. These stages are the legacies of both the Pax Britannica, which is responsible basically for the emergence of the Heckscher-Ohlin (textiles) and nondifferentiated Smithian (iron and steel) phases, and the Pax Americana, which is responsible for the last three higher phases (cars, computers, and the Internet) (Ozawa, 2003a,b).

In each sequential stage of industrial upgrading—except the latest IT-based industries, which are still inchoate in development—Japan emerged as the world's most formidable exporters by capturing large market shares in the world economy, as witnessed initially in textiles, then in steel, and later in cars and consumer electronics. However, Japan was not able to retain competitiveness in each captured market for long. Two basic mechanisms were involved in this decline: (1) an inevitable rise in wages and (2) a sharp appreciation of the yen (up to 1985, when the yen once recorded the unprecedented appreciation of 80 yens to the dollar from the fixed rate of 360 yen to the dollar under the Bretton Woods regime). In fact, the more successful Japan was in climbing the ladder of industrial upgrading, the stronger these self-altering mechanisms once proved to be (that is, before the onset of the present post-bubble stagnation in 1990).

As a consequence, Japan's step-by-step industrial upgrading has had an enormous impact on the industrialization pattern of other East Asian countries. As Japan lost comparative advantages in low-productivity tiers of industry or low-end goods at each tier, it transplanted via FDI those disadvantaged industries or activities to other Asian economies (first to the NIEs, then to ASEAN-4, and most recently to China) where they were still able to produce competitively because of relatively low wages.

What made the region so vibrant, moreover, is that the NIEs themselves began to shift their comparatively disadvantaged industries to the lower-echelon countries—first to ASEAN-4 and now increasingly to China. In other words, the NIEs themselves became "lead geese" for the lower-ranking countries. Consequently, in each round of industrial transplantation, the host countries' exports and output have increased and the United States has been serving as the major demand provider by absorbing manufactured imports from Asia's rapidly industrializing countries. (In this regard, this is the prime example and mechanism of "trade as aid," which may be identified as a privatized form of foreign economic aid from the United States.)

It is worth noting that when a country loses a comparative/competitive advantage in a particular activity, two types of assets/resources are released from the contracting sector: (1) those readily transferable to the expanding sector (namely, homogeneous, nonsector-specific resources, such as land and labor); and (2) those specific to the contracting sector and, therefore, nontransferable to the expanding sector (for example, industry/firm-specific technology, knowledge, and experiences). Most resources of the first type, however, are nontransferable to other countries because of institutional or physical constraints. On the other hand, the second type of resources released will be wasted at home unless they are transferred to and employed in other countries where such industry/firm-specific resources are needed to develop comparatively advantaged industries. Hence, comparative advantage recycling reflects an FDI-mediated recycling of productive resources/assets which otherwise would be simply wasted at home. Through this mechanism the resources released from the contracting sector at home are reused (instead of being left unused) and transformed into dividends from FDI operations. The end result is a rise in output and economic welfare.

Aside from the investing (home) country's point of view, the host countries can grow faster thanks to the same mechanism for two major reasons: (1) the inflows of technology and sector-specific other resources will spark and magnify the host country's comparative advantage. This is the "trade-augmentation" effect of FDI (Kojima and Ozawa, 1984); and (2) the demands (markets) needed by the newly created or strengthened export industries in the host countries are guaranteed by the home country that loses comparative advantage and therefore now imports those goods it once and hitherto produced.

In this regard, export-focused industrialization is a misnomer, since the host countries are necessarily importing the critical sector-specific technology and capital goods, which enable them to develop exports quickly and earn foreign exchange (hard currency). This in turn assures the investing foreign multinationals for profit repatriation—hence, a paradigm of "import- and export-led growth," as mentioned earlier.

Japan As a Key Capacity Augmenter

Japan has become the most significant supplier of industrial inputs for other Asian economies, particularly in assembly-based industries, such as electronics and automobiles—that is, starting with the components-intensive, assembly-based, nondifferentiated Smithian stage of industrial upgrading. For instance, Park and Park (1991, p. 93) makes a pertinent observation:

> [The NIEs] have relied on Japan as their main supplier of capital and intermediate goods. . . . Almost 80 percent of [their] imports from Japan in the 1980s included capital- and technology-intensive manufactures. This dependence on Japan for capital and technology has increased in recent years. In 1987, [the NIEs] obtained from Japan almost 50 percent of their total imports of technology-intensive manufactures (up from about 41 percent in 1980) as compared to 26 percent from the United States.

Similarly, Thurow (1996, p. 207) observes:

> On the Pacific Rim, countries run big trade deficits with Japan, which they finance out of their trade surplus with the United States . . . China's 1995 trade surplus with Japan is . . . misleading since it sells Japanese components that are installed on products that are exported to Europe and America.

In fact, Sinohara (1987) much earlier argued that Japan interacts with the rest of East Asia more strongly from the supply side (i.e., as a capacity augmenter) than from the demand side (i.e., as a market provider). Nakamura and Matsuzaki (1997) similarly demonstrated Japan's role as a capacity augmenter by way of an international input-output analysis, and concluded that Japan developed more of a supply-side relationship with the rest of East Asia.

In short, then, it is not amiss to argue that without Japan as a capacity augmenter—via provision of capital goods, inputs, and technology most often in connection with Japanese multinationals' investments—other Asian economies could not have been able to develop export competitiveness in such assembly-based industries.

Yet the developing host countries are not likely to remain as final assemblers forever. They will eventually move into local production of those capital goods and intermediate inputs once imported by way of "import substitution." The strategy of "import- and export-led growth" thus eventually (and almost ineluctably) turns into the "import substitution and local production" phase for intermediate goods. In fact, this process itself is encouraged by the suppliers of capital goods and intermediate inputs themselves once they begin to shift overseas and locate the production of intermediate goods in close proximity to their major customers. For example, Toyota's or Honda's assembly operations in Thailand and China are increasingly accompanied by localization of parts production in those host countries, and these parent companies at home are procuring overseas and importing foreign-made parts from their host countries. In other words, not only final assembly operations but also production of some capital goods and intermediate inputs are destined to move out of the home country to the host countries. Indeed, the sudden recent growth of "pure" Chinese electronics manufacturers and carmakers are said to be fostered by the local availability of modular components and individual parts now increasingly produced by foreign multinationals (Goto, 2003).

One outcome of this development is the phenomenon of so-called "production process fragmentation" across borders (inter alia, Jones, 2000). Vertical production is fragmented "in the sense that a final manufactured good will consist of parts that have been manufactured in a variety of different countries" (Bond, 2001, p. 358). The phenomenon of fragmentation is thus an outcome of comparative advantage recycling, which fosters regionalized cluster growth in East Asia.

The evolving flows of final goods, technology, and intermediate goods based on the "import-supported export drive" targeted at the U.S. markets by the follower geese economies are schematically summarized in Figure 3.2.

Demanufacturization and Tertiarization in the United States

As observed by Colin Clark (1935), economic development is typically characterized by the relative decline of the primary sector (agriculture, forestry, mining, and fishery), the rise of the secondary sector (manufacturing and construction), and the growth of the tertiary sector (services)—all in a continuous sequence over time. In this respect, the United States has experienced a rapid pace of tertialization in recent decades, causing fears of deindustrialization or "hollowing out." In fact, "the deindustrialization wave" (Bluestone and Harrison, 1982) began to erode the soil of industrial America, starting noticeably in the 1970s. In many instances, domestic factories were closed and American firms moved their manufacturing facilities outside the country. This trend continued unabated into the 1980s—so much so that in a special report, *Business Week* (Jonas et al., 1986, magazine's front page) warned of a transformation of U.S. manufacturing companies into "hollow corporations." It observed that "a new kind of company is evolving in the U.S.—manufacturing companies that do little manufacturing. Instead, they import components or products from low-wage countries, slap their own names on them, and sell them in America."

Most recently, moreover, this hollowing has moved up the corporate chain of value-added activities, and American corporations are now actively shifting overseas such white-collar jobs as "chip design, engineering, basic research—even financial analysis," as warned in a recent *Business Week* special report (Engardio et al., 2003, p. 50). These are the types of services heretofore considered "nontradable"

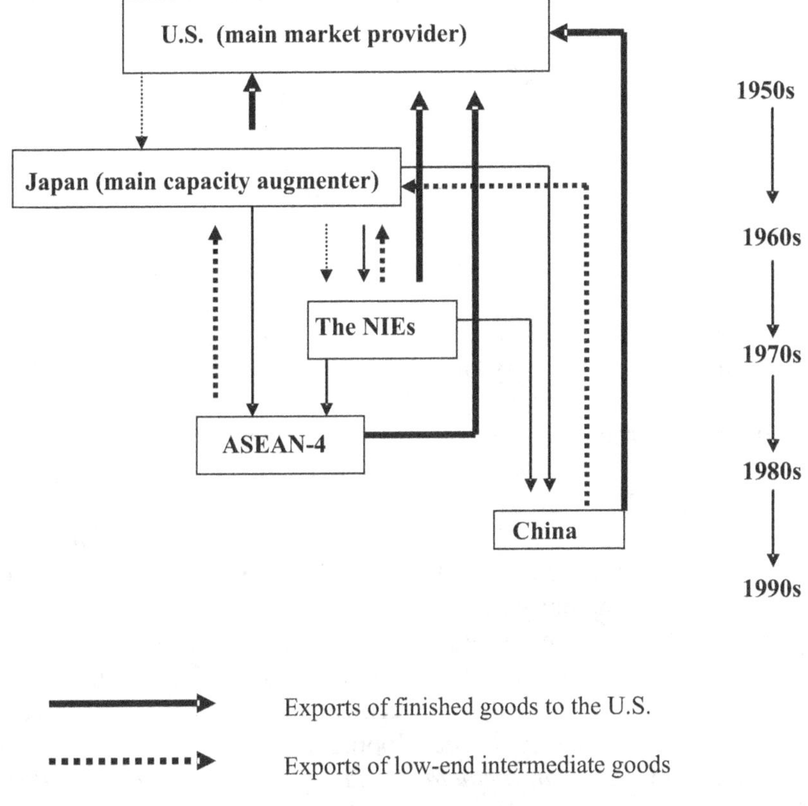

FIGURE 3.2. Comparative advantage recycling and import-supported export drive.

and secluded from foreign competition. The IT revolution and its accompanied new round of globalization (also sparked by stepped-up liberalization of trade and investment around the world) have exposed these once-protected jobs to competition in low-wage—but increasingly skilled—developing and transition economies. One estimate predicts that "at least 3.3 million white-collar jobs and $136 billion in wages will shift from the United States to low-cost countries by 2015" (as cited in Engardio et al., 2003, p. 52).

Furthermore, America's tertialization, culminating in the emergence of the New Economy and the recent equity bubble (during the latter half of the 1990s), has been accompanied—and facilitated—by rising trade (and current account) deficits. One important cause of the current account deterioration is the rapid transfer of manufacturing and services overseas, while American firms increasingly concentrate on knowledge creation (via R&D) and entrepreneurial ventures, especially in financial services, in the postindustrial economy.

The beginning of this structural change was captured early in the product-cycle (PC) theory of trade and investment (Vernon, 1966; Hirsch, 1967). It describes (1) why new high-income products and labor-saving processes are first innovated in, and exported from, the United States ahead of other countries, (2) why such U.S. exports are to be soon replaced by overseas production once the technology involved was perfected and standardized, making it easy for the follower firms in other countries to imitate, and (3) that in the end, the United States is actually to wind up importing these goods, the very goods it has initially innovated and exported. Thus, the PC theory can be reinterpreted as a theory of "demanufacturization" (if not precisely deindustrialization, since the most critical upstream operations, R&D activities and product/market development, are still retained at home) because it describes *an ineluctable market-driven process of industrial migration from home and propagation abroad.*

In addition to this PC theory-Type I, Vernon (1979) introduced the PC theory-Type II, in which R&D activities are, in turn, widely dispersed throughout the world via networks of multinational subsidiaries—instead of being centered in the United States only. The PC theory-Type II thus can be reinterpreted as a theory of R&D capability dispersion overseas. A full range of R&D activities (from basic research to commercialization, involving product/process engineering, designing, and development) are still controlled and managed by U.S. multinationals, but they are now carried out across borders. This dispersion facilitates immediate local production overseas—without the prolonged sequence of innovations at home → exports → technology transfers and production transplantation → imports as depicted in the PC theory-Type I.

In this connection, another version of PC theory (i.e., the PC theory-Type III) should be proposed to describe how in the *early* stages of R&D activities American firms are often induced to sell basic/seed technologies abroad through licensing agreements or other nonequity transactions—instead of fully developing and commercializing such technologies first at home. The PC theory-Type III is, for example, quite relevant to Japan's postwar strategy to acquire the latest Western technologies in crude/unapplied forms under licensing and commercialize them into successful products. As rapidly catching-up economies (such as the NIEs and China) develop R&D capabilities of their own, the Japanese experience is most likely to be replicated. In sum, all three types of the PC model illustrate the *high* propensity of the United States, the hegmon economy, to propagate newly introduced products and R&D capacities, as well as seed knowledge itself, abroad.

America's New Economy has been—and still is—driven by what may be characterized as "financialization" (a phenomenon of tertialization), a phase of capitalism in which the engine of growth shifts from manufacturing to financial activities, such as securities investment, mergers and acquisitions, initial public offerings, and creation/trading of derivatives. As Mandel (2000, p. 16) put it, "Technology is the engine, finance is the fuel." Many new financial products and transactions have been innovated in the United States, and they have begun to similarly go through the product-cycle process of spreading to other countries.

As expected, the innovative U.S. financial markets have attracted huge inflows of capital from overseas (estimated to be about $2 billion a day at one time prior to the sudden tanking of the U.S. stock market in July 2002—but now about $1.5 billion a day), leading to a large capital account surplus, which in turn caused a highly overvalued dollar and an equally large current account deficit. Consequently, the McLuhan phase of the U.S. economy has again been transmitting growth stimuli abroad, especially to East Asia, currently the main supplier of IT hardware and software (programming, data processing, chip design, call centers, and business back-office work), as the United States absorbs large amounts of imports from East Asia and elsewhere. The United States recorded a $432 billion trade deficit in its 2002 trade balance.

THE KRUGMAN AND SACHS PUZZLES

Widely cited is Paul Krugman's (1994) observation about the East Asian Miracle. He argued that the region's fast growth could be characterized and dismissed as "input driven," but not as total factor productivity (TFP) (efficiency)-driven, and that measurable factor inputs of capital and labor can explain it. He likened it to the former Soviet Union's rapid growth, which was achieved by mobilizing workers and capital for employment on a massive national scale. However, the Soviet Union's input-driven growth soon encountered a slow and stagnated growth (that is, it fell victim to the law of diminishing returns). Hence, Krugman predicted that East Asia would likewise meet the same fate eventually, and contended that there was no need to invoke any other special mechanism—such as a miracle—to account for the high rates of growth.

In a follow-up article, Krugman (1997, p. 27) replaced "input-driven" with "perspiration," and "efficiency" with "inspiration":

> If you conclude that [Asian growth's due mainly to] perspiration—that efficiency is not soaring—then the brilliance of Asian industrial policies becomes a lot less obvious. The other unwelcome implication of the perspiration theory was that the pace of Asia's growth was likely to slow.

Krugman's view is, however, in line with the neoclassical canon of growth that emphasizes inputs and capital accumulation, and treats technological progress as *exogenous* (that is, like manna from heaven). His observation has a nuance that input- or perspiration-driven growth is inferior to efficiency- or inspiration-driven growth. However these two different orientations of growth have their *own* appropriateness and utility to a *particular* stage of development in which a country is operating at the moment. In the early stages of development the country must provide job opportunities (sustenance) for the unemployed, uneducated, and unskilled masses, as well as skill-enhancing opportunities (human capital formation).

In this respect, export-propelled and labor-driven industrialization is the first necessary step to pursue, either autonomously (as Japan did) or in collaboration with foreign multinationals in the Heckscher-Ohlin industries (as China is currently doing). Perspiration is *exactly* what developing countries need to lift their standard of living. It is, indeed, their perspirations that made Singapore's and Hong Kong's per capita income higher than that of their former "mother" country, England (at least in terms of the World Bank's official statistics). Inspiration is needed in any country, but *especially* in advanced countries since they can no longer count on perspiration.

Reacting to Krugman's observation, Sachs (1995) counterargued that unlike the Soviet Union, Singapore is highly export oriented, and its continuous high investment (nearly 40 percent of GDP) has shown no sign of diminishing returns (as cited in Rodrigo, 2001). In fact, East Asia's strategy of export-propelled industrialization facilitated by FDI, both inward and outward, is the driving mechanism of regionally endogenized growth.

The questions raised by these two noted economists are thus: whether technological progress in East Asia is really exogenous and not endogenous; and why Singapore—for that matter, other NIEs—has been so much more export efficient and able to maintain such a high level of investment year after year. The concept and logic of comparative advantage recycling introduced earlier can answer these questions easily. Technological progress in the Pacific (inclusive of the United States) has been regionally endogenous, in the sense

1. that the U.S. initially provided both markets and technologies,
2. that Japan then quickly introduced a large number of significant improvements in imported technologies, both technical and organizational,
3. that standardized and "renovated" technologies (often embodied in capital goods, intermediate inputs, and FDI) have been relayed to other Asian economies during the course of comparative advantage recycling, and
4. that the NIEs in turn are replicating Japan's experiences in technological progress and transfer to the rest of Asia.

Indeed, these features of East Asian growth are the essence of the FG model of tandem growth.

FINAL REMARKS

Whether they like it or not, all of the economies in the world are ineluctably under the forces of open-market capitalism unleashed under the Pax Americana. But why has rapid industrialization and growth so far been concentrated so intensively in East Asia? The possible answer is that East Asia has been blessed, first by the presence of the United States, the hegemon of the post–World War II global economic system, as the major provider of industrial knowledge and markets, and second by the role of Japan as a structural intermediator and capacity augmenter, the role which the NIEs themselves in turn have recently begun to play. The existence of these robust secondary geese and the lower-echelon (follower) geese's eagerness to exploit the favorable external environment with a lot of "perspiration" are what has made a regionally clustered growth possible in, and endemic to, East Asia.

Is the East Asian case so unique that a similar clustered growth cannot be replicated in other regions such as Central and Eastern Europe, Latin America, and Africa? This chapter demonstrates the importance of the existence of strong second-goose economies. Their absence is doubtless one critical missing factor in other regions, accounting for failed catch-up. After all, it is *not* an already advanced economy (whose growth rate is low) that can actively shed lower-echelon industries (especially labor-intensive production) overseas, since it has already lost comparative advantages in such industries, and whatever survives at home tends to be protected. Instead it is a *rapidly catching-up economy* whose wage and currency rise quickly, compelling it to transplant low-cost, labor-dependent production in its neighboring lower-wage countries.

In this respect, a rapid rise in wages (that is, the Stolper-Samuelson effect of factor price magnification) is not a threat but a powerful stimulus to the process of structural transformation. Japan and the NIEs are often criticized for their restrictions on labor immigration—say in sharp contrast with European Union countries, which are said to be more open to foreign workers. If labor inflows are permitted, labor shortages and the upward pressure on wages are attenuated in the short run, but the additional supply of low-wage, unskilled labor merely prolongs the existence of advantage-losing industries at home. In other words, the decline of those domestic industries that would otherwise quickly lose competitiveness is put off and prolonged. To this extent, therefore, comparative advantage recycling is hindered. Labor movement and trade are good substitutes.

Furthermore, Japan and the NIEs either had relatively small rural hinterlands that could supply only a limited amount of cheap labor or lacked such a labor source totally. Hence, wages rose sharply, and rising incomes created an ever-growing crave/demand for education in East Asia's Confucianism-oriented culture and tradition. Growth has thus been accompanied by an increase in the supply of better-educated workers, reinforcing the favorable interactions between growth and human capital formation.

In contrast, China has a vast, underdeveloped inland with a massive reservoir of potential industrial workers, while its coastal regions have been rapidly industrialized with the help of inward FDI. As wages rise in the latter, emigration from the hinterland to the industrial coast is naturally motivated. Arthur Lewis's (1954) growth model of "unlimited labor supply" is quite applicable in this case—but only if free labor movement is permitted. In reality, the Chinese government restricts internal labor migration. Hence, as wages rise in the coastal areas without immigration (that is, a "segmented" factor price magnification occurs), a rising interregional income gap inevitably appears, creating socially and politically unsettling problems. However, if free migration is allowed, the coastal areas will be flooded with unskilled labor. This strains housing, public services, and other infrastructural facilities.

This type of geographical disparity may be construed as a misallocation of labor by static neoclassical analysis, but it may serve as a powerful dynamic force for spreading industrial activities inward over time from a more advanced region to less developed regions in the hinterland. In other words, migration controls may actually lead to an internal FG formation in which the coastal regions serve as the lead geese for the hinterland. That is to say, China will organize its *own* flock of geese internally—flying gradually from the coastal to the inland areas. The former will develop into, and serve as, the supply source of key components and other intermediate and capital goods, while the inland is increasingly engaged in labor-intensive assembly-type activities at lower stages of development. The upshot is that a new intracountry, interregional division of labor will be created as a new hierarchy of subregions emerges, and the economies of concatenation can be exploited. China's miracle is in the works as it capitalizes on the forces of the Pax Americana–led macroclustering, which generate opportunities for FG-style comparative advantage recycling.

REFERENCES

Akamatsu, K. (1935). "Wagakuni yomo kogyohin no susei" [Trend of Japan's wooden product industry], *Shogyo Keizai Ronso,* 13: 129-212.

Akamatsu, K. (1962). "A historical pattern of economic growth in developing countries," *Developing Economies,* 1: 1-23.

Asian Development Bank (1999). *Asian Development Outlook 1999.* Manila: ADB.

Berri, D. and Ozawa T. (1997). "Pax Americana and Asian exports: Revealed trends of comparative advantage recycling," *International Trade Journal,* 11 (1): 39-67.

Bluestone, B. and Harrison, B. (1982). *The Deindustrialization of America: Plant Closings, Community Abandonment, and the Dismantling of Basic Industry.* New York: Basic Books.

Bond, E.W. (2001). "Commercial policy in a 'fragmented' world," *American Economic Review,* 91 (2): 358-362.

Caldwell, A.J. (1972). "The evolution of Japanese economic cooperation, 1950-1970." In Malmgren, H.B. (Ed.), *Pacific Basin Development.* Lexington, MA: Heath, pp. 23-60.

Clark, C. (1935). *The Conditions of Economic Progress.* London: Macmillan.

Cutler, H., Berri, D., and Ozawa, T. (2003). "Market recycling in labor-intensive goods, flying-geese style: An empirical analysis of East Asian exports," *Journal of Asian Economics,* 14: 35-50.

Dunning, J.H. (2000). *Regions, Globalization, and the Knowledge-Based Economy.* Oxford: Oxford University Press.

Dutta, M. (1999). *Economic Regionalization in the Asia-Pacific.* Cheltenham, UK: Edward Elgar.

Dutta, M. (2000). "The Euro revolution and the European Union: Monetary and economic cooperation in the Asia-Pacific region," *Journal of Asian Economics,* 11: 65-88.

Engardio, P., Bernstein, A., and Kripalani, M. (2003). "Is your job next?" *Business Week,* February 3: 50-60.

Goto, Y. (2003) "China's 'pure' auto industry expanding with foreign help," *Nikkei Weekly,* February 17: 19.

Harrison, A. (1996). "Openness and growth: A time-series, cross-country analysis for developing countries," *Journal of Developing Economies,* 48: 419-447.

Hirsch, S. (1967). *Location of Industry and International Competitiveness.* Oxford: Oxford University Press.

Jonas, N. et. al. (1986). "The Hollow Corporation," *Business Week,* March 3: 57-85.

Jones, R.W. (2000). *Globalization and the Theory of Input Trade.* Cambridge, MA: MIT Press.

Klien, L. (1990). "Can export-led growth continue indefinitely? An Asian-Pacific perspective," *Journal of Asian Economics,* 1: 1-12.

Kojima, K. (2000). "The 'flying-geese' model of Asian economic development: Origin, theoretical extensions, and regional policy implications," *Journal of Asian Economics,* 11: 375-401.

Kojima, K. (2003). *Gankogata Keizai Hattenron* [The Flying-Geese Theory of Economic Development], Vol. 1. Tokyo: Bunshindo.

Kojima, K. (2004). *Gankogata Keizai Hattenron* [The Flying-Geese Theory of Economic Development], Vol. 2. Tokyo: Bunshindo.

Kojima, K. and Ozawa, T. (1984). "Micro- and macro-economic models of direct foreign investment: Toward a synthesis," *Hitotsubashi Journal of Economics,* 25 (1): 1-20.

Kojima, K. and Ozawa, T. (1985). "Toward a theory of industrial restructuring and dynamic comparative advantage," *Hitotsubashi Journal of Economics,* 26 (2): 135-145.

Krugman, P. (1991). *Geography and Trade.* Cambridge, MA: MIT Press.

Krugman, P. (1994). "The myth of Asia's miracle," *Foreign Affairs,* 73 (6): 412-416.

Krugman, P. (1997). "What ever happened to the Asian Miracle?" *Fortune,* 136 (4): 26-29.

Lewis, A. (1954). "Economic development with unlimited supplies of labour," *Manchester School of Economics and Social Studies,* 12: 139-191.

Mandel, M. (2000). *The Coming Internet Depression.* New York: Basic Books.

Markusen, A. (1996). "Sticky places in slippery space: A typology of industrial district," *Economic Geography,* 72 (3): 293-313.

Nachum, L. (1999). *The Origins of the International Competitiveness of Firms.* Cheltenham, UK: Edward Elgar.

Nakamura, Y. and Matsuzaki, I. (1997). "Economic interdependence: Japan, Asia, and the world," *Journal of Asian Economics,* 8 (2): 199-224.

Ozawa, T. (1974). *Japan's Technological Challenge to the West: Motivation and Accomplishment.* Cambridge: MIT Press.

Ozawa, T. (1992). "Foreign direct investment and economic development," *Transnational Corporations,* 1 (1): 27-54.

Ozawa, T. (1993). "Foreign direct investment and structural transformation: Japan as a recycler of market and industry," *Business & the Contemporary World,* 5: 129-150.

Ozawa, T. (2000). "The 'flying-geese' paradigm: Toward a co-evolutionary theory of MNC-assisted growth." In Fatemi, K. (Ed.), *The New World Order: Internationalism, Regionalism, and the Multinational Corporations.* Amsterdam: Pergamon, pp. 209-223.

Ozawa, T. (2001a). "The 'hidden' side of the 'flying-geese' catch-up model: Japan's dirigiste institutional set-up and a deepening financial morass," *Journal of Asian Economics,* 12: 471-491.

Ozawa, T. (2001b). "The Internet revolution, networking, and the 'flying-geese' paradigm of structural upgrading," *Global Economy Quarterly,* 11: 1-18.

Ozawa, T. (2003a). "Pax Americana-led macro-clustering and flying-geese-style catch-up in East Asia: Mechanisms of regionalized endogenous growth," *Journal of Asian Economics,* 13 (6): 699-713.

Ozawa, T. (2003b). "Toward a theory of hegemon-led macro-clustering." In Gray, P. (Ed.), *Extending the Eclectic Paradigm in International Business.* Cheltenham, UK: Edward Elgar, 201-225.

Ozawa, T. (2005). *Institutions, Industrial Upgrading, and Economic Performance in Japan: The "Flying-Geese" Paradigm of Catch-up Growth.* Cheltenham, UK: Elgar.

Park, Y.C. and Park, W.-A. (1991) "Changing Japanese trade patterns and the East Asian NICs." In Krugman, P. (Ed.), *Trade with Japan: Has the Door Opened Wider?* Chicago: University of Chicago Press, pp. 85-115.

Piore, M.J. and Sabel, C.F. (1984). *The Second Industrial Divide: Possibilities for Prosperity.* New York: Basic Books.

Porter, M.E. (1990). *The Competitive Advantage of Nations.* New York: Free Press.

Rodrigo, G.C. (2001). *Technology, Economic Growth, and Crises in East Asia.* Cheltenham, UK: Edward Elgar.

Rodrik, D. (2000). "How far will international economic integration go?" *Journal of Economic Perspective,* 14 (1): 177-186.

Sachs, J.D. (1995). "It keeps economy ahead of pack." *The Straits Times,* September 21: 5.

Schumpeter, J. (1934). *The Theory of Economic Development.* New York: Oxford University Press.

Sinohara, M. (1987). "Patterns and backgrounds of dynamics in the Asia-Pacific economies." In Dutta, M. (Ed.), *Asia-Pacific Economies: Promises and Challenges.* Greenwich, CT: JAI Press, pp. 23-48.

Shinohara, M. (1996). "The flying geese model revisited: Foreign direct investment, trade in machinery, and the boomerang effect." *Journal of the Asia Pacific Economy,* 1: 411-419.

Thurow, L.C. (1996). *The Future of Capitalism: How Today's Economic Forces Shape Tomorrow's World.* New York: William Morrow.

United Nations Conference on Trade and Development (1995). *World Investment Report 1995.* Geneva: UN.

United Nations Conference on Trade and Development (1998). *World Investment Report 1998: Trends and Determinants.* Geneva: UN.

Vernon, R. (1966). "International investment and international trade in the product cycle," *Quarterly Journal of Economics,* 80: 190-207.

Vernon, R. (1979). "The product cycle hypothesis in the new international environment," *Oxford Bulletin of Economics and Statistics,* 41: 255-268.

World Bank (1993). *The East Asian Miracle: Economic Growth and Public Policy.* New York: Oxford University Press.

World Bank (2001). "Globalization, growth, and poverty." World Bank policy research report, December.

Yamazawa, I. (1990). *Economic Development and International Trade: The Japanese Model.* Honolulu: East-West Center.

Zhang, K.H. (2001). "Does foreign direct investment promote economic growth? Evidence from East Asia and Latin America," *Contemporary Economic Policy,* 19 (2): 175-185.

Chapter 4

The Relative Efficiencies of U.S. and Pacific Rim Industries: The Case of the Four Dragons

Parviz Asheghian

INTRODUCTION

The onset of the financial crisis in Asia was one of the most notable—and troubling—developments in the world economy during 1997. The currency crisis began in midyear and deepened over the remainder of the year, permeating the real sectors of the distressed economies as well as the rest of the globe. Nevertheless, Asia as a whole continued to experience economic growth. In 2000, largely driven by strong exports to the United States, real gross domestic product growth across Asia (excluding Japan) averaged about 7.3 percent. Most notably among these nations, Singapore, South Korea, Hong Kong, and Taiwan, facetiously referred to as the "four dragons" or the "Gang of Four," continued to forge ahead with impressive economic performance and maintained their status as models of economic development by other developing nations. Table 4.1 provides data on the economic growth of these nations and the United States for the years 1999 and 2000. According to this table the average combined rate of economic growth of these nations as a group was 6.25 percent in 1999, which was higher than the growth rate of 4.08 percent for the United States in the same year. What is even more remarkable is that the projected average rate of growth of these coun-

Globalization and East Asia: Opportunities and Challenges

doi:10.1300/5463_04

TABLE 4.1. The Rate of Growth of Real GDP for the United States and the Four Dragons

Nations	1999	2000
The United States	4.08	4.14
Hong Kong	3.00	10.15
Singapore	5.40	10.10
South Korea	10.90	8.80
Taiwan	6.00	6.00

Source: Data for the Four Tigers were derived from Deutsche Bank Research On Line, and data for the United States were derived from Economagic. Com: Economic Time Series Page On Line.

tries is 8.85 percent, which is much higher than the United States' rate of growth of 4.14 percent.

Given the unprecedented growth of the four dragons (FD), there is a growing interest to examine the relative efficiencies, measured in terms of profitability, of the United States and FD industries. Although the literature on the measurement of efficiency of U.S. industries is extensive (see for example, Buckley et al., 1978; Shapiro, 1983; Kumar, 1984; Haar, 1972), one area of research that has not attracted the attention that it deserves is the overall efficiency of FD industries as compared to U.S. industries. The purpose of this chapter is to evaluate the relative efficiency and leveraging of assets of eight matched-pair U.S. and FD industries.

In this study, the notion of efficiency is defined in terms of profitability and is measured by return on equity (net income divided by equity, where equity is the cash value of the stock of each firm), and the leveraging of an asset is measured by asset turnover (revenue divided by total assets). In addition to primary measures, two secondary measures exist. Return on investment is used as a somewhat inferior measure of efficiency and is considered to have a minor importance in a theoretical framework. The equity multiplier (asset divided by equity) is a secondary measure of leveraging, wherein the greater the leveraging, the higher the equity multiplier.

The following five financial ratios are used in the analysis:

1. ROE: Return on Equity (net income/common equity);
2. ROA: Return on Assets (net income/assets);
3. ROS: Return on Sales (net income/total sales);
4. ATO: Asset Turnover (sales/assets); and
5. EM: Equity Margin (assets/equity).

The efficiency ratios that include ROS, ROA, and ROE show the combined effects of liquidity, asset management, and debt management on operating results. ATO ratio measures how effectively the firms use their total assets, and EM ratio portrays a firm's financial leverage.

THE LIMITATIONS OF THE STUDY AND THE SAMPLE SIZE

The problems of measurement in comparative analysis have been discussed by a number of researchers (Lary, 1968; Dunning, 1970). Measurement problems, as related to interindustry comparison, center around two main issues: First, the choice of industries, and second the kind of data. As for the first issue, ideally the two groups of industries should be similar with regard to product heterogeneity and size. They should also operate in a similar environment and market structure. However, the limitations of the sample size in most of the empirical studies call for restriction in choosing industries for comparison.

The second question has to do with accounting differences that exist between countries. These differences might lead to biases in the measurement of the ratios employed in the analysis. For example, measurement problems could arise because the two countries may use different procedures for the valuation of income-producing assets that affects income statements. In one country, marketable securities may be treated at the lower of cost or market value, whereas cost method could be utilized in another country. These differences might affect comparability of the two countries with regard to asset turnover and profitability ratios.

In the case of our study, both the FD and the United States adhere to the strict application of historical cost and conservatism in their accounting practices. Revenue recognition between the two countries' systems is comparable. As a result, the comparison of financial ratios in this study should not be affected significantly. Following the most acceptable criteria set by empirical studies, each pair of industry chosen in this study consists of one U.S. industry and one FD industry producing similar products and having approximately the same size.

All the data for the study were compiled by the author from the *Global Company Handbook* (CIFAR, 1996), *CD Rom Disclosure/ World Scope* (1998), and *Mergent Online* (www.fisonline.com). These include asset, equity, sales, and net income for eight U.S. industries and the eight FD industries for the years 1983 through 2000. Table 4.2 shows the industrial sectors of these matched pairs.

THE TESTING OF HYPOTHESES

Paired comparison is used to compare the relative efficiency and the leveraging of assets of U.S. and FD industries. Five hypotheses are tested on the basis of ROE, ROA, ROS, ATO, and EM. In all of these cases the null hypothesis states that no difference exists between U.S. and FD industries with regard to the ratio that is being compared. The alternative hypothesis explains that these ratios are higher for U.S. industries as compared to FD industries. Since matched pairs are used, an appropriate test is the Wilcoxon matched-pairs signed-rank test. This test is ideal because it is a nonparametric test, not requiring a large sample size. The Wilcoxon test gives more weight to pairs that show a large difference than to pairs indicating

TABLE 4.2. The Industrial Sectors of the Matched Pairs Used in This Study

Pair Number	Industrial Sector
1	Banking
2	Chemical
3	Food & beverage
4	Construction
5	Metal
6	Electronics
7	Textiles
8	Auto

small ones. In this manner the Wilcoxon test is similar to the t-test but it deals with ordinal data. This test is one of the most powerful nonparametric test. Even for small samples its power is about 95 percent of that of the t-tests (Asheghian and Foote, 1985; Mendenhall et al., 1977; Siegel, 1956).

To conduct the Wilcoxon test, differences between each pair, with regard to the ratios that are being compared, are computed first. Then these differences are ranked on the basis of their absolute values. Next, the sum of the ranks of the negative differences is used as the test statistic T.

The results of the test are shown in Tables 4.3 through 4.7. The values of the test statistics (T) in these tables indicate that all of the null hypotheses can be rejected at the 5 percent level of significance.

TABLE 4.3. The Wilcoxon Test for the Comparison of the ROE Ratios of U.S. and FD Industries

INDUSTRY	$\sum_{i=1}^{n} ROEUS_{KI}$	$\sum_{i=1}^{n} ROEFD_{KI}$	DK	RD	NRS
1	16.00	11.25	4.75	4.00	
2	28.30	17.28	11.02	7.00	
3	8.30	9.18	–0.88	1.00	1.00
4	8.90	13.03	–4.13	3.00	3.00
5	1.00	14.00	–13.00	8.00	8.00
6	12.60	13.88	–1.28	20.0	2.00
7	24.08	15.78	8.30	5.00	
8	15.03	4.08	10.95	6.00	
					T = 14

Sources: Calculated from the data provided by CIFAR (1996) Disclosure/World Scope (1998), and Mergent Online.

Note: $ROEUS_{KI}$ = ROE of the kth U.S. industry in the ith year
$ROEFD_{KI}$ = ROE of the kth FD's industry in the ith year
$i = 1 \ldots 8$; $k = 1 \ldots 7$

$$DK = \sum_{i=1}^{n} ROEUS_{SI} - \sum_{i=1}^{n} ROEFD_{KI}$$

RD = Rank of DK
NRS = Negative rank sum

TABLE 4.4. The Wilcoxon Test for the Comparison of the ROA Ratios of U.S. and FD Industries

INDUSTRY	$\sum_{i=1}^{n} ROAUS_{KI}$	$\sum_{i=1}^{n} ROAFD_{KI}$	DK	RD	NRS
1	3.90	2.60	1.30	1.00	
2	7.70	9.35	–1.65	2.00	2.00
3	10.20	5.23	4.97	5.00	
4	0.90	4.60	–3.70	3.00	3.00
5	–1.50	5.34	–6.93	6.00	
6	5.60	13.70	–8.10	8.00	8.00
7	14.40	6.58	7.82	7.00	
8	5.34	1.52	–3.82	4.00	
					T = 13

Sources: Calculated from the data provided by CIFAR (1996), *Disclosure/ World Scope* (1998), and Mergent Online.

Note: $ROAUS_{KI}$ = ROA of the kth U.S. industry in the ith year
$ROAFDA_{KI}$ = ROA of the kth FD industry in the ith year
$i = 1 \ldots 8$; $k = 1 \ldots 7$

$$DK = \sum_{i=1}^{n} ROAUS_{KI} - \sum_{i=1}^{n} ROADFD_{KI}$$

RD = Rank of DK
NRS = Negative rank sum

TABLE 4.5. The Wilcoxon Test for the Comparison of the ROS Ratios of U.S. and FD Industries

Industry	$\sum_{i=1}^{n} ROSUS_{KI}$	$\sum_{i=1}^{n} ROSFD_{KI}$	DK	RD	NRS
1	5.40	21.05	–15.65	7.00	7.00
2	10.70	12.74	–2.04	1.00	1.00
3	147.40	9.25	138.15	8.00	
4	2.24	8.78	–6.54	5.00	5.00
5	7.65	–4.00	11.65	6.00	
6	8.90	5.70	3.20	2.00	
7	3.82	9.05	–5.32	4.00	4.00

TABLE 4.5 *(continued)*

Industry	$\sum_{i=1}^{n} ROSUS_{KI}$	$\sum_{i=1}^{n} ROSFD_{KI}$	DK	RD	NRS
8	0.71	4.32	–3.61	3.00	3.00
					T = 20

Sources: Calculated from the data provided by CIFAR (1996), *Disclosure/ World Scope* (1998), and Mergent Online.

Note: $ROSUS_{KI}$ = ROS of the kth U.S. industry in the ith year
$ROSFD_{KI}$ = ROS of the kth FD industry in the ith year
$i = 1 \ldots 8;\ k = 1 \ldots 7$

$$DK = \sum_{i=1}^{n} ROSUS_{KI} - \sum_{i=1}^{n} ROSFD_{KI}$$

RD = Rank of DK
NRS = Negative rank sum

TABLE 4.6. The Wilcoxon Test for the Comparison of the ATO Ratios of U.S. and FD Industries

Industry	$\sum_{i=1}^{n} ATOUS_{KI}$	$\sum_{i=1}^{n} ATOFD_{KI}$	DK	RD	NRS
1	0.72	0.12	0.60	4.00	
2	0.72	0.73	–0.01	1.00	1.00
3	0.07	0.57	–0.50	3.00	3.00
4	0.40	0.52	–0.12	2.00	2.00
5	–0.20	–1.36	1.16	5.00	4.00
6	0.63	2.40	–1.77	6.00	6.00
7	3.77	0.73	3.04	7.00	
8	7.52	0.53	7.17	8.00	
					T = 16

Sources: Calculated from the data provided by CIFAR (1996), *Disclosure/ World Scope* (1998), and Mergent Online.

Note: $ATOUS_{KI}$ = ATO of the kth U.S. industry in the ith year
$ATOFD_{KI}$ = ATO of the kth FD industry in the ith year
$i = 1 \ldots 8;\ k = 1 \ldots 7$

$$DK = \sum_{i=1}^{n} ATOUS_{KI} - \sum_{i=1}^{n} ATOFD_{KI}$$

RD = Rank of DK
NRS = Negative rank sum

TABLE 4.7. The Wilcoxon Test for the Comparison of the EM Ratios of U.S. and FD Industries

Industry	$\sum_{i=1}^{n} EMUS_{KI}$	$\sum_{i=1}^{n} EMFD_{KI}$	DK	RD	NRS
1	4.10	4.33	–0.22	2.00	2.00
2	3.68	1.85	1.83	6.00	
3	0.81	1.76	–0.94	4.00	4.00
4	9.89	2.83	7.06	8.00	
5	–0.67	2.58	–3.24	7.00	7.00
6	2.25	1.01	1.24	5.00	
7	1.67	2.40	–0.73	3.00	3.00
8	2.81	2.68	0.13	1.00	2.00
					T = 18

Sources: Calculated from the data provided by CIFAR (1996), *Disclosure/World Scope* (1998), and Mergent Online.

Note: $EMUS_{KI}$ = EM of the kth U.S. industry in the ith year
$EMFD_{KI}$ = EM of the kth FD industry in the ith year
$i = 1 \ldots 8; k = 1 \ldots 7$
$DK = \sum_{i=1}^{n} EMUS_{KI} - \sum_{i=1}^{n} EMFD_{KI}$
RD = Rank of DK
NRS = Negative rank sum

CONCLUDING REMARKS

To the extent that the data are not biased in the context of the limitations set in this study, the foregoing analysis suggests the following conclusions:

1. The absence of statically significance differences between the ROE of the U.S. and the ROE of the FD industries suggests that they are similar to each other with respect to their efficiency, as measured by the rate of return on equity.

2. The absence of statically significant differences between the ROA of the U.S. and the ROA of the FD industries suggests that they are similar to each other in terms of asset utilization.
3. The absence of statistically significant differences between the ROS of U.S. industries and similar FD industries implies that U.S. industries and FD industries are similar with respect to the efficiency by which they produce their products.
4. The absence of statistically significant differences between the ATO of U.S. industries and similar FD industries implies that U.S. industries and FD industries are similar with respect to the efficiency by which they utilize their plants.
5. The absence of statistically significance differences between the EM of U.S. industries and similar FD industries implies that these industries are similar with respect to their financial leveraging.

Given the aforementioned results, it is no wonder that the four dragons had been forging ahead with such an impressive growth rate, far exceeding those of Japan, the United States, and Europe.

This study examined the comparative efficiencies of the FD and the U.S. industries in terms of profitability, portraying the relative effectiveness of the executives of these industries in managing their finances. It would be helpful to compare production efficiencies of the FD with the U.S. industries to see whether FD industries are as efficient as their counterparts in the United States in managing their production process. This would require the measurement of total factor productivity, capital productivity, and labor productivity, and could be the subject of further research in this area.

REFERENCES

Asheghian, P. and Foote, W. (1985). The productivities of U.S. multinationals in the industrial sector of the Canadian economy. *Eastern Economic Journal,* April-June, pp. 123-133.

Buckley, P., Dunning, J.H., and Pearce, R.D. (1978). The influence of firm size, nationality, and degree of multinationality on the growth and profitability of the world's largest firms. *Welwirtschaftliches Archiv* 114, No. 2, pp. 243-257.

CIFAR (1996). *Global Company Handbook.* Princeton, NJ: Center for International Finance and Research.

Deutsche Bank Research. Online database. Available at http://www.dbresearch.com/.

Disclosure/World Scope (1998). CD-ROM. W/D Partners.

Dunning, J.H. (1970). *Studies in International Investment.* London: George Allen and Unwin.

Economagic: Economic Time Series Page. Online database. Available at http://www.economagic.com.

Haar, J. (1972). A comparative analysis of the profitability performance of the largest U.S., European, and Japanese multinational enterprises. *Management International Review,* Vol. 54, pp. 130-140.

Lary, H.B. (1968). *Imports of Manufactures from Less Developed Countries.* New York: Columbia Press.

Mendenhall, W., McClave, J.T., and Ramey, M. (1977). *Statistics for Psychology,* 2nd ed. Boston, MA: Dubury Press.

Mergent Online. Online database. Available at http://www.fisonline.com.

Shapiro, A.C. (1983). *Multinational Financial Management.* London: Allyn and Bacon.

Sigel, S. (1956). *Nonparametric Statistics for the Behavioral Sciences.* New York: McGraw-Hill.

Chapter 5

Asian Structural Differences and Comparative Economic Performance

Vincent Dropsy
Dennis Pollard

INTRODUCTION

Following three decades of exceptional economic growth, most Asian nations suffered a severe financial and economic crisis in 1997-1998. A large body of literature has been dedicated to understand the causes of this new type of crisis (cf. Cartapanis et al., 2002; IMF, 2000; World Bank, 1998), and it appears that "a combination of macroeconomic imbalances, external developments, and weakness in financial and corporate systems" (IMF, 2000) is responsible for the severity of the Asian crisis. Although the economic recovery in the region has been relatively strong in aggregate terms, it has also varied on an individual country basis and depending on the topical indicators.

The objective of this chapter is to shed some light on the economic and political differences that could explain and potentially predict the variations in the speed and magnitude of economic recovery between major Asian countries. First, some groupings are offered to reflect these structural differences: (1) the "pragmatic" group (China, Hong Kong, Taiwan, Singapore); (2) the "oligopolistic" group (Japan, South Korea); (3) the "authoritarian" group (Indonesia, Malaysia); and (4) the "versatile" group (Thailand, the Philippines). Second, various models are proposed to test the effects of structural differences on standards of living and economic growth. Third, these models are estimated on more than 100 nations (using cross-sectional regressions or panel error correction models). Finally, out-of-sample forecasts (1995-2000) of

Globalization and East Asia: Opportunities and Challenges

doi:10.1300/5463_05

short-term and long-term economic growth rates for Asian countries are generated and compared with actual growth rates to come to a conclusion about the nature of the Asian crisis and the potential for a sustained recovery.

STRUCTURAL DIFFERENCES IN ASIA

Despite major differences in economic structure, political institutions, and cultural attributes, most Asian nations have been victims of the Asian crisis. However, the severity of the economic and financial crisis, as well as the nature of the recovery, has varied from country to country. Zaman (2000) argues that "the recovery of the Asian economies is contingent upon the restoration of growth of the Japanese economy" (p. 180). DeOcampo (2000), chairman of Asia-Pacific Economic Cooperation (APEC) Finance Ministers Meeting in 1997, wonders whether the economic recovery is sustainable. Some of the insights in this chapter come from discussions with this former "Finance Minister of the Year" (from *Euromoney* in 1995 and 1996, and from *Asiamoney* in 1997). It appears to Park (2001) that Asian countries are turning to a strategy of "growing out," rather than "restructuring out," with the risk of a future economic slowdown. Gray (2000) also highlights the role of socioeconomic (e.g., legal, educational, technological, financial, cultural, governmental, political) infrastructures for economic development.

In an effort to better understand the differences in sustainability of economic growth between the major Asian countries, the latter are categorized into the following "business thinking" groups:

1. the "pragmatic" group (China, Hong Kong, Taiwan, Singapore), which is dominated by the Chinese approach to business, where small and medium enterprises, often family ventures, are preferred, and where discipline, order, but also flexibility and pragmatism are prevalent;
2. the "oligopolistic" group (Japan, South Korea), which is characterized by large conglomerates, where companies, banks and the government often work hand in hand to create economies of scale and thus oligopolies;
3. the "authoritarian" group (Indonesia, Malaysia), whose "dirigiste" governments have so far successfully united and con-

trolled their respective countries, which are rich in ethnic diversity and in economic resources (e.g., oil);

4. the "versatile" group (Thailand, the Philippines), which combines Westernized and traditional values, blends democracy and corruption, with easy adaptability.

These oversimplified groups give a preliminary insight of the economic, political, and cultural differences between Asian nations before refining the analysis of individual and group characteristics. To gain a better understanding of the strengths and weaknesses of these various countries or groups, a series of indicators are presented as statistical evidence to support this analysis before regression analysis is performed on panel data of more than 100 countries.

Most Asian economies experienced very strong growth over the three decades preceding the Asian crisis in 1997-1998. The traditional economic indicator of "per capita real GDP growth" in Table 5.1 reflects this exceptional performance, with some notable exceptions: the Chinese economy began to grow very rapidly only after liberalization in 1978-1979, and the Filipino economy is still functioning below par. The data also clearly shows the collapse in economic growth due to the Asian financial crisis. However, China has not been significantly affected by the Asian crisis (due to strict capital controls) and has had the best record of growth in the first five years of the twenty-first century.

When analyzed in groupings, the pragmatic (Chinese) group also appears to have been the least affected by the crisis (with an average 0.3 percent positive growth in 1998, and the best ranking in terms of growth between 1996 and 2000), although per capita real GDP growth fell by 5 percent between 1997 and 1998. The oligopolistic group (Japan, Korea) ranked second (with an average 5.1 percent drop in per capita output in 1998). The versatile group (Thailand, Philippines) came third (with an average fall of 7.0 percent of its per capita real GDP), whereas the authoritarian group (Indonesia, Malaysia) was the hardest hit (with an average 11.5 percent decline in its per capita output).

In terms of economic recovery, the Chinese thinking group grew 4 percent in 1999 and 7.7 percent in 2000 (with the best record among the four groups). The oligopolistic group had a sharp turnaround of 9.6 percent (as the average growth went from –5.1 percent to +4.5 percent), but the year 2000 brought about an average growth of 3.6

TABLE 5.1. Per Capita Real GDP Annual Growth and Ranking

Country	1976-80	1981-85	1986-90	1991-95	1996	1997	1998	1999	2000	Ranking (1996-2000)
China	4.1%	9.4%	6.2%	10.9%	8.5%	7.8%	6.8%	6.1%	7.1%	1
Hong Kong	9.1%	4.1%	6.7%	3.8%	2.0%	2.0%	–7.3%	1.8%	10.0%	6
Singapore	6.2%	3.8%	6.4%	6.8%	5.3%	6.1%	–1.6%	3.5%	8.1%	3
Taiwan	8.7%	5.4%	8.1%	6.0%	5.1%	5.5%	3.4%	4.8%	5.7%	2
Average	7.1%	5.7%	6.8%	6.9%	5.2%	5.3%	0.3%	4.0%	7.7%	G1
Japan	3.5%	2.7%	4.2%	1.1%	4.8%	1.3%	–2.8%	0.1%	1.1%	8
Korea	5.2%	6.6%	7.3%	4.3%	3.4%	1.7%	–7.4%	9.0%	6.1%	5
Average	4.4%	4.6%	5.7%	2.7%	4.1%	1.5%	–5.1%	4.5%	3.6%	G2
Indonesia	5.7%	3.8%	5.4%	6.1%	6.2%	3.1%	–14.6%	–1.3%	2.6%	10
Malaysia	7.0%	3.8%	5.9%	8.5%	8.8%	6.3%	–8.3%	4.9%	7.1%	4
Average	6.3%	3.8%	5.6%	7.3%	7.5%	4.7%	–11.5%	1.8%	4.9%	G3
Philippines	3.8%	–3.7%	1.8%	–0.3%	3.4%	2.7%	–3.1%	0.8%	1.5%	7
Thailand	5.6%	3.6%	8.7%	7.5%	5.3%	–2.3%	–10.9%	3.4%	3.6%	9
Average	4.7%	–0.1%	5.2%	3.6%	4.3%	0.2%	–7.0%	2.1%	2.6%	G4

Source: World Bank, *World Economic Report.* Various issues.

percent (less than one-half of the Chinese thinking group). The authoritarian group had an average turnaround of 13.3 percent, (from a 11.5 percent drop in 1998 to a 1.8 percent rise in 1999), and the year 2000 brought an average increase of 4.9 percent (still well below the Chinese thinking group). The versatile group had the slowest turnaround with an increase of average per capita real GDP growth by 9.2 percent (from –7.0 percent in 1998 to +2.1 percent in 1999), and the year 2000 returned to a more normal growth rate of 2.6 percent.

Differences in standards of living among nations are often analyzed by comparing their per capita GDP, but one potential pitfall comes from the translation of that economic variable in the same currency (usually the U.S. dollar). It is well known that exchange rates are often misaligned, sometimes for long periods. However, the World Bank provides estimates of per capita real GDP translated in

U.S. dollars at purchasing power parity, derived from extensive international price comparisons. Table 5.2 illustrates the large differences between such appropriate measurement (first columns) and per capita real GDP translated at 1995 exchange rates (last columns), especially for poor countries. Economic theory predicts that poorer nations will grow faster than richer nations when converging exponentially toward their steady state. Yet this "catch-up" effect is not obvious for most countries, and even less for groupings when comparing their ranking in Tables 5.1 and 5.2. Therefore, factors other than initial standards of living must also affect economic growth. Some of these factors are examined later.

TABLE 5.2. Per Capita Real GDP (in US$) and Ranking

	Translated in US$ at PPP (World Bank)							Ranking (in 1995 US$)	
Country	**1975**	**1980**	**1985**	**1990**	**1995**	**1999**	**Raking (1996-99)**	**1999**	**1996-99**
China	$273	$465	$839	$1,400	$2,681	$3,617	10	$769	10
Hong Kong	$3,234	$6,896	$9,730	$16,665	$22,166	$22,090	2	$22,185	3
Singapore	$2,856	$5,894	$7,602	$12,843	$19,406	$20,767	3	$26,460	2
Taiwan	$964	$2,344	$3,297	$8,111	$12,686	$13,235	5	$14,216	4
Average	$1,832	$3,900	$5,367	$9,755	$14,235	$14,927	G2	$15,907	G2
Japan	$5,955	$9,885	$13,079	$19,913	$23,725	$24,898	1	$42,318	1
Korea	$1,613	$2,988	$4,792	$8,923	$13,759	$15,712	4	$12,086	5
Average	$3,784	$6,437	$8,935	$14,418	$18,742	$20,305	G1	$27,202	G1
Indonesia	$468	$871	$1,244	$1,960	$2,911	$2,857	8	$962	9
Malaysia	$1,278	$2,412	$3,280	$4,763	$7,491	$8,209	6	$4,526	6
Average	$873	$1,642	$2,262	$3,361	$5,201	$5,533	G3	$2,744	G3
Philippines	$809	$1,482	$2,072	$3,863	$6,260	$6,132	7	$1,138	8
Thailand	$1,469	$2,459	$2,435	$3,368	$3,633	$3,805	9	$2,717	7
Average	$1,139	$1,971	$2,253	$3,615	$4,947	$4,969	G4	$1,928	G4

Source: World Bank, *World Development Report*. Various issues.

The Human Development Index (HDI, from the United Nations), presented in Table 5.3, is often cited as a better indicator of standards of living, since it embodies not only per capita GDP, but also life expectancy and literacy. This multifaceted index also reflects the social efforts (e.g., public education) to create an atmosphere for development. A brief analysis of these results indicates that the government-aided economies of the oligopolistic group have the resources to focus on human development with large social commitments from both the private and public sectors. The pragmatic group, even including mainland China (last in the individual ranking), is second in the ranking on human development, with both limited government involvement and high private sector involvement in Hong Kong and Singapore (and probably in Taiwan, though figures are not available). The versatile group is now moving more toward this development

TABLE 5.3. Human Development Index (0 = lowest, 1 = highest)

Country	1975	1980	1985	1990	1995	1996	1997	1998	1999	Ranking (1996-99)
China	0.52	0.55	0.59	0.62	0.68	0.68	0.70	0.71	0.72	10
Hong Kong	0.75	0.79	0.82	0.86	0.88	0.88	0.88	0.87	0.88	2
Singapore	0.72	0.75	0.78	0.82	0.86	0.73	0.74	0.88	0.88	5
Taiwan	NA	NA	NA	NA	NA	NA	NA	NA	NA	6
Average	0.67	0.70	0.73	0.77	0.80	0.76	0.77	0.82	0.82	G2
Japan	0.85	0.88	0.89	0.91	0.92	0.92	0.92	0.92	0.93	1
Korea	0.69	0.73	0.77	0.81	0.85	0.87	0.89	0.85	0.88	3
Average	0.77	0.80	0.83	0.86	0.89	0.90	0.91	0.89	0.90	G1
Indonesia	0.47	0.53	0.58	0.62	0.66	0.67	0.68	0.67	0.68	9
Malaysia	0.61	0.66	0.69	0.72	0.76	0.84	0.85	0.77	0.77	4
Average	0.54	0.59	0.64	0.67	0.71	0.75	0.77	0.72	0.73	G4
Philippines	0.65	0.68	0.69	0.72	0.73	0.76	0.77	0.74	0.75	7
Thailand	0.66	0.68	0.69	0.72	0.74	0.75	0.75	0.74	0.76	8
Average	0.65	0.68	0.69	0.72	0.74	0.75	0.76	0.74	0.75	G3

Source: United Nations, *Human Development Index.* Various years.

effort, with Thailand enacting laws that offer free education to the ninth grade (future to high school) and the Philippines attempting to reduce corruption so that monies will be available for education, training, and development. The authoritarian group continues to struggle with society mores somewhat linked to past traditions that impede development, particularly relative to women. These conditions may have contributed to the deeper plunge and somewhat slower recovery and growth rate of Indonesia, although political factors played an important role.

Human capital is an important engine of growth and development. Literacy (one of the components of the HDI), is a good proxy for human growth, and is illustrated in Table 5.4. Most Asian nations and groups have made tremendous progress in this area. Only China, Indonesia, and Malaysia have not yet reached the 90 percent literacy ratio, although it appears to be a question of years rather than decades.

TABLE 5.4. Literacy (% of the population above 15 years old)

Country	1975	1980	1985	1990	1995	1996	1997	1998	1999	Ranking (1996-99)
China	58%	66%	72%	77%	81%	82%	82%	83%	84%	10
Hong Kong	82%	86%	88%	90%	92%	92%	93%	93%	93%	6
Singapore	79%	83%	86%	89%	91%	91%	92%	92%	92%	7
Taiwan (est.)	81%	85%	88%	91%	92%	94%	95%	95%	95%	4
Average	73%	78%	82%	87%	89%	90%	90%	91%	91%	G3
Japan (est.)	99%	99%	99%	99%	99%	99%	99%	99%	99%	1
Korea	90%	93%	95%	96%	97%	97%	97%	98%	98%	2
Average	95%	96%	97%	97%	98%	98%	98%	98%	98%	G1
Indonesia	63%	69%	75%	80%	84%	84%	85%	86%	86%	9
Malaysia	65%	71%	77%	81%	84%	85%	86%	86%	87%	8
Average	64%	70%	76%	80%	84%	85%	85%	86%	87%	G4
Philippines	87%	89%	91%	93%	94%	94%	95%	95%	95%	5
Thailand	85%	88%	90%	92%	94%	94%	95%	95%	95%	3
Average	86%	88%	91%	92%	94%	94%	95%	95%	95%	G2

Source: World Bank, *World Development Report.* Various issues.

In Table 5.5, a compilation of key factors results in a single index of world competitiveness (created by the Institute for Management Development) averaged over the period 1995-1999. Again, the desire to be competitive and succeed relates to the methods in which countries and cultures view their needs to compete in all areas of human endeavor. Clearly, the pragmatic (Chinese) group is the most competitive group in terms of the weighted average key index and with the three most competitive economies (Singapore, Hong Kong, and Taiwan) in Asia. This shows the ability of the culture to adapt and meet competitive situations in both domestic and international settings. Japan and Korea, perhaps due to its "group societal" structure, are less competitive and more "group" dependent. The two least competitive groups appear to be slower in adopting a competitive attitude relative to most key elements required in maintaining a competitive edge.

TABLE 5.5. World Competitiveness Index (0 = lowest , 1 = highest) and Ranking

	World Competitiveness		Economic Performance		Government Efficiency		Business Efficiency		Infrastructure	
Country	**1995-99**	**Rank**	**1995-99**	**Rank**	**1995-99**	**Rank**	**1995-99**	**Rank**	**1995-99**	**Rank**
China	0.41	6	0.90	1	0.40	5	0.25	8	0.24	7
Hong Kong	0.86	2	0.71	4	0.95	2	0.80	2	0.72	2
Singapore	0.96	1	0.90	2	0.98	1	0.86	1	0.94	1
Taiwan	0.64	3	0.53	6	0.62	3	0.66	3	0.59	4
Average	0.74	G1	0.84	G1	0.78	G1	0.64	G1	0.63	G1
Japan	0.53	4	0.76	3	0.38	7	0.40	5	0.66	3
Korea	0.31	7	0.52	7	0.20	9	0.31	6	0.27	6
Average	0.42	G2	0.64	G2	0.29	G4	0.36	G2	0.47	G2
Indonesia	0.07	10	0.18	10	0.15	10	0.06	10	0.03	10
Malaysia	0.50	5	0.67	5	0.63	3	0.43	4	0.38	5
Average	0.29	G3	0.42	G3	0.39	G2	0.24	G3	0.20	G3
Philippines	0.28	8	0.28	9	0.38	6	0.25	7	0.21	8
Thailand	0.23	9	0.44	8	0.34	8	0.13	9	0.17	9
Average	0.26	G4	0.36	G4	0.36	G3	0.19	G4	0.19	G4

Increasing evidence demonstrates that the economic performance of a country is also related to the well-functioning of its markets. Table 5.6 presents an index of economic freedom (from the Fraser Institute) as a measure of governmental and societal control. Once again, even with the addition of mainland China (last in the ranking, but progressing), the pragmatic group leads the oligopolistic group, closely followed by the versatile group.

In terms of the bitter with the sweet, Table 5.7 introduces the corruption perception index (from Transparency International), for which the group ranking is similar (high freedom corresponding to low corruption). It is interesting to note that the past 20 years during which China has experienced high growth, have also been a period of progress in terms of economic freedom and reduction in corruption. It appears, therefore, that pragmatism may be more powerful than ideology in the long run.

TABLE 5.6. Economic Freedom Index (0 = control, 1 = freedom)

Country	1975	1980	1985	1990	1995	1996	1997	1998	1999	2000	Ranking (1995-99)
China	0.20	0.32	0.43	0.37	0.51	NA	NA	NA	0.58	NA	10
Hong Kong	0.94	0.97	0.93	0.92	0.97	NA	NA	NA	0.94	NA	1
Singapore	0.76	0.80	0.84	0.90	0.94	NA	NA	NA	0.93	NA	2
Taiwan	0.60	0.68	0.71	0.74	0.74	NA	NA	NA	0.73	NA	5
Average	0.62	0.70	0.73	0.73	0.81	NA	NA	NA	0.82	NA	G1
Japan	0.69	0.75	0.76	0.81	0.81	NA	NA	NA	0.79	NA	3
Korea	0.57	0.58	0.58	0.63	0.70	NA	NA	NA	0.71	NA	8
Average	0.63	0.66	0.67	0.72	0.75	NA	NA	NA	0.75	NA	G1
Indonesia	0.50	0.52	0.62	0.67	0.68	NA	NA	NA	0.62	NA	9
Malaysia	0.63	0.70	0.70	0.75	0.74	NA	NA	NA	0.67	NA	6
Average	0.56	0.61	0.66	0.71	0.71	NA	NA	NA	0.65	NA	G4
Philippines	0.47	0.50	0.50	0.56	0.72	NA	NA	NA	0.76	NA	4
Thailand	0.56	0.58	0.60	0.66	0.73	NA	NA	NA	0.68	NA	7
Average	0.52	0.54	0.55	0.61	0.73	NA	NA	NA	0.72	NA	G3

TABLE 5.7. Corruption Perceptions Index (0 = corrupt, 1 = clean)

Country	1975	1980	1985	1990	1995	1996	1997	1998	1999	2000	Ranking (1996-2000)
China	NA	0.51	NA	0.47	0.29	0.35	0.34	0.31	0.35	0.35	7
Hong Kong	NA	0.74	NA	0.69	0.73	0.78	0.77	0.77	0.79	0.79	2
Singapore	NA	0.84	NA	0.92	0.87	0.91	0.91	0.91	0.92	0.92	1
Taiwan	NA	0.60	NA	0.51	0.50	0.53	0.56	0.55	0.59	0.59	4
Average	NA	0.70	NA	0.69	0.63	0.68	0.67	0.66	0.69	0.69	G1
Japan	NA	0.78	NA	0.73	0.66	0.58	0.60	0.64	0.71	0.71	3
Korea	NA	0.39	NA	0.35	0.43	0.42	0.38	0.40	0.42	0.42	6
Average	NA	0.58	NA	0.54	0.54	0.50	0.49	0.52	0.57	0.57	G2
Indonesia	NA	0.02	NA	0.06	0.27	0.20	0.17	0.17	0.19	0.19	10
Malaysia	NA	0.63	NA	0.51	0.50	0.53	0.51	0.48	0.50	0.50	5
Average	NA	0.32	NA	0.28	0.39	0.37	0.34	0.33	0.35	0.35	G3
Philippines	NA	0.10	NA	0.20	0.31	0.33	0.36	0.28	0.29	0.29	9
Thailand	NA	0.24	NA	0.19	0.31	0.30	0.32	0.32	0.32	0.32	8
Average	NA	0.17	NA	0.19	0.31	0.32	0.34	0.30	0.31	0.31	G4

METHODOLOGY

New growth theories, surveyed by Temple (1999), stress the role of knowledge and human capital accumulation, such as in the model introduced and tested by Mankiw et al. (1992). On a balanced growth path (indicated by a "*"), income per effective labor (stationary by definition) is given by:

$$\text{Log}(y^*) = \frac{\alpha}{1-\alpha-\beta}\text{Log}\left(\frac{s_K{}^*}{n^*+g^*+\delta}\right) + \frac{\beta}{1-\alpha-\beta}\text{Log}\left(\frac{s_H{}^*}{n^*+g^*+\delta}\right) \tag{5.1}$$

where y = output per unit of effective labor (Y/AL), n = growth rate of labor (L), g = growth rate of effectiveness of labor (A), s_K and s_H are the respective investment rates in physical capital (K) and human capital (H), and δ is the common depreciation rate.

This model has been extensively tested. For example, Bernanke and Gurkaynak (2001) conclude that "Mankiw, Romer and Weil's basic estimation framework is broadly consistent with any growth model that admits a balanced growth path—a category that includes virtually all the growth models in the literature." For econometric reasons, the following cross-sectional equation, derived from Equation 5.1, is regressed:

$$\text{Log}(y^*) = \text{A} + B_K \cdot \text{Log}(s_K^*) + B_H \cdot \text{Log}(s_H^*) + B_n \cdot \text{Log}(n^*) \quad (5.2)$$

Similarly, the effects of these explanatory variables (except human capital, which was not significant) on long-run economic growth g^* (annual average over 1975-1999) are also estimated:

$$g^* = \text{C} + D_K \cdot \text{Log}(s_K^*) + D_n \cdot \text{Log}(n^*) \quad (5.3)$$

Mankiw et al.'s (1992) model has also been augmented to take into account other factors in other studies. Barro (2001) confirms the importance of human capital, as well as policy and institutional factors. In addition, the effects of trade and financial liberalization have recently received a lot of attention. For example, Van den Berg and Lewer (2001) discover that trade promotes faster growth among developing countries when they follow their comparative advantage by importing capital goods and exporting consumption goods. Williamson and Mahar (1998) survey the theoretical literature on financial liberalization and conclude that some evidence exists of favorable effects of liberalization on economic growth. Kahn and Sendhadji (2000) review the empirical literature and find new evidence in favor of a positive effect of financial development on growth. Krol (2001) also finds evidence of a positive effect of capital account liberalization on economic growth. More general, Gwartney, Lawson, and Samida (2001) create (and update) an index of economic freedom and provide statistical evidence of its correlation with per capita GDP growth. This index of economic freedom covers seven major areas:

1. size of government,
2. economic structure and use of markets,

3. monetary policy and price stability,
4. freedom to use alternative currencies,
5. legal structure and security of private ownership,
6. freedom to trade with foreigners, and
7. freedom of exchange in capital markets.

Clark et al. (2001) also find evidence of a positive impact of economic freedom on economic growth and stability.

In the empirical analysis, the following four political (economy) factors are focused on:

1. trade openness (proxied by the sum of exports and imports of goods and services over GDP),
2. financial liberalization (proxied by the seventh component of the economic freedom index),
3. government size (proxied by the ratio of government consumption to GDP), and
4. legal structure (proxied by the fifth component of the economic freedom index).

The corruption perception index (cf. Table 5.7) is also considered, but the small number of observations and problem of multicollinearity prevented the inclusion of this factor in the empirical work. As a result, the following cross-sectional equations were originally planned for regression analysis:

$$\begin{aligned}\text{Log}(y^*) = A &+ B_{TO}\cdot\text{Trade Openness}^* \\ &+ B_{FL}\cdot\text{Financial Liberalization}^* \\ &+ B_{GS}\cdot\text{Government Size}^* + B_{LS}\cdot\text{Legal Structure}^*\end{aligned} \tag{5.4}$$

$$\begin{aligned}g^* = C &+ D_{TO}\cdot\text{Trade Openness}^* \\ &+ D_{FL}\cdot\text{Financial Liberalization}^* \\ &+ D_{GS}\cdot\text{Government Size}^* + D_{LS}\cdot\text{Legal Structure}^*\end{aligned} \tag{5.5}$$

However, it has been argued that the explanatory variables might be endogenous to the level of economic development (and/or the rate of economic growth). As a result, it is possible that the econometric estimates suffer from a simultaneity bias. In order to remedy this problem, panel data is used in the form of a dynamic error correction model (ECM), such as:

$$d\text{Log}(y_t) = \delta\cdot[\,\text{Log}(y_{t-1}) - \alpha - \beta\,\text{Log}(x_{t-1})\,] \tag{5.6}$$

where $\text{Log}(y^*) = \alpha + \beta\ \text{Log}(x^*)$ represents the long-run relationship (i.e., "cointegration" if the variables were not stationary), and the coefficient measures the speed of convergence toward this long-run equilibrium ("mean reversion").

Since the ECM's explanatory variables are all lagged, endogeneity problems disappear. The ECM structure also eliminates the econometric problems related to dynamic panel data estimation. Indeed, Breusch-Godfrey tests (not reported) confirm the absence of serial correlation in the models (after adding an autoregressive [AR] term). As a result, the panel data ECM versions of Equations 5.4 and 5.5 become:

$$\begin{aligned} d\text{Log}(y_t) = \delta\cdot[\,&\text{Log}(y_{t-1}) - A - B_{TO}\cdot\text{Trade Openness}_{t-1} \\ &- B_{FL}\cdot\text{Financial Liberalization}_{t-1} \\ &- B_{GS}\cdot\text{Government Size}_{t-1} \\ &- B_{LS}\cdot\text{Legal Structure}_{t-1}\,] + \text{AR}(1) \end{aligned} \tag{5.7}$$

$$\begin{aligned} g_t = \delta\cdot[\,&g_{t-1} - \text{C} - D_{TO}\cdot\text{Trade Openness}_{t-1} \\ &- D_{FL}\cdot\text{Financial Liberalization}_{t-1} \\ &- D_{GS}\cdot\text{Government Size}_{t-1} \\ &- D_{LS}\cdot\text{Legal Structure}_{t-1}\,] + \text{AR}(1) \end{aligned} \tag{5.8}$$

Other factors are also likely to significantly affect standards of living and economic growth. In particular, one can differentiate between the political (economy) factors examined earlier and the economic resources and policies investigated in the paragraphs to follow. Preliminary investigation revealed evidence of multicollinearity between these two types of factors (political versus economic), which prevented their simultaneous inclusion in the same equation.

First, countries have different endowments, which are important to develop comparative advantages, according to Heckscher-Ohlin theory, and thus to promote economic growth. For example, demographic factors, such as population density, affect the quantity of labor available and thus its price. One would expect that low-wage countries tend to grow faster ("catch-up" effect) and population density to be positively related to economic growth. The availability of primary resource endowments, such as arable land, mineral and oil reserves, and indirectly, a country's reliance on traded primary goods, can also influence its growth through price volatility. Since petroleum is a major energetic resource, we constructed a proxy for a nation's sensitivity to oil shocks, i.e., the product of real oil prices and the difference between the shares of oil in total exports and in total imports. When real oil prices rise, this index will rise for oil exporters and decrease for oil importers. As a result, this proxy should be positively correlated with economic growth. Another related factor is a country's vulnerability to terms of trade shocks, for which we built a proxy equal to the difference between the shares of agricultural and food products, fuel, and ores in total exports and in total imports. Greater reliance on trade of these primary goods tends to be the source of higher economic volatility and lower growth, leading to a negative correlation between the proxy and economic growth.

Second, national macroeconomic strategies and policies also impact standards of living and economic growth rates. In particular, financial vulnerabilities have become an important source of worries after a series of first-generation (1980s) and second-generation (1990s) financial crises. As a result, we constructed various indicators of financial weakness or strength. The ratio of short-term to total external debt is a proxy for the vulnerability to liquidity risk, and is expected to be negatively related to economic growth. Vice versa, the share of foreign direct investment (FDI) in total foreign investment is an indicator, which is expected to be positively correlated with growth, since FDI is much less volatile than its counterpart, foreign portfolio investment. A large amount of foreign exchange reserves, measured in months of imports, is a sign of financial strength when faced with speculative attacks, and is also expected to be positively correlated with growth. Fiscal and monetary policies, respectively proxied by the government's budget balance over GDP and the percentage change in money supply M2, tend to have opposite effects in the short and long run. In the short run, expansionary policies tend to boost GDP, but in the long run, they tend to raise interest and inflation rates, and thus lower GDP. Similarly, one can argue that trade barriers, proxied by the ratio of import duties to imports, tend to protect domestic industries and elevate GDP in the short run, but also reduce efficiency and GDP in the long run. Finally, the ratio of M3 to GDP is used as a proxy for dollarization (or exchange rate policy), and the debate over its benefits relative to its costs in terms of growth has restarted without a consensus emerging. Other economic factors were considered (age distribution, degree of urbanization, dependence on imported energy, eternal debt sustainability, nominal exchange rate flexibility, telecommunication infrastructure, openness to tourism), but were rejected due to lack of significance or collinearity.

For the same econometric reasons discussed earlier (for political factors), a panel ECM is used for the estimation of these economic effects on standards of living and economic growth:

$$\begin{aligned} d\text{Log}(y_t) = \delta\cdot[&\text{Log}(y_{t-1}) - \text{A} - B_{PD}\cdot\text{Population Density}_{t-1} \\ &- B_{SOS}\cdot\text{Sensitivity to Oil Shocks}_{t-1} \\ &- B_{TTV}\cdot\text{Terms of Trade Vulnerability}_{t-1} \\ &- B_{STD}\cdot\text{Short-Term Debt Ratio}_{t-1} \\ &- B_{FDI}\cdot\text{FDI Share}_{t-1} \\ &- B_{FXR}\cdot\text{FX Reserves/Imports}_{t-1} \\ &- B_{BB}\cdot\text{Budget Balance/GDP}_{t-1} \\ &- B_{DM2}\cdot d\text{Log(M2)}_{t-1} \\ &- B_{ID}\cdot\text{Import Duties/Imports}_{t-1} \\ &- B_{BMP}\cdot\text{FX Black Market Premium}_{t-1} \\ &- \text{B}_{\text{M3}}\cdot\text{M3/GDP}_{t-1}] + \text{AR(1)} \end{aligned} \tag{5.9}$$

$$\begin{aligned} g_t = \delta\cdot[&g_{t-1} - \text{C} - D_{PD}\cdot\text{Population Density}_{t-1} \\ &- D_{SOS}\cdot\text{Sensitivity to Oil Shocks}_{t-1} \\ &- D_{TTV}\cdot\text{Terms of Trade Vulnerability}_{t-1} \\ &- D_{STD}\cdot\text{Short-Term Debt Ratio}_{\text{t}-1} \\ &- D_{FDI}\cdot\text{FDI Share}_{t-1} - D_{FXR}\cdot\text{FX Reserves/Imports}_{t-1} \\ &- D_{BB}\cdot\text{Budget Balance/GDP}_{t-1} \\ &- D_{DM2}\cdot d\text{Log(M2)}_{t-1} - D_{ID}\cdot\text{Import Duties/Imports}_{t-1} \\ &- D_{BMP}\cdot\text{FX Black Market Premium}_{t-1} \\ &- D_{M3}\cdot\text{M3/GDP}_{t-1}] + \text{AR(1)} \end{aligned} \tag{5.10}$$

EMPIRICAL RESULTS

The economic data is based on a cross-section of 207 countries and annual time series over 25 years (1975-1999), obtained from the World Development Indicators (World Bank, 2001), and the Economic Freedom of the World Report (Gwartney, Lawson, and Samida, 2001). Due to incomplete data for many countries and/or time series, the empirical analysis was restricted to an available dataset of various sizes (indicated in the tables). The following stationary variables were created to estimate the models described in the previous section and avoid econometric issues related to nonstationarity in panel data: (1) y = output per unit of effective labor (Y/AL), proxied by the ratio of per capita GDP (Y/L, expressed in constant 1995 US$) to an exponential trend, whose growth rate is the per capita GDP growth rate over the sample 1975-1999 (variable g below). By construction, this series is stationary and expressed in logarithmic terms, representing a measure of standards of living; (2) g = rate of growth of GDP per unit of labor (Y/L), proxied by the logarithmic change in per capita real GDP defined earlier. (The definitions and sources of the other variables are available from the authors upon request.)

The empirical results of the cross-sectional regressions are presented in Table 5.8 for the traditional Mankiw et al. (1992) model, and in Table 5.9 for the political model, for both standards of living and economic growth as the dependent variable. The traditional model yields significant coefficients and the estimated average shares of physical and human capital (and labor) in the world economy can be derived as respectively 40 percent and 28 percent (and 32 percent), according to the standards of living equation. The political model produces a higher goodness of fit, and most coefficients are significant: trade openness, financial liberalization, a small government size, and a strong legal structure are beneficial for standards of living and/or economic growth.

TABLE 5.8. Traditional Factors of Standards of Living and Economic Growth (Cross-Sectional Averages: 1980-99)

Dependent Variable	**Standards of Living**	**Economic Growth**
Constant	7.57	–0.02
(t-statistics)	(5.05)	(2.72)
Log (physical investment)	1.27	0.19
(t-statistics)	(1.97)	(6.17)
Log (human investment)	0.88	
(t-statistics)	(2.35)	
Log (population growth)	–1.22	–0.49
(t-statistics)	(9.31)	(3.35)
R2	62.1%	44.3%
Adjusted R2	60.1%	43.0%
Number of cross-sections	60	91

TABLE 5.9. Political Factors of Standards of Living and Economic Growth (Cross-Sectional Averages: 1980-99)

Dependent Variable	Standards of Living	Economic Growth
Constant	3.67	–0.007
(t-statistics)	(12.48)	(1.09)
Trade openness	–0.03	0.007
(t-statistics)	(0.20)	(2.55)
Financial liberalization	0.21	0.001
(t-statistics)	(3.27)	(1.31)
Government size	4.22	–0.098
(t-statistics)	(2.24)	(2.57)
Legal structure	0.43	0.004
(t-statistics)	(8.79)	(5.08)
R2	78.0%	35.1%
Adjusted R2	76.7%	31.3%
Number of cross-sections	72	73

The next step in the empirical analysis consists of using the panel data error correction model to investigate the mean-reversion properties of standards of living and economic growth, and the implicit long-run effects of economic and political factors. Empirical results are presented in Table 5.10 for the political model, and in Table 5.11 for the economic model. In both models, and for both standards of living and economic growth as the dependent variable, the mean reversion coefficient is significant, indicating convergence toward the long-run steady state. Most of the coefficients of the political model are even more significant than for the cross-sectional regression (cf. Table 5.9), and the goodness of fit reaches only 4.5 percent for the standards of living equation, but 36.2 percent for the growth equation. The economic model produces a higher R^2, even in adjusted terms (for degrees of freedom), for both equations (more than double for the first one), and most of the coefficients are significant. Higher population density, greater sensitivity for oil shocks (differentiating for exporters and importers), less terms of trade vulnerability, less reliance on short-term external debt and on portfolio investment, greater amount of foreign exchange reserves, an improved government budget balance, higher growth of money supply, less protectionism, less foreign exchange controls, and a lower degree of dollarization, tend to significantly raise standards of living and/or economic growth.

TABLE 5.10. Political Factors of Standards of Living and Economic Growth (Panel Data:1975-99)

Dependent Variable	Standards of Living	Economic Growth
Constant (t-statistics)	0.005 (0.73)	–0.005 (1.61)
Log (per effective capita real GDP) (–1) (t-statistics)	–0.003 (1.85)	
Log (real per capita GDP growth) (–1) (t-statistics)		–0.59 (11.08)
Trade openness (–1) (t-statistics)	0.002 (1.15)	0.005 (3.40)
Financial liberalization (–1) (t-statistics)	0.001 (2.23)	0.001 (3.25)
Government size (–1) (t-statistics)	–0.028 (1.23)	–0.055 (3.60)
Legal structure (–1) (t-statistics)	0.002 (2.11)	0.002 (4.06)
AR(1) (t-statistics)	0.18 (4.91)	–0.13 (2.09)
R2 (Adjusted R2) Number of cross-sections (# obs.)	4.5% (4.2%) 92 (1807)	36.2% 111 (2014)

Most of these coefficient signs were expected, except perhaps for monetary growth.

Ultimately, out-of-sample growth forecasts were generated from these panel-data (Table 5.12) and cross-sectional (Table 5.13) models for the ten Asian countries selected. The traditional, political and economic models were reestimated with a shorter sample from 1980 to 1994, and out-of-sample forecasts were obtained for 1995 to 2000. None of these forecasts appear to be consistent with the 1997-1998 Asian crisis, reinforcing the notion that self-fulfilling panics rather than bad fundamentals were responsible for the financial crisis. However, most of the short-term growth-rate forecasts (Table 5.12) are lower than the long-term growth rates (Table 5.13), indicating that the Asian miracle was overstated, and perhaps unsustainable. In terms of individual performance, China should have grown at around 6 percent per annum, according to the economic model, but much less for the other models. Hong Kong and Singapore still yield high politically

TABLE 5.11. Economic Factors of Standards of Living and Economic Growth (Panel Data: 1975-99)

Dependent Variable	**Standards of Living**		**Economic Growth**	
Constant (t-statistics)	0.065	(3.17)	0.024	(2.86)
Log (per effective capita real GDP) (–1)	–0.007	(2.85)		
Log (real per capita GDP growth) (–1)			–1.07	(10.1)
Population density (–1)	0.00002	(1.11)	0.00004	(2.50)
Sensitivity to oil shocks (–1)	0.00009	(2.67)	0.00009	(2.17)
Terms of trade vulnerability (–1)	–0.013	(1.47)	–0.033	(3.33)
Short-term/total ext. debt (–1)	–0.034	(1.50)	–0.047	(1.82)
FDI share of foreign invt. (–1)	0.019	(1.87)	0.022	(1.89)
FX reserves/imports (–1)	0.003	(3.23)	0.003	(3.23)
Budget balance/GDP (–1)	0.10	(2.59)	0.12	(2.92)
Change (percent) in M2 (–1)	0.0004	(2.03)	0.0003	(1.37)
Import duties/imports (–1)	–0.041	(1.78)	–0.014	(0.58)
FX black market premium (–1)	–0.008	(1.67)	–0.009	(1.64)
M3/GDP (–1)	–0.027	(2.50)	–0.005	(0.43)
AR(1)	0.15	(2.96)	0.32	(3.25)
R2 (Adjusted R2)	10.5%	(8.9%)	41.1%	(40.0%)
Number of cross-sections (# obs.)	63	(713)	78	(780)

forecasted growth rates, given their respective trade and financial openness, small government size, and good legal structure, but less according to the traditional model, raising the question: is the model missing something about the so-called Asian miracle, or is this miracle a myth? The forecasted growth rates for the other countries (except Japan) are also lower than their actual long-term rates for most of the models. On the other hand, Japan appears to perform subpar relative to its potential: this can be explained by its dismal performance in the 1990s relative to strong growth in the previous decades.

TABLE 5.12. Per Capita Economic Growth Out-of-Sample Forecast, 1995-2000

Country		1994	1995	1996	1997	1998	1999	2000
China	Actual Data	11.6%	9.3%	8.5%	7.8%	6.8%	6.1%	7.1%
	Political Forecast		4.6%	2.6%	1.6%	1.0%	0.6%	1.2%
	Economic Forecast		7.1%	6.4%	6.4%	6.2%	6.3%	NA
Hong Kong	Actual Data	3.7%	1.2%	2.0%	2.0%	–7.3%	1.8%	10.0%
	Political Forecast		5.3%	6.1%	5.8%	5.1%	4.3%	5.2%
	Economic Forecast		NA	NA	NA	NA	NA	NA
Singapore	Actual Data	8.0%	4.8%	5.3%	6.1%	–1.6%	3.5%	8.1%
	Political Forecast		7.2%	7.0%	6.4%	5.6%	4.8%	5.7%
	Economic Forecast		NA	NA	NA	NA	NA	NA
Taiwan	Actual Data	5.8%	5.4%	5.1%	5.4%	3.3%	4.7%	5.6%
	Political Forecast		3.9%	3.3%	3.0%	3.0%	2.9%	2.9%
	Economic Forecast		NA	NA	NA	NA	NA	NA
Japan	Actual Data	0.3%	1.1%	4.8%	1.3%	–2.8%	0.1%	1.1%
	Political Forecast		2.0%	2.5%	2.4%	2.0%	1.5%	2.2%
	Economic Forecast		NA	NA	NA	NA	NA	NA
Korea	Actual Data	7.3%	7.6%	3.4%	1.7%	–7.4%	9.7%	6.1%
	Political Forecast		3.9%	3.0%	2.3%	1.8%	1.4%	2.2%
	Economic Forecast		4.3%	2.8%	2.3%	3.1%	NA	NA
Indonesia	Actual Data	5.8%	6.5%	6.2%	3.1%	–14.6%	–1.3%	2.6%
	Political Forecast		2.9%	2.0%	1.5%	1.1%	1.0%	1.2%
	Economic Forecast		3.8%	3.6%	3.6%	3.0%	3.7%	NA
Malaysia	Actual Data	6.5%	7.1%	8.8%	6.3%	–8.3%	4.9%	7.1%
	Political Forecast		4.4%	3.8%	3.3%	2.8%	2.5%	3.1%
	Economic Forecast		4.8%	4.2%	3.8%	3.3%	NA	NA
Philippines	Actual Data	1.9%	2.2%	3.4%	2.7%	–3.1%	0.8%	1.5%
	Political Forecast		1.7%	1.8%	1.7%	1.4%	1.1%	2.0%
	Economic Forecast		3.7%	4.0%	3.7%	3.2%	4.2%	4.4%

TABLE 5.12 *(continued)*

Country		1994	1995	1996	1997	1998	1999	2000
Thailand	Actual Data	8.1%	8.3%	5.3%	–2.3%	–10.9%	3.4%	3.6%
	Political Forecast		4.4%	3.3%	2.6%	2.2%	1.7%	2.3%
	Economic Forecast		3.1%	2.2%	2.2%	2.0%	2.7%	2.8%

TABLE 5.13. Per Capita Economic Growth Predictions

Country	Actual Data	Traditional Forecast	Political Forecast
China	8.4%	2.9%	0.8%
Hong Kong	5.3%	2.4%	4.6%
Singapore	5.6%	4.0%	5.8%
Taiwan	6.5%	1.9%	2.8%
Japan	2.7%	3.4%	2.6%
Korea	6.6%	3.6%	1.5%
Indonesia	5.0%	1.7%	0.7%
Malaysia	4.2%	2.5%	2.3%
Philippines	–0.3%	0.9%	0.2%
Thailand	6.1%	3.3%	1.9%

CONCLUSIONS

The goal of this chapter was to analyze economic, political, and cultural characteristics of ten individual Asian countries to reveal their respective potential for a sustained economic recovery following the 1997-1998 Asian crisis. Utilizing various topical indicators, country groups were constructed to reflect these structural differences: (1) the "pragmatic" group (China, Hong Kong, Taiwan, Singapore); (2) the "oligopolistic" group (Japan, South Korea); (3) the "authoritarian" group (Indonesia, Malaysia); and (4) the "versatile" group (Thailand, the Philippines). Preliminary analysis showed that the pragmatic Chinese group ranked ahead of the other three groups in terms of initial economic turnaround as well as in terms of political and cultural factors (even with the inclusion of mainland China).

The oligopolistic group was a reasonably close second (if not first in some categories), whereas the authoritarian group and versatile group lagged well behind in both economic turnaround and cultural factors.

Different types of models were then proposed to estimate the effects of these economic and political differences on standards of living and economic growth, with a panel of more than hundred nations over 25 years. Empirical results confirmed the traditional economic model, but also unveiled the significance of other political factors. In particular, economic liberalization, smaller governments, and stronger legal structures tend to significantly improve standards of living and/or economic growth. Finally, out-of-sample forecasts (1995-2000) were generated for the economic growth rates of the ten Asian countries and then compared with the actual growth rates. These results indicate that the severity of the Asian crisis was virtually unpredictable and unwarranted, but also that the potential for a return to pre-crisis growth levels was unlikely.

REFERENCES

Barro, R. (2001). Human capital and growth. *American Economic Review, 91,* May, pp. 12-17.

Bernanke, B. and Gurkaynak, R. (2001). Is Growth exogenous? Taking Mankiw, Romer, and Weil seriously. *NBER Macroeconomics Annual.*

Cartapanis, A., Dropsy, V., and Mametz, S. (1999). The Asian currency crises: Vulnerability, contagion, or unsustainability? *Review of International Economics, 10,* February, pp. 79-91.

Clark, E., Dropsy, V., and Jokung, O. (2001). Economic growth, volatility, and policy intervention. mimeo.

DeOcampo, R. (2000). Economic recovery in the Asia Pacific: Is it sustainable? Speech made at the Pacific Basin Economic Council 33rd annual International General Meeting, retrieved from www.pbec.org/newhorizons/speeches/deocmpo.htm.

Gray, H.P. (2000). Globalization and economic development. *Global Economy Quarterly, 1* (1), pp. 71-96.

Gwartney, J. and Lawson, R. (with Samida, D.) (2001). *Economic Freedom of the World: 2001 Annual Report.* Vancouver: The Fraser Institute, retrieved from www.freetheworld.com.

International Monetary Fund (2000). Recovery from the Asian crisis and the role of the IMF. *IMF Issues Brief,* June.

Kahn, M. and Sendhadji, A. (2000). Financial development and economic growth: An overview. IMF Working Paper WP/00/209, December.

Krol, R. (2001). Cross-country evidence on capital account liberalization and economic growth. *Global Economy Quarterly, 2,* pp. 39-64.

Mankiw, G., Romer, D., and Weil, D. (1992). A contribution to the empirics of economic growth. *Quarterly Journal of Economics, 107,* May, pp. 407-437.

Park, Y.C. (2001). The East Asian dilemma: Restructuring out or growing out? *Essays in International Economics,* No. 223, August.

Temple, J. (1999). The new growth evidence. *Journal of Economic Literature, 37,* March, pp. 112-156.

Transparency International (2001). Corruption Perceptions Index, retrieved from www.transparency.org/documents/cpi/index.html.

United Nations (2001). Human Development Report, retrieved from www.undp.org/hdro/.

Van den Berg, H. and Lewer, J. (2001). Do capital-importing countries really grow faster? *Global Economy Quarterly, 2* (1), pp. 19-38.

Williamson, J. and Mahar, M. (1998). A survey of financial liberalization. *Essays in International Economics,* No. 211, November.

World Bank (1998). East Asia's financial crisis: Causes, evolution, and prospects. *Global Development Finance,* pp. 29-48.

World Bank (2001). *World Development Indicators.* Washington, DC: World Bank.

Zaman, R. (2000). Restoring Asian economies after the financial markets collapse of 1997-98. *Global Economy Quarterly, 1,* pp. 179-190.

Chapter 6

The Asian Influence: An Analysis of Trade Flows Between the United States and Thailand in the Home Furnishings Industry

Kennita Kind

INTRODUCTION

As is the case with the fashion industry, the home furnishings industry is often driven by trends. A recent trend that has been quite visible in home furnishing stores, magazines, books, and advertising is Asian-influenced interior decorating. Interiors filled with richly colored silks, ceramics, wood, rattan, bamboo and wicker have become very trendy in homes across America, Western Europe, and other non-Asian countries. The Asian influence on home furnishings usually leads to simplified lines and natural, muted tones with bursts of color in furniture, textiles, and tableware.

In 2000 and 2001, several books were published that focused solely on the Asian style in Western and European interiors. One of these books, De Bure and Morellec's (2000) *Asian Style,* not only depicts striking images of interiors influenced by Asian style, but also includes a buyer's guide listing numerous international resources for materials shown in the book. Some of these source countries are China, Thailand, Malaysia and Taiwan.

Another book, Na Ayudhya and Doughty's (2001) *Contemporary Thai,* focused solely on the influence that Thailand has played on Western interior décor as well as the rest of the world. In addition, the Asian influence has been noted in the American popular press. For

Globalization and East Asia: Opportunities and Challenges

doi:10.1300/5463_06

example, the March 2001 issue of *Architectural Digest* (Lutfy, 2001) included a feature on Thai garden landscapes and décor.

PURPOSE

The purpose of this research was to serve as an exploratory analysis of trade flows between the United States and Thailand in the home furnishings industry. The primary objective of this research was to gain an understanding of the home furnishings industry of Thailand and its significance to the U.S. home furnishings industry. Unfortunately, at this time, there are no empirical studies relating to the international trade of home furnishings between the United States and the Asia-Pacific region. This research seeks to fill that void and provide a foundation on which to build a research base in home furnishings trade flows worldwide.

PART I

Methodology

The home furnishings industry is comprised of numerous products, such as electronics, appliances, carpeting, textiles, furniture, lighting, tabletop accessories, plumbing fixtures, and some construction materials. For this exploratory research the following home furnishings items were selected for this initial analysis: furniture and furniture products; wicker baskets; ceramic tableware; and metal tableware, tabletop accessories, and lighting. Future research is warranted in the other categories. Secondary data from the U.S. Census Bureau (2001) were collected based on four-digit Standard Industrialized Trade Classification (SITC) codes for 1996, 1998, and 2000 in the aforementioned categories.

Thailand was selected for a trade-flow analysis with the United States for several reasons. The Asian influence in Western interiors is currently a lucrative market in the home furnishings industry. In addition, Thailand is a leading exporter of furniture and wooden home furnishings products in the Asia-Pacific region; whereas other countries of the region are facing economic instability, lack of natural resources, and political turmoil. Finally, for more than 200 years, wooden products made of Thai teak were highly regarded worldwide. Historically, Thailand was, and continues to be, a country known for its wooden furniture and quality construction.

Results

Home Furnishings Industry (Aggregate)

All of the industries mentioned previously (furniture and furniture products; wicker baskets; ceramic tableware; metal tableware, tabletop accessories, and lighting) were grouped together to obtain the aggregate totals for trade flows between Thailand and the United States in the home furnishing industry in order to gain an initial understanding of overall trade flows. This analysis revealed that U.S. exports to Thailand have been falling from $15 million in 1996 to $10 million in 1998 and $8.5 million in 2000 in the home furnishings industry. In contrast, U.S. imports from Thailand in aggregated home furnishings categories have risen from $389 million in 1996 to $433 million in 1998 and $445 million in 2000. These results are shown in Table 6.1.

The results clearly show that the trade flows in the home furnishings industry between Thailand and the United States are imbalanced, and lead to several research questions:

1. What are the leading exports from Thailand in the home furnishings industry to the United States?
2. What are the leading imports to Thailand in the home furnishings industry from the United States?
3. Are trade flows completely one-sided in virtually all of the trade categories used in this analysis? If not, what categories are balanced?
4. What natural resources are important to the Thai home furnishings industry and do these resources influence trade flows?

To answer these questions, more in-depth analyses of the different trade categories in home furnishings were conducted.

TABLE 6.1. Aggregate Home Furnishings Trade Flows (in U.S. Dollars)

Year	U.S.-Thailand Relationship
U.S. exports to Thailand	
1996	$15,682,495
1998	$10,199,142
2000	$8,505,184
U.S. imports from Thailand	
1996	$389,020,249
1998	$433,551,608

Source: U.S. Census Bureau, 2001.

Furniture Industry

The home furnishings industry, particularly furniture, is a significant part of Thailand's economy. At present, furniture is one of Thailand's top 20 leading export markets (CorporateInformation.com, 2002; Thailand.com, 2002b). Natural resources and international demand for Asian-inspired design, detailing, workmanship, and cultural influence have led to the popularity of Thai furniture for hundreds of years. In addition, the stability of Thailand's economy and political climate (as compared to other Asian countries) have also contributed to the importance of Thai furniture.

The Thai government and furniture industry representatives understand the importance that furniture plays on the national economy and are working to increase its prominence in the world furniture market. For example, in 1996 ten manufacturers from the Thai home furnishings industry were featured at the High Point International Furnishings Market in North Carolina (Thaitrade.com, 2001). In addition, numerous Web sites are available that market Thai furniture to American importers.

The importance of Thai furniture on the world furniture market is nothing new. Western-styled wooden furniture imported from France was introduced into Thailand more than 200 years ago (Thailand.com, 2002b). The Western designs were in high demand by wealthy Thai citizens and members of the nobility. Consequently, local craftsmen became highly skilled in reproducing Western designs using locally grown teakwood. Over a period of 100 years, Thai furniture became very unique. The furniture was heavily influenced by Western designs, but still adhered to Southeast Asian culture and materials. These pieces were generally sold locally and within the region, but began to be exported to the world market. In addition, Thailand became known for its products made of teak. Teak was demanded worldwide for furniture as well as flooring and shipbuilding, and became a highly regarded material in terms of quality and natural beauty (Thailand.com, 2002b).

Throughout the twentieth century, Thai furniture manufacturers enjoyed strong worldwide demand, especially for products made of teak. However, in 1989, the Thai government imposed a hardwood logging ban due to the deforestation and environmental degradation of lands in northern Thailand. In order to remain productive and to survive, the furniture industry quickly shifted production to utilize parawood.

Parawood, which is abundant in Thailand, is made from old rubber trees that no longer produce sufficient quantities of sap. Thailand is a leading producer of rubber, thus leading to a limitless supply of rubber trees for furniture manufacturers. Today, more than 80 percent of Thailand's wood furniture exports are made of parawood, which is often treated to mimic teak. Due to the government ban on teakwood, some furniture manufacturers shifted production away from wood and are producing furniture made of metal, wicker, and rattan with great success (Thai Furniture Industries, 2002).

Based on data from the U.S. Census Bureau (2001), U.S. exports of furniture to Thailand fell from $13 million in 1996 to just under $7 million in 2000, with a majority of the exports to Thailand in SITC code 9404 (mattresses). On the contrary, U.S. imports of Thai furniture (SITC codes 9401, 9403, and 9404) have grown significantly from $172 million in 1996 to $229 million in 2000. These results are depicted in Table 6.2.

In 1996, 1998, and 2000, a significant trade imbalance existed between the United States and Thailand in the furniture industry, with U.S. exports decreasing, whereas Thai exports to the United States continued to grow. Future research is warranted to determine factors that influence these levels.

TABLE 6.2. Furniture Trade Flows (in U.S. Dollars)

Year	U.S.-Thailand Relationship
U.S. exports to Thailand	
1996	$13,141,789
1998	$8,038,203
2000	$6,921,714
U.S. imports from Thailand	
1996	$172,724,980
1998	$209,912,239

Source: U.S. Census Bureau, 2001.

Ceramics Industry

This study of the Thai home furnishings industry also included an analysis of trade flows in the ceramics industry (SITC 6911–6914). Thailand's ceramic industry, which has been in existence for more than 50 years, is located in northern Thailand, where natural resources are located that are utilized in the production of ceramic products. These natural resources are kaolin, kaolinite, and feldspar (Thailand.com, 2002a).

Recently, the Thai ceramic industry has also been successful in repositioning itself in the export market. Exports of Thai ceramics were previously known for the famous "blue and white" tabletop accessories, but that has changed in the past several years. Industry leaders have repositioned Thai ceramics to the upper segment of the market through innovative product development. Items that sold previously for as little as 50 cents in the United States are now being priced at $10. Ceramics are popular souvenirs for the tourist industry, and can be found in many import stores in the Western hemisphere. These pieces are usually made of celadon, which is a glazed, dark-blue jade; cobalt blue ceramic pieces; bencharong (five-color porcelain); and earthenware.

The Thai ceramic industry's main competitors are ceramic manufacturers in other Asia-Pacific countries. The industry has made significant gains in the past several years, and the Thailand Industrial Promotion Department believes that Thailand's ceramic industry has the "highest potential for expansion and export growth among small to medium enterprise industries" (Thailand.com, 2002a).

The in-depth study of trade flows in the ceramics industry between the United States and Thailand, based on data from the U.S. Census Bureau (2001), revealed that U.S. exports to Thailand of ceramics rose significantly to almost $1 million in 1998 and fell drastically to $277,000 in 2000. This trend in the data is perplexing, particularly with the significant peak in 1998. More research is needed to ascertain the reasons for this peak. In addition, a significant trade imbalance exists in this industry as U.S. imports of Thai ceramics exceeded $102 million in 1996, rose slightly in 1998, and fell to $91 million in 2000. These results are shown in Table 6.3.

Tabletop Accessories Industry

The United States is also the leading importer of Thai-produced tabletop accessories (SITC 3924, 4419–4420). These accessories may be manufactured of plastic, wood, or other materials, however, many of the wooden tableware items are now manufactured of parawood rather than teak. These accessories include such items as wooden bowls, vases, kitchen utensils, wooden boxes, and candle holders.

The trade-flow analysis revealed a large trade imbalance in the tabletop accessories industry based on data from the U.S. Census Bureau (2001). As shown in Table 6.4, there were no U.S. exports in this industry in 1996 and 1998, whereas only $12,000 of tabletop acces-

TABLE 6.3. Ceramics Trade Flows (in U.S. Dollars)

Year	**U.S.-Thailand Relationship**
U.S. exports to Thailand	
1996	$421,809
1998	$935,243
2000	$277,116
U.S. imports from Thailand	
1996	$102,435,720
1998	$103,242,828

Source: U.S. Census Bureau, 2001.

TABLE 6.4. Tabletop Accessories Trade Flows (in U.S. Dollars)

Year	U.S.-Thailand Relationship
U.S. exports to Thailand	
1996	$0
1998	$0
2000	$12,562
U.S. imports from Thailand	
1996	$49,490,293
1998	$43,841,101
2000	$50,946,163

Source: U.S. Census Bureau, 2001.

sories were exported to Thailand in 2000. Thai exports of tabletop accessories to the United States were $49 million in 1996, fell slightly in 1998, and topped $50 million in 2000. This is a significant export market for Thailand, especially to the United States.

Metal Tableware Industry

The metal tableware industry (SITC 7323 and 8215) is an important export market for Thailand. Thailand is not particularly known for one specific metal in this industry, as many metals are used in the manufacture of metal tableware, such as aluminum, stainless steel, iron, brass, tin, bronze, and silver. Many of the more expensive products are usually made of any of the aforementioned metals, but it is the intricate, skilled, handmade pieces that are marketed to the higher end market.

Results of this analysis revealed that the United States exported $2.1 million of metal tableware in 1996 and $1.2 million in 1998 and 2000 to Thailand (U.S. Census Bureau, 2001). However, in 1996, Thai metal tableware exports to the United States were close to $50 million and grew to over $63 million in 2000. This is another industry expected to make significant gains in the next few years. These results are shown in Table 6.5.

TABLE 6.5. Metal Tableware Trade Flows (in U.S. Dollars)

Year	U.S.-Thailand Relationship
U.S. exports to Thailand	
1996	$2,118,897
1998	$1,225,696
2000	$1,293,792
U.S. imports from Thailand	
1996	$48,430,290
1998	$59,480,557
2000	$63,439,238

Source: U.S. Census Bureau, 2001.

Wicker Basket Industry

The trade analysis for the wicker basket industry (SITC 4602) and lighting industry (SITC 9405) provided some interesting results. Data collected from the U.S. Census Bureau (2001) for the wicker basket industry revealed that the trade between the United States and Thailand in both industries was completely one sided, as depicted in Table 6.6.

The United States exported nothing to Thailand in 1996, 1998, and 2000 in either category. However, the U.S. imports from Thailand in the wicker basket industry rose from $439,000 in 1996 to $1.4 million in 2000. The outlook for this industry is very optimistic. This industry, which consists of baskets and similar pieces made of wicker, bamboo, rattan, and, most recently, water hyacinth, has had significant increases in the past several years, and the United States is a lucrative market for Thailand as many of these products are popular in American import stores.

Lighting Industry

Export levels to Thailand for U.S. home furnishings products in the lighting industry were similar to those in the wicker basket industry, that is they were completely one-sided. As shown in Table 6.7,

TABLE 6.6. Wicker Baskets Trade Flows (in U.S. Dollars)

Year	U.S.-Thailand Relationship
U.S. exports to Thailand	
1996	$0
1998	$0
2000	$0
U.S. imports from Thailand	
1996	$439,343
1998	$306,766
2000	$1,401,902

Source: U.S. Census Bureau, 2001.

TABLE 6.7. Lighting Trade Flows (in U.S. Dollars)

Year	U.S.-Thailand Relationship
U.S. exports to Thailand	
1996	$0
1998	$0
2000	$0
U.S. imports from Thailand	
1996	$15,499,623
1998	$16,768,117
2000	$8,925,292

Source: U.S. Census Bureau, 2001.

The United States had no exports in the lighting industry to Thailand from 1996 to 2000. In fact, U.S. imports from Thailand fell significantly from $16 million in 1998 to $8.9 million in 2000 (U.S. Census Bureau, 2001). These results were not expected. Further research is warranted to determine the reasons behind this significant decline and completely one-sided imbalance.

Conclusions

In general, this analysis of trade flows between the United State and Thailand revealed a strong trade imbalance in the home furnishings industry. The trade imbalance between the two countries for the aggregated home furnishings industry was 0.92 in 1996, 0.95 in 1998, and 0.96 in 2000. At this point in the analysis it was determined to further this research and investigate Thai trade export levels in the home furnishings industry to countries other than the United States. Three additional research questions emerged: (1) What countries other than the United States are leading import markets for Thai home furnishing products? (2) Is the United States the leading importer of Thai home furnishings goods? (3) If not, what other countries are lucrative markets?

PART II

Methodology

Although the data available from Thailand are somewhat limited, some data was available to gain a better understanding in this exploratory analysis of the questions asked earlier. Worldwide trade export data from Thailand were obtained for the furniture industry, ceramics industry, and the tabletop accessories industry (Thailand.com, 2002a,b,c). Although different categorical estimates exist, the figures are somewhat similar to the data obtained from the United States Census Bureau for its trade analysis of Thailand and United States. However, the following results do provide some insight into world markets for Thai home furnishings. Hopefully, more complete data will become available in the future, as Thailand improves its international trade prominence and further research could be conducted in this area.

Results

Thai Furniture Exports

Based on the data available from Thailand.com (2002b), Thai furniture exports continue to play a significant role in the world's furniture market, particularly western cultures. Thai furniture exports (wood and metal) amounted to $959.0 million in 2000. Japan was the largest importer of Thai furniture ($387.8 million), whereas the United States was the second largest ($277.7 million). These two countries alone account for almost 70 percent of the total furniture exports from Thailand in 2000 (Thailand.com, 2002b). The remaining top countries of exports were from Western Europe in general, as depicted in Table 6.8. The data clearly show that Thai furniture plays a significant role in the home furnishings markets of many Western countries. These trade flows may be influenced by home furnishings trends, retail price, quality, and availability. Further research is warranted to explore variables that influence this industry.

With regard to Thai ceramics, the United States was the leading importer for the first three quarters of 2000 based on data from Thailand.com (2002a). U.S. imports of ceramic products were $49.6 million, followed by Japanese imports at $16.4 million. The other leading import markets for Thai ceramics are Asia-Pacific countries and some Westernized nations, although the United States accounts for one-third of the Thai export market. These results are shown in Table 6.9.

TABLE 6.8. Thai Exports of Furniture, 2000 (in Millions of US$)

Country	Amount
Japan	$387.8
United States	277.7
United Kingdom	47.5
Germany	26.2
Australia	22.8
Canada	22.8
France	23.5
Netherlands	14.0
Sweden	6.6
Italy	7.9
Other	122.4
Total	959.2

Source: Adapted from Thailand.com, 2002b.

TABLE 6.9. Thai Exports of Ceramics, 2000 (in Millions of US$)

Country	Amount
United States	$49.6
Japan	16.4
Hong Kong	11.5
Australia	7.5
United Kingdom	6.3
Myanmar	5.9
Germany	5.3
Laos	5.2
Canada	4.7
Cambodia	3.8
Other	39.8
Total	156.0

Source: Adapted from Thailand.com, 2002a. Data from January-August, 2000.

Based on Thai trade data (Thailand.com, 2002c), the United States is the leading importer of Thai tabletop accessories. The United States imported $156.8 million of tabletop goods for the first three quarters of 2000. U.S. imports account for nearly half of all Thai exports of tabletop goods. The other leading export markets are listed in Table 6.10.

Conclusions

This analysis was conducted to gain a general understanding of trade flows in the home furnishings industry between the United States and Thailand. The results have revealed that the outlook for Thai home furnishings is very optimistic. Due to economic uncertainty, many Americans are more frugal in regard to their disposable income. Many analysts believe that U.S. consumers will not be purchasing big ticket items, rather they will be "cocooning" and spending time at home with family and friends (Zisko, 2002). If this is the case, it is believed that consumers will be purchasing small items for their homes, such as furniture, tabletop accessories, and other items,

TABLE 6.10. Thai Exports of Tabletop Accessories, 2000 (in Millions of US$)

Country	Amount
United States	$156.8
Japan	31.2
United Kingdom	25.2
Germany	14.4
France	11.6
Italy	8.9
Canada	8.9
Belgium	7.4
Australia	6.9
Netherlands	6.5
Other	65.5
Total	343.3

Source: Adapted from Thailand.com, 2002c. Data from January-August, 2000.

rather than purchasing big ticket items such as automobiles or spending money on expensive vacations. This is promising news for the home furnishings industry, and if the trend toward Asian influence continues, this is promising news for the Thailand home furnishings industry as well.

IMPLICATIONS FOR FUTURE RESEARCH

Although, this analysis has been informative, more extensive research is warranted. Future studies are being planned to expand this research to more countries of the Asia-Pacific region. In addition, research that investigates trade flows between trading blocks of the Asia-Pacific region is warranted. Based on the preliminary results of this study, more extensive research is needed as it is an area that has been overlooked in empirical studies. The results from this study and future studies in the area would prove to be very beneficial to the home furnishings industries in the Asia-Pacific region and the rest of the world.

REFERENCES

CorporateInformation.com (2002). *Industry Analysis, Thailand: Furniture,* retrieved from www.corporateinformation.com/thsector/Furniture.html.

De Bure, G. and Morellec, F. (2000). *Asian Style.* Paris: Flammarion.

Lutfy, C. (2001). Taste for the tropics: A landscape designer's love for Asia is reflected in his Bangkok garden sanctuary. *Architectural Digest, 58,* March, 226-231.

Thaitrade.com (2001). *Made in Thailand . . . A Label of Distinction,* retrieved from www.thaitrade.com/hppress.html.

Na Ayudhya, W.D. and Doughty, J.M. (2001). *Contemporary Thai.* Boston: Tuttle Publishing.

Thai Furniture Industries (2002). *Furniture Export Helps Boost Thailand's Economy,* retrieved from www.furnituresthai.com/tfa/html/articles/html/ articles02.html.

Thailand.com (2002a). *Industry Outlook: Ceramics,* retrieved from www.thailand .com/exports/html/industry_iocermaics.htm.

Thailand.com (2002b). *Industry Outlook: Furniture,* retrieved from www.thailand .com/exports/html/industry_iofurniture.htm.

Thailand.com (2002c). *Industry Outlook: Table Kitchenware,* retrieved from www .thailand.com/exports/html/industry_housetablekit.htm.

U.S. Census Bureau (2001). *U.S. Imports and Exports History, Historical Summary 1996-2000* [CD-ROM]. Washington, DC: U.S. Department of Commerce.

Zisko, A. (2002). Housewares show provides vendors with a fresh start. *Home Furnishings Magazine,* January 14, 55, 58.

Chapter 7

Trade and Environment Issues in APEC

Antonina Ivanova
Manuel Angeles

INTRODUCTION

The Asia-Pacific Economic Cooperation (APEC) is a unique intergovernmental process. The process that began in November 1989 with a meeting in Canberra, Australia, and attended by ministers from 12 Asia-Pacific countries has come a long way. APEC's unique characteristics can be understood and appreciated against the background of the region's diversity and the various attempts at promoting regionalism and regional economic cooperation over some 25 years prior to that historic meeting in Canberra (Soesastro, 1994a, b). As a process of cooperation, and as a forum for consultations, APEC definitely has undergone a significant evolution. APEC's evolution has been influenced by three major developments, namely: (1) expansion of membership, (2) gradual institutionalization, and (3) widening and deepening of the cooperation agenda.

Let us briefly review past developments on those three fronts that have influenced APEC's evolution, beginning with the expansion of APEC membership. The process began in 1989 with the involvement of 12 member economies, namely the six ASEAN countries (Brunei, Indonesia, Malaysia, the Philippines, Singapore, and Thailand), South Korea, the five Pacific Organisation for Economic Co-operation and Development (OECD) countries (Australia, Canada, Japan, New Zealand, and the United States), and three Latin American economies (Mexico, Chile, and Peru). From the outset, the composition of APEC's membership has been seen as a novel arrangement as it has

Globalization and East Asia: Opportunities and Challenges

doi:10.1300/5463_07

brought together developing, newly industrializing, and advanced industrial economies into a process of regional consultation and cooperation.

Many environmentalists and citizen groups throughout the Asia-Pacific region worry about APEC's "sweeping vision." Despite some first steps to "green" APEC, free-trade diplomacy has to date taken little consideration of the environment. Yet economic openness generates new and specific pressures on environmental policymaking. With economic interdependence, the policies and norms of one country become deeply entangled with those of its trading partners. The scope for unilateral action is reduced, even as trade-induced economic growth increases pressures on resources and ecosystems.

This chapter will address these basic concerns by examining the process and progress in the area of APEC's environmental cooperation. The central argument of this paper is that regional economic integration must be complemented by the creation of regional frameworks for environmental management. Beyond working to expand market access, APEC countries must cooperate to create conditions that provide incentives for sustainable resource and ecosystem use. In this way, trade and environmental policies can mutually reinforce each other. In one way or another, it is likely that environmental issues will be on the agenda. The crucial issue is how deep and broad the integration of trade and environmental concerns will be. This chapter suggests some guiding principles and innovative strategies.

TRADE LIBERALIZATION, ECONOMIC INTEGRATION, AND THE ENVIRONMENT

The relationship between trade liberalization, economic growth, and the environment in the Asia-Pacific region has not yet been charted (Strutt and Anderson, 1998). Conceptual frameworks and evidence from other regions suggest first, that trade openness has both positive and negative impacts on the environment; and second, that economic integration constrains national environmental policymaking. When regions are highly integrated economically, they must develop common frameworks to govern the trade-environment interface.

APEC encompasses one of the most highly integrated economic regions in the world. Nearly 70 percent of total APEC trade is intraregional, much of it between East Asia and North America and between Southeast Asia and Japan. The subregion of East Asia, which excludes APEC's North and South American and Australasian members, is also highly integrated. About 45 percent of total East Asian trade is with other East Asian countries.

Total trade statistics mask the importance of economic size and do not measure a "bias factor," viz, the tendency for countries to favor particular trade partners. Another measure of trade interdependence, the gravity model, adjusts for size by dividing the share of two-way trade by the partner's share in world trade. Under a gravity model, the intensity of regional trade in East Asia outstrips the intensity of Pacific-region trade by some 25 percent. Indeed, the intensity of East Asian trade is the highest in the world (Petri, 1997).

Economic integration within East Asia, as well as on a trans-Pacific basis, is also evident in rising foreign direct investment (FDI). Between 1988 and 2000, the stock of FDI in East Asia grew by nearly 22 percent. Investors from North America and Japan, as well as Hong Kong, Taiwan, and South Korea, have targeted Southeast Asia and China as growth poles.

Spurred by market opening in China, Russia, and potentially North Korea, economic integration within the subregion of Northeast Asia is likely to grow rapidly in the coming decade. Rent by ideological and military divides for 50 years, Northeast Asian trade has been skewed away from the high level of integration that has emerged in other regions where borders are friendly. With the end of the Cold War and increasing economic openness, trade and investment flows within the region are predicted to boom. According to one estimate, the value of trade flows within the Northeast Asian region will more than triple by 2010 (Jeong et al., 1995).

ENVIRONMENTAL COSTS OF RAPID GROWTH

The rapid industrialization of the Asia-Pacific region has produced an environmental situation that can only be described as a situation bordering on crisis. Rapid growth, fueled largely by foreign investment and trade openness, has made East Asia the economic success story of the world. Economic success, however, has come at the expense of severe and rising ecological degradation, including the pollution of water and air systems, rapid depletion of resources such as forests, wetlands and fisheries, and loss of flora and fauna (Ban, 2000). Ecological degradation imposes large financial costs in the Asia-Pacific region and globally. Moreover, some losses in ecosystem goods and services may be irreversible.

The costs of environmentally unconstrained, export-oriented economic growth are not limited to the rapidly industrializing and developing countries of APEC. In Canada, unsustainable management, including inappropriate pricing, undermines forest sustainability. In California, water subsidies promote the cultivation of water-intensive crops, such as rice, in arid areas, with negative impacts on water salinity, soil microorganisms, and flora and fauna. In Australia, farming and grazing practices in some states generate soil erosion and the decline of water tables.

High rates of environmental degradation are also evident throughout Southeast and Northeast Asia, as well as Mexico and Chile. Environmental groups in Indonesia, for example, predict that, at current rates of logging, Indonesian forests will be exhausted within ten years (Pangestu, 1994). In Thailand, the huge inflow of unregulated flows of foreign investment have made a nightmare of Bangkok and severely widened the gaps between urban and rural Thais (Zarsky, 1994).

Some analysts consider environmental degradation to be the "cost of development" and suggest that "grow now, pay later" is the only way to overcome poverty and achieve industrialization. Attention to environmental concerns, they posit, will come at the cost of gross national product (GNP) growth, which will itself generate the resources for future clean up and restoration. However, the financial, let alone social and ecological, costs of environmental carelessness are likely to be large in terms of damage to human health, loss of resource productivity, and degradation of ecosystem services.

The lack of environmental care is already imposing costs on development. The Tumen River, for example, site of a major Northeast Asian development project, is so polluted that cleanup and restoration is required before site preparation. Not even treated water is useable for human consumption, and agricultural lands irrigated by the Tumen have declined in productivity due to toxic contamination. Even industrial polluters along the Tumen have suffered declining productivity because their water input is below required standards (Yamasawa, 1997).

The way to calculate potential trade-offs between environment and development is not the absolute, additional cost of environmental investment but the net cost, that is, the additional cost minus the benefit (Lucas et al., 1992). Additional costs are often easy to calculate. A recent study, for example, calculated that reducing acid-rain-causing sulfur emissions in Asia by half over the next 25 years requires an annual investment of $432 per ton of sulfur dioxide emitted per year. For China this would mean an annual extra cost of $4-6 billion per year (Leavitt Siak, 2000).

So much for additional cost. But what is the benefit? In financial terms, the benefit amounts to the cost of not making the investment, that is, the cost of the environmental and health damage. According to a recent study, the annual damage of uncontrolled emissions of a single 600-MW coal-fired power plant in northern China totaled more than $39 billion per year (Leavitt Siak, 2000).

EVOLUTION OF APEC'S ENVIRONMENTAL AGENDA

How central has the environment and sustainable development been in the APEC agenda?

Although sustainable development found its way into various documents prior to 1993, it was only when the APEC countries' environmental ministers met in Vancouver in March 1994 that the environment was given serious consideration (Chia Siow, 1994). The resulting "Environmental Vision Statement" emphasized the following points that:

- There were "inseparable linkages between environment protection and economic growth" in the creation of "an enduring foundation for sustainable development."
- APEC should take the lead in "addressing global [environmental] problems and solutions in line with the global consensus reached at UNCED."
- The "market can be an efficient and flexible means of allocating resources but that market outcomes do not always take into full account relevant environmental concerns. The challenge is to achieve sustainable development while taking advantage of the dynamism that market economies provide" (APEC EPG, 1994).

At first, the impetus from the Vancouver meeting seemed to pay off as the August 1994 report of the Eminent Persons Group (EPG), the quasi-official body that served as APEC's intellectual shepherd in the early 1990s, encouraged member economies "to harmonize national product standards, develop and share pro-environmental technologies, jointly fund environmentally sound development projects, and seek international acceptance of the principle of the internalization of the costs of environmental protection" (APEC EPG, 1994).

However, as Dua (1997) points out, the environment was given short shrift in the next few years. The Bogor Declaration was almost totally focused on the goal of creating a free trade area and hardly mentioned sustainable development. Prior to the Osaka Summit in November 1995, in the third and last report of the EPG, environmental concerns "were conspicuous by their absence." The Osaka Summit itself resulted in the creation, at the direction of the leaders, of a food, energy, economic growth, and population or FEEP task force that would consider "cross-cutting issues." But more important was the decision not to create new working groups, which, as Dua affirms, "effectively rules out an APEC committee or working group on trade and the environment" (p.73).

APEC appeared to regain its interest in an environmental agenda in mid-1996, during the second meeting of environmental ministers in Manila. President Fidel Ramos of the Philippines seemed to strike the appropriate note when he warned, "We finally stand on the threshold of unprecedented growth and change. That threshold—unless we watch our step and look when we cross—could very well be the brink of environmental disaster." Such an outcome would be a result of mismanaging the "critical and often competing claims of environmental protection and economic growth," thus making it imperative to continue "pushing the limits of what we can do to harmonize these concerns" (Pacific Economic Cooperation Council, 1996).

The results of the meeting, however, did not match Ramos's (some would say, largely rhetorical) note of urgency. At this meeting, three proposals were mooted as areas of joint cooperation in environmental matters: a "Clean Pacific" initiative that was intended as a "regional cooperative effort to improve and improve the health of the Pacific Ocean by the year 2020"; a "Clean Production" initiative that emphasized "non-regulatory, market-based approaches to achieving cleaner production, involving the mobilization of partnerships among and between government and the private sector"; and a "Sustainable Cities" program to counter the "negative environmental and social impacts such as reduced air and water quality and increased health risks" in the growing urban centers of the Asia-Pacific region (Drusdale et al., 1998).

The problem with these initiatives was that they were very general and thus relatively noncontroversial and not backed by concrete commitments of funds. Moreover, they were skimpy in detail, revealing that they had not really been thought through. The "Sustainable Cities" initiative, for instance, had not gone much beyond Japan's proposal at the Vancouver Conference to build "eco-cities," which would be "self-sustaining by being more efficient" in the consumption of water and energy, in protecting and promoting green areas, and in involving individuals and private industry in the solution of local problems.

The Manila Summit, although dominated by trade concerns, nevertheless struck the note of "sustainable development" more frequently than previous summit statements.

Point 3 of the Manila declaration refers to the leaders' commitment to "sustainable growth and equitable development." Point 16 asserts that

> as an essential complement to our trade and investment agenda, economic and technical cooperation helps APEC members to participate more fully in and benefit from an open global trading environment, thus ensuring that liberalized trade contributes to sustainable growth and equitable development and to a reduction in economic disparities.

Point 19 affirms "promoting rapid economic growth that ensures a healthy environment and improves the quality of life of our citizens is a fundamental challenge."

Finally, Point 20 directs the senior ministers of the APEC countries "to develop specific initiatives to implement an initial work program for sustainable development in APEC that includes the themes of the sustainability of the marine environment, clean technology and clean production, and sustainable cities."

But juxtaposing the Manila Declaration and the Collective Action Plan approved at the same time reveals the gap between rhetoric and reality that marks APEC's approach to the environment. Of the three initiatives receiving special mention by the leaders, the only one that was touched on by some concrete proposals in the Collective Action Plan was the marine environment. The "Marine Resources Conservation Working Group" completed by the year 2000 "a program to provide training, infrastructure, and oversight measures necessary to establish harmony in policies, procedures, and capabilities to enable the export/import of fishery products without concern for algal toxins" (Ferrantino, 2000, p. 67).

The marine environment was also the focus of another working group, the Fisheries Working Group (FWG), but from its list of accomplishments in 2000, it was clear that exploitation of the sea was much more on the mind of the committee than the conservation of sea life. The FWG completed six projects:

> a) the publication of a Who's Who in Fisheries Inspection in the region; b) a feasibility study on improving market information on seafood trade in APEC; c) an inventory of fisheries management administrations and organizations in the region; d) several technical workshops on seafood health and quality rules; e) a technical workshop on Hazard Analysis and Critical Control Point-based seafood inspection; and f) a technical workshop on quality assurance in seafood inspection laboratories.

The Collective Action Plan underlined, among other things, the consequences of the absence of a committee on the environment. Not only did the initiatives mooted by the leaders lack an institutional home that could process and implement them, but the environmental problems threatening the region could not be addressed in a comprehensive fashion. This situation was in marked contrast to the World Trade Organization (WTO) that, for all its shortcomings when it came to the environment, did have a Committee on Trade and the Environment (CTE). This, in turn, reflects the fact that even more than in the case of the WTO, the environment has not been integrated into the trade agenda of APEC, as have other areas such as energy, transportation, agricultural and technical cooperation, and telecommunications and information, on which working groups meet regularly.

THE TRADE-ENVIRONMENT INTERFACE

Dimensions of the Problem

As Ban (2000) notes over the last three decades, APEC economies have been the mayor source of world pollution. In fact, the world's top three emitters of greenhouse gases are in the region. Carbon dioxide emissions from the region are expected to rise 1.7 to 3.2 times in the next few decades, from the current 25 percent of the world's total to 36 percent by 2025. Sulphur dioxide and nitrous oxide emissions are expected to increase two to three times.

China's industrialization, with most of its energy dependent on the burning of high sulfur coal, poses a massive environmental threat. The Korean rapid industrialization has made the sulfur dioxide content of Seoul's air one of the highest in the world and caused close to 70 percent of the rain falling on the city to be so acidic as to pose a threat to human health. Seoul's air pollution is not unique in being a serious health hazard. In Taiwan, cancer rates have doubled since 1960, and children in Bangkok have among the highest levels of lead in their blood, largely attributable to air pollution.

"Water pollution," says the Australian APEC Study Center, "is the most widespread environmental problem in Asia" (O'Connor, 1999, p. 98). Levels of dissolved mercury in Asian rivers far exceed recommended World Health Organization (WHO) standards. A few examples underline the gravity of the situation: a Malaysian government report (O'Connor, 1997) ranked only 27 percent of 116 surveyed rivers in Peninsular Malaysia as "pollution free"—the others being ranked as "biologically dead" or "dying." In Taiwan, the lower reaches of virtually all of the island's rivers are biologically dead. In Bangkok, key sections of the Chao Phraya River "are either biologically dead or very close to being so," owing to uncontrolled dumping of both industrial and human waste; and animal species that populated the length of the river declined from 121 in the late sixties to 31 in recent times (Leavitt Siak, 2000).

Deforestation is uncontrolled. The highest rate of deforestation in the world in the period 1981-1990 was in mainland Southeast Asia, followed by island Southeast Asia. From more than 50 percent in 1950, the portion of the Philippines covered by forests dropped to less than 25 percent by 1990. Seventy percent of Thailand was virgin forest in 1932; by 1990, only 17 percent of the country was forested. In the Malaysian state of Sarawak, loggers eliminated 30 percent of the forest area in barely 23 years, 1962 to 1985. And in just eight years, 1982 to 1990, a third of the forests of the island of Sumatra, in Indonesia, have disappeared (Strutt and Anderson, 1998).

Large tracts of agricultural land are being degraded by chemical intensive agrotechnology and erosion or are being converted indiscriminately into urban real estate. China, where estimates of loss range from 50 million to 100 million acres since the 1950s (out of a total of 272 million to 346 million acres), is probably the worst case (Easterly et al., 1999).

These figures paint a bleak scenario that justifies Andre Dua's (1997) comment that "Nowhere else in the world are huge and growing markets juxtaposed with such serious and worsening environmental degradation."

Is trade openness itself responsible for environmental degradation? Or should the blame—and the solution—be put squarely with national governments? Put simply, is environmental degradation the result of market or government failures? Openness to trade and foreign investment has both positive and negative impacts on the environment (Ivanova Boncheva, 1998). Positive impacts include

- the transfer of more efficient, cleaner production technologies and consumer goods via foreign direct investment and imports;
- the learning and norm building that occur through crossborder exchange of goods, services, capital, and ideas;
- the transmission of higher environmental standards via import requirements by "large market" countries; and
- a more efficient allocation of production activity, with potential reductions in energy and materials use per unit of output (Corona Guzman, 1994).

If the goal of good environmental management is not simply ecosystem and resource conservation but sustainable human development, then the benefits of growth-inducing trade openness would also include rises in per capita income and consumption (Zarsky, 1998).

On the negative side, trade openness subjects national economies to rising market demand and the pressures of international market prices, which rarely include any, let alone full, calculation of environmental damage. With environmental degradation simply outside the market equation, market signals do not give information about the true costs of production (Grossman and Krueger, 1992). As a result, global production and consumption patterns could be grossly inefficient, in both narrowly economic and ecological terms.

Moreover, trade openness subjects national policymaking to competitive pressures. A country that attempts to internalize its own environmental costs will be priced out of markets. In this way, trade openness can be a transmission belt not for high and rising but for low and immoveable environmental standards. For example, the United States will not enact a tax on the carbon content of energy until the European Union does—and vice versa. Indeed, the failure of studies to find any significant impact on competitiveness of environmental standards is most likely due to the fact that market pressures sit heavily on domestic standards.

Economic integration means that firms compete across jurisdictional boundaries. Property rights and regulatory regimes in different countries specify different rights and obligations of resource users, including firms (Garnaut, 1996). Regulatory regimes, in turn, affect competitiveness. But firms compete in common markets. Through competitive markets, producers with the lowest private costs of production win the sale, whereas producers with higher private cost go out of business. Yet the difference between high- and low-cost producers may reflect, at least in part, differences in the property rights regimes under which they operate. Low-cost producers, for example, may create social costs including pollution, resource depletion, and irreversible ecological losses.

International market competition, in other words, is not just between firms but also between systems of rules. The rules that generate the lowest private costs will dominate. Rules systems in other countries limit a government's control over its own national resources. Through economic integration, ecological resources within national boundaries acquire the characteristics of a crossborder, common property resource such as an ocean or the ozone layer. Actions by one country to incur costs in order to sustainably utilize a resource exposed to international trade will be irrational unless every other country does so as well. On the other hand, each country's attempt to maximize its own advantage undermines the collective good by depleting the resource. This is the essence of the "prisoner's dilemma" problem in economics.

"Growth" may be a poor measure of improvements in human welfare. Recent studies have established the relationship between growth-induced resource depletion and rural poverty throughout Asia (Wee and Heyzer, 1995). In many cases, women have been the most impoverished by market-oriented depletion of forests, watersheds, fisheries, etc., since they are traditionally the most directly dependent on natural resources for livelihood. In other words, the very same development process that is depleting resources to generate economic growth is also generating poverty by undermining livelihood resources.

What, then, is the path to sustainable trade and development? Clearly, neither old-fashioned protectionism and export-maximizing growth, nor environmentally unconstrained, "bulldozer" trade openness offers the route. A third way aims to channel markets toward eco-efficient and resource-conserving production and consumption. When countries are highly integrated in economic terms, they must build the channels together.

While conceding short-term ecological degradation, some analysts argue that no formal governance of the trade-environment interface is needed because trade openness is good for the environment in the long term. This is because trade openness speeds growth and national income, which provides financial resources for environmental clean-up, restoration and management, and helps to replace inefficient, obsolete producer and consumer goods with newer, cleaner goods.

Experience and empirical data increasingly show that the costs of environment-blind economic growth are likely to be higher than development paths that build in environmental protection. The experiences of the Philippines and South Korea, for example, show that "grow now, pay later" imposes high financial, social, and ecological costs (Zarsky, 1994). Development strategies that promote income growth while preventing or minimizing pollution and ecosystem degradation could generate an entirely different relationship between economic growth and environmental quality. It could be less negative or even positive if strong environment protection policies promote product and process innovation and enhance investment in environmental infrastructure.

The point is that without explicit environmental disciplines and constraints, trade and investment liberalization will not unambiguously promote sustainable use of resources and ecosystems. A host of rules and disciplines have been erected to frame the architecture of the world's trading system. To protect the environment, countries must likewise develop norms and rules-setting limits and guidelines—not through at-the-border trade restrictions—but through the creation of common, transnational, environment management frameworks.

ECONOMIC INTEGRATION AND THE HARMONIZATION OF ENVIRONMENTAL POLICY

If governments do not act together to develop common environmental frameworks, markets and unilateral state actions will do it for them. The problem is that neither markets nor unilateral action are likely to deliver adequate and appropriate environmental protection.

Economic integration subjects states to two kind of external pressures on domestic policymaking: (1) competitive market pressures that create "prisoner's dilemma" problems for national resource and ecosystem management and (2) regulatory pressures to adopt the environmental standards and policies of large-market countries (Zarsky and Drake-Brockman, 1994). In the absence of supranational governance, environmental standards governing trade-exposed sectors will gravitate either toward those of the most competitive producer or the largest market country.

Market pressures for harmonization in environmental standards are transmitted in a number of ways. The traditional way is via competition for export markets. As argued earlier, states are typically reluctant to (knowingly) impose regulatory costs on domestic producers that dull their competitive edge. Competition for foreign investment is another gravitational pull toward similar practices and standards. Multinational corporations (MNCs) are themselves often a vehicle for convergence.

For large MNCs, which operate in dozens of countries, learning about and complying with standards that differ from country to country can be a high-cost strategy. Moreover, liability laws may make them vulnerable to being sued in their home countries even when the damage occurs overseas (Klitgaard and Sciele, 2000). For these reasons, many MNCs set company-wide standards that apply wherever they operate. Moreover, MNCs often support international standards and norms such as the International Organization for Standardization (ISO) 14000 series on environmental management.

Beyond competitive market forces, harmonization among trade and investment partners is driven by national regulatory policies. Large-market countries set product requirements for imports, including environmental, health, and safety requirements. Large-market states, which tend to be politically powerful, have also taken initiatives to institutionalize convergence in environmental policy in the context of negotiations over trade liberalization, including in the European Union and North America. Convergence lowers transaction costs of trade that stem from a patchwork of differing national environmental requirements. It also reduces the likelihood that environment policies will be used as a protectionist device.

Harmonization can be driven politically as well as through markets by large-market countries either through unilateral action, especially threats of trade sanctions, or via bilateral, regional, and global trade agreements. The best-known instance of unilateral action was the threat of the United States to restrict imports from Mexico of tuna caught with kill rates that exceeded those of U.S. standards. The EC also threatened to ban imports of tropical timber from Southeast Asia. Indeed, free-trade proponents consider the use of the threat to use unilateral trade sanctions in support of environmental objectives as the primary issue in the trade-environment interface.

Some analysts have concluded that market-driven economic integration is beneficial for the environment because large-market countries tend to have high standards. Markets acts as transmission belts, disseminating domestic standards and driving up the standards of trading partners (Vogel, 1995). However, these studies are based primarily on Europe, where Germany is the large-market country. German environmental standards in manufacturing tend to be high. Moreover, a host of environmental institutions have been created in the process of European economic integration.

The "large-market" convergence process in APEC will be complicated by the fact that there are two large-market countries within APEC—the United States and Japan. With their very different industrial structures and resource endowments, the United States and Japan tend to have different environmental concerns and standards. Moreover, the ASEAN countries, combined with East Asian newly industrializing economies (South Korea, Taiwan, and Hong Kong) represent a significant economic force. Finally, China is already an important site for foreign investment and will emerge as a large-market country over the next decade (Elek, 1998). China is growing at the rate of about 12 percent per year, and by 2010 its GNP is expected to triple that of Japan. Without environmental constraints, increasing integration with China would likely pull environment standards down as foreign companies compete for market share.

Some APEC governments and citizen groups have condemned the use of unilateral environment-related trade restrictions as "eco-imperialism." They charge that the environmental issue is a mask for old-fashioned protectionism by the rich countries and a means of retarding industrialization. By the same logic, some countries have condemned any environment-related trade disciplines and argue that "national sovereignty" alone should prevail over environment and resource policy.

These arguments miss the point. Economic integration sets in train both market and political pressures to move toward the same environmental standards and management practices—at least within industry sectors. There is little doubt that rich and powerful countries promote their own interests in international trade fora, and that, in some cases at least, trade sanctions have seemed to protect domestic producers at least as much as the environment. Nonetheless, the heart of the issue is that market-driven economic integration itself erodes "national sovereignty." By the same token, economic interdependence erodes the effectiveness of unilateral sanctions by rich and powerful countries.

From an ecological standpoint, the problem with harmonization is two-fold. First, nowhere in the world are environmental standards good enough. Market-driven and government-driven harmonization could lock countries into a relatively low ceiling on environmental commitment (Ferrantino, 2000). Second, whether driven by markets or diplomacy, whether standards rise or fall, the same standards cannot be ecologically appropriate everywhere.

Ecosystems (and social priorities) differ enormously by specific locale—even within countries' borders. Standards imported from elsewhere may be too low, too high, or simply irrelevant to the sustainable functioning of a local ecosystem or the sustainable harvesting of local resources. Moreover, the use of scarce local resources to meet standards developed elsewhere may mean that more pressing local priorities are neglected. Even within countries (the United States, for example) there is increasing dissatisfaction with rigid, national standards (Duchin, 1997).

The main problem in the trade-environment interface in APEC is the need to create common regional frameworks to govern resource and ecosystem use, while at the same time promoting local diversity and rising environmental commitments (Brandon and Ramankutty, 1993). This will require navigating between the tendency by powerful, developed countries to simply impose their own standards and concerns and the tendency of newly industrializing countries to resist environmental constraints on fast-track growth.

It also suggests an approach that aims toward convergence in principles and policy guidelines, rather than harmonization of standards. Most important, it suggests the need for formal and informal institutions and processes that maximize opportunities for learning, incorporating new information, resolving disputes, and generating solutions.

TOWARD COMMON PRINCIPLES IN APEC'S ENVIRONMENTAL AGENDA

As mentioned in earlier, most APEC countries took steps in the 1990s to improve environmental management and reduce the ecological costs of rapid growth. At a regional level, however, joint environmental discussion and action is in its infancy. The role of analysts and activists could be pivotal in the next few years. The environmental agenda is very much in the development stage and the political will to discuss environmental issues at APEC is just emerging. Without external pressure, governments are likely to focus on narrow environmental concerns, such as the harmonization of product standards, which are heavily influenced by their national economic interests. It is up to citizen groups, scientists, analysts, and other nongovernmental stakeholders to articulate regional common interests and to press for a broader environmental agenda (Zarsky, 1998).

The first step is to develop common principles to guide the governance of the trade-environment interface. Key first principles might be:

1. *Integration of trade and environment:* The very first principle is the recognition that trade and environment impacts and policies are interlinked, both at the national and regional levels. Trade and investment policies should maintain the environmental integrity of ecosystems.
2. *Cooperation:* Common rules, guidelines, and frameworks for environmental management should be developed through processes of regional discussion and consensus building. The more powerful countries should eschew the use of unilateral trade sanctions to impose environmental conditionalities, except in the context of international or regional agreements. Ample opportunities must be created for environmental concerns to be articulated by all members of APEC.
3. *Mutual responsibility:* No APEC country can claim the moral high ground as the guardian of ecologically sound development. The embrace of regional mechanisms that promote environmentally sound trade patterns will require all APEC countries to make changes in their existing domestic policies and to enact new policies.
4. *Efficiency, eco-efficiency, and cost internalization:* One of the central aims of regional trade-environment cooperation is to generate market prices that take ecological costs into account. The reverse is also important: environment policies should promote economic efficiency and aim to ensure that scarce financial resources are well spent.
5. *Scientist and stakeholder participation:* The creation of sound approaches to regional environmental management requires APEC to open its doors to scientists, especially ecological scientists, citizen groups, and other stakeholders. Scientists and stakeholders should receive ongoing opportunities to participate in the design and implementation of regional trade, investment, and environment policies. Stakeholders include community, consumer, environment, and development groups, labor unions, farmers, businesses, and others.
6. *Diversity and commonality:* The general approach of APEC should be to promote common guidelines and frameworks while leaving micromanagement to national and subnational governments. Rather than prevailing standards, for example, APEC could aim to standardize information gathering and testing pro-

cedures, as well as standard-setting methodologies such as environmental and health impact and risk assessment. Harmonization of standards should be pursued where appropriate.

A broad environmental agenda aims to embed an environmental rationality into APEC's fundamental goals and institutions—and to do so in a way that does not create a low ceiling on mutual environmental commitments. Among the issues that a regional citizen group coalition should address are the following (Zarsky, 1998).

Integration of Environment in the Trade Liberalization Process

Without doubt, the centerpiece of APEC diplomacy in Osaka was the implementation of the Bogor "free trade" Agreement. APEC economies have been free to develop their own implementation plans. In the future, a common principle approach will be required.

On the environment side, the key issue will be whether environmental issues should be incorporated within the process of trade liberalization or treated in parallel. Trade proponents tend to argue for the parallel-track approach since building and sustaining momentum for trade liberalization is politically difficult. The inclusion of environmental issues could muddy the waters, they fear, especially if championed by countries whose commitments to liberalization are lukewarm. The Western countries, including the United States, Canada, and Australia, are keen to press ahead with trade liberalization. Southeast Asian countries, especially Malaysia, are more reticent, and Japan tries to stay in the middle.

From an environmental point of view, the ecological impacts of trade liberalization should be considered before trade barriers are lowered and environmental policies put in place in tandem with liberalization. This means that environmental issues should be integrated into national targets and timelines for liberalization. Integration could mean that mitigation policies at either the national or regional level should be in place concurrently with the liberalization; or, if environmental costs are severe, that goals and timelines of liberalization should be changed. On the other hand, in cases where liberalization brings environmental benefits, timelines could be speeded up.

Integration of trade and environment diplomacy could also mean that all APEC nations make a common commitment to internalize environmental costs and maintain ecosystem health. Operationalizing such commitments could be undertaken regionally or, more likely, in the spirit of diversity, left to national governments. At a minimum, each APEC nation should be required to submit environment management plans concurrently with its national free-trade implementation plans.

Integration of the trade and environmental agendas does not exhaust the range of beneficial regional cooperation. Parallel track initiatives are important in building human and technological capacities, generating and incorporating new information, and developing common norms for regional environmental management. The crucial point is that the new patterns of trade that will be created as a result of trade liberalization are shaped by an ecological, as well as a narrowly economic, rationality.

Resource Management: A Sectoral Approach

Environmental issues in trade agreements are typically treated as a problem of "standards," which refer primarily to ambient air and water quality or to product health and safety issues, such as pesticide residues. The crucial issues for sustainable development, however, are bound up with the processes of production. Regional guidelines should aim to promote ecologically sustainable production and harvesting processes. Different ecological issues arise in the production of different kinds of goods and services. Rather than an across-the-board approach to environmental standards, APEC should approach trade-environment linkages on a sector-specific basis. This would allow a greater level of management specificity.

A sector-specific approach could aim to develop common guidelines for sectoral management policies, including resource use, allowable subsidies, the use of economic instruments, Energy Information Administration requirements, labeling, and other policy tools. In the manufacturing sector, environmental guidelines could be considered in light of work being undertaken by the ISO to develop environment management standards (i.e., ISO 14000). One advantage is that trade discussions are often structured around sectors.

The sectoral approach might be especially effective for resource-intensive sectors. Tourism, for example, is the fastest-growing industry in the region. Without a common floor for environmental management, regional competition could undermine the long-term value of tourism assets. A set of common guidelines could set a broad framework for environmental responsibilities, including environmental impact assessment, biodiversity and waste management plans, and environment loading. Micromanagement would be left to national and/or local governments.

Other resource-intensive sectors in which regional guidelines would be helpful include forest and forest products, shrimp aquaculture, and mining.

Sustainable Agriculture

Agricultural liberalization is a highly contentious issue in APEC, with the United States and other Western states pressing East Asian states to open markets. The environmental impacts of liberalization, however, have not been considered. Moreover, the trade impacts of current resource management policies that affect agriculture have also been ignored. For example, California's water subsidies not only deplete soils and water tables, they also distort international trade patterns.

APEC should establish an agriculture working group to study the interrelationship between agricultural, resource management, trade and environmental policies and impacts. The group should consider broad, trade-related environmental disciplines, such as for input and resource subsidies, that aim to promote sustainable agriculture.

Environmental Provisions with the Investment Code

Foreign direct investment flows are central to the process of economic growth in the Asia-Pacific region. APEC's recognition of the importance of FDI was made apparent in the adoption of a set of nonbinding investment principles. The principles aimed primarily at facilitating foreign investment by promoting "free trade" principles, i.e., national treatment, transparency, and most-favored-nation status. However, one article in the principles called for nations not to use low environmental standards as a way to attract foreign investment.

Eschewing "pollution havens" is a good start, although it falls short of providing a framework that proactively promotes environmentally sound foreign investment. Currently, there is no regional or international investment code that would necessarily promote environmentally beneficial technology transfers through foreign direct investment. In China, for example, anecdotal evidence suggests that to reduce costs local partners or purchasers have asked foreign investors and exporters to strip away safety and environment protection components of their investments. Environmental provisions within a regional investment code should specify the responsibilities of investors, home and host countries, and include methods of accountability.

Regional Environmental Implications of WTO's IPR Regime

The World Trade Organization has embraced a new regime on intellectual property rights (IPR) that was negotiated during the Uruguay Round. Many environmentalists and developing country analysts have raised concerns that the regime will undermine crop genetic biodiversity and/or expropriate small farmers of potentially valuable IPR assets. Another IPR-related issue is whether the new regime will speed or retard the process of environmental technology transfer, dissemination, and development. These and other issues need to be explored in the context of APEC.

"Green Financing" Mechanisms

Many APEC countries have large financing needs for infrastructure and human resource development. The embrace of new and rising environmental commitments will add to demands for capital. APEC members should consider innovative financing methods for environmental infrastructure and capacity building. These might include educating and mobilizing banks and other private-sector lenders, perhaps through a regional banker's sustainable development code (potentially modeled after the United Nations Environmental Program code) the creation of an APEC environmental trust fund and the creation of an environment investment window at the Asian Development Bank.

An APEC Environmental Commission

APEC has few central institutions and operates largely on the basis of formal and informal committees and working groups. The day-today process of making decisions and building consensus is headed by the Senior Officials Meeting, which includes the senior officials of foreign affairs and trade ministries. Below the SOM are two economic committees and 11 working groups. In addition, APEC functions via a range of "fast track" processes, including summit meetings of APEC heads of state, sectoral ministerial meetings, and task-specific groups, such as the Eminent Persons Group and Pacific Business Forum. Finally, there are subregional meetings, most importantly of ASEAN, and non-governmental groups. The only NGO that currently has observer status at APEC is the Pacific Economic Cooperation Committee (PECC). The inclusion of more environmentally minded NGOs is highly recommendable.

All these groups have a role in promoting sustainable development in APEC. The central question, however, is whether environmental issues can be adequately pursued without a separate institutional home. On the one hand, an environmental institution could provide oversight and guidance to APEC's environmental work. On the other hand, an institutional home far from the central economic action, such as an Environment Working Group, would only marginalize environmental issues. A commission on environment and sustainable development, however, might be effective in interfacing with other APEC groups and with a broader public. The input of scientists and citizen groups is especially important in developing what will of necessity be an unfolding agenda in coming years.

CONCLUSION

The low institutionalization of the environment in APEC is all the more noteworthy since, unlike the WTO, it has been conceived as being more than a trade grouping but as a body for multidimensional trans-Pacific cooperation.

In any event, more than ten years after APEC's founding, the not very attractive reality of the status of the environment in its member countries is summed up by a report by the Nautilus Institute for Security and Sustainable Development: The seeds of environmental cooperation at APEC are still germinating; little has yet blossomed in terms of implementation of initiatives, let alone measurable improvements in environmental performance. Significant areas of sustainable resource management, including agriculture, are not yet on the agenda, there is resistance to discussing policy change, and institutional mechanisms to coordinate environmental work and to interface with environmental NGOs are lacking. Most important, the trade "track" remains largely separate from, rather than integrated with, sustainable development objectives and environmental diplomacy (Zarsky and Hunter, 1995).

In other words, much further action is needed. First, the United States, APEC's prime actor, is not sympathetic to any effort within APEC that might detract from the primacy of free trade. Free trade within APEC and the use of APEC to advance the global free-trade agenda remains uppermost in the U.S. agenda for APEC. To Washington, the environmental agenda within APEC is in many ways like the aid agenda, one that threatens to deflect APEC from its main goal of promoting trade liberalization. In 1995, the Japanese effort to upgrade the "economic cooperation" leg of APEC—which would include aid for environmental programs—received the rebuke from Washington that Tokyo was trying to convert APEC into an aid agency.

Second, the U.S. corporations that are backing APEC's free-trade agenda in order to reassert a U.S. trade and investment presence in the Western Pacific are not sympathetic to a serious environmental program that would add to their costs of doing business in the region, and this would be the same for other Asia-Pacific corporate elites.

Third, many developing-country elites have pursued the NIC development model, which sees no need to invest in pollution control and externalizes environmental costs. They would be loath to sacrifice their immediate economic gains to transnational environmental controls. Some leaders, such as Malaysia's former Prime Minister Mahathir bin Mohamad, further see environmental measures as a way of hobbling development in the south.

Finally, there is the question of the future direction of APEC's institutional evolution. The previous examination helps identify a number of issues that should be examined by APEC. First is the role of the leaders meetings. As shown in the past, the APEC process can be accelerated by a boost from the leaders, such as can be produced by a summit meeting. Therefore, APEC leaders meetings should be re-engineered, to return to free-wheeling format without a preset agenda, as, indeed, they were originally conceived. In this way the leaders meetings function as a "guiding spirit" in the APEC process. The G-7 (G-8) approach may be the closest model.

The intergovernmental process, APEC proper or the so-called "first track" of APEC, definitely needs to be further institutionalized to be able to meet the challenges of developing new cooperative arrangements, such as would be needed to give serious and effective consideration to environmental issues. This would probably lead to the development of an OECD type of organization for the region.

The third element in the institutional evolution of APEC is the development of mechanisms that could accommodate a role for "second track" activities (PECC, Pacific Basin Economic Council, etc.) as well as the "third track" (NGOs) in APEC's agenda setting. This is clear and imperative if the development-environment duality is to be properly operationalized, but no model for it exists as yet.

To ensure that any APEC environmental efforts draw on the widest possible range of interests and skills, it would be useful to set up an environmental advisory committee along the model of the existing APEC Business Advisory Committee (ABAC). Such a group would provide an established mechanism for receiving input from NGOs, the business community, and others. By drawing a diverse set of environmental, business, consumer, and non-governmental organizations into the APEC "trade and environment" process, it is likely that environmental problems will be identified earlier, better policy responses will be crafted, and the enforcement of commitments will be more vigilant.

Serious pursuit of economic integration makes environmental cooperation an imperative. However, translating the rhetorical environmental commitment of the APEC leaders into a serious program for sustainable development poses a significant challenge.

REFERENCES

Asia-Pacific Economic Cooperation Eminent Persons Group (1994). Achieving the APEC vision—Free and open trade in the Asia Pacific. Second Report of the Eminent Persons Group to APEC Ministers, August.

Ban, K. (2000). Application of CGE modeling to analysis of environmental measures in APEC. In Yamazawa, I. (Ed.), *Asia Pacific Economic Cooperation: Challenges and Tasks for the Twenty-First Century.* London: Routledge, pp. 280-297.

Brandon, C. and Ramankutty, R. (1993). Toward an environmental strategy for Asia. World Bank Discussion Papers, No. 224. Washington, DC: World Bank.

Chia Siow, Y. (1994). Asia-Pacific foreign direct investment. In Chia Siow, Y. (Ed.), *APEC: Challenges and Opportunities.* Singapore: Institute of Southeast Asian Studies.

Corona Guzman, R. (1994). Comercio y ambiente: Armonización y sanciones en el ambito multilateral. *Comercio Exterior,* Vol. 44, No. 5, Mayo, pp. 402-411.

Drusdale, P., Elek, A., and Soesastro, H. (1998). Open regionalism: The nature of Asia Pacific Integration. In Drysdale, P. and Vines, D. (Eds.), *Europe, East Asia, and APEC—A Shared Global Agenda?* Cambridge: Cambridge University Press.

Dua, A. (1997). *Sustaining the Asian Pacific Miracle: Economic Protection and Environment Integration.* San Francisco, CA: Institute for International Economics.

Duchin, F. (1997). Ecological economics: The second stage. In Costanza, R., Segura, O., and Martinez-Alier, J. (Eds.), *Down to Earth: Practical Applications of Ecological Economics.* Covelo, CA: Island Press.

Easterly, W., Islam, R., and Stiglitz, J.E. (1999) Shaken and stirred: Volatility and macroeconomic paradigms for rich and poor countries. In M. Bruno Lecture, XIIth World Congress of the International Economic Association, Buenos Aires, August 27.

Elek, A. (1998). ECOTECH at the heart of APEC: Economic and technical co-operation for financial sector recovery and trade and investment liberalization and facilitation in the Asia Pacific. Paper presented at an international conference on APEC and Liberalization of the Chinese Economy, organized by the APEC Policy research Center of the Chinese Academy of Social Sciences, Beijing, October 7.

Ferrantino, M.J. (2000). International trade, environmental quality, and public policy. In King, P. (Ed.), *International Economics and International Policy.* Boston, MA: McGraw-Hill, pp. 87-110.

Garnaut, R. (1996). *Open Regionalism and Trade Liberalization.* Singapore: Institute of Southeast Asian Studies.

Grossman, G. and Krueger, A. (1992). *Income Increase and Rates of Contamination.* National Bureau of Economic Research Study.

Ivanova Boncheva, A. (1998). Libre comercio y medio ambiente. *Paradigmas,* April-June, pp. 37-47.

Jeong, K., Kubayashi, S., and Takahasi, H. (1995). International trade in NEA: Past, present, and future. Working Paper Number 1, Project on Economic Cooperation in Northeast Asia, Sasakawa Peace Foundation.

Klitgaard, T. and Sciele, K. (2000). Free versus fair trade: The dumping issue. In King, P. (Ed.), *International Economics and International Policy.* Boston, MA: McGraw-Hill, pp. 30-37.

Leavitt Siak, N. (2000). Environment, energy management top APEC concerns. *ASEAN Economic Bulletin,* No. 4, pp. 163-173.

Lucas, G., Wheeler, N., and Hettige, R. (1992). The inflexion point of manufacture industries. In *International Trade and Environment,* World Bank Discussion Papers, No. 148. Washington, DC: World Bank, pp. 98-112.

O'Connor, D. (1999). *Managing the Environment with Rapid Industrialization: Lessons from the East Asian Experience.* Paris: OECD.

Pacific Economic Cooperation Council (1996). *Perspectives on the Manila Action Plan for APEC.* Report prepared in cooperation with the Philippine Institute for development Studies and The Asia Foundation (November).

Pangestu, M. (1994). APEC and Investment facilitation. In Soesastro, H. (Ed.), *Indonesian Perspectives on APEC and Regional Cooperation in Asia Pacific.* Jakarta: Center for Strategic and International Studies.

Petri, P. (1997). Measuring and comparing progress in APEC. Mimeograph.

Soesastro, H. (1994a). Pacific economic cooperation: The history of an idea. In Garnaut, R. and Drysdale, P. (Eds.), *Asian Pacific Regionalism—Readings in International Economic Relations.* Pymble, Australia: Harper Educational Publishers, pp. 77-88.

Soesastro, H. (1994b). The Pan-Pacific movement: An interpretative history. In Bundy, B.K. et al. (Eds.), *The Future of the Pacific Rim.* Westport, CT: Praeger, pp. 9-24.

Strutt, A. and Anderson, K. (1998) *Will Uruguay round and APEC trade liberalization harm the environment in Indonesia?* Working Paper No. 98.02, ACIAR Indonesia Research Project founded by the Australian Center for International Agricultural Research, Adelaide, Australia.

Vogel, D. (1995). *The Greening of Trade Policy: National Regulation in a Global Economy.* Cambridge: Harvard University Press.

Wee, V. and Heyzer, N. (1995). *Gender, Poverty, and Sustainable Development.* Singapore: Center for Environment, Gender, and Development.

Yamazawa, I. (1997). APEC's progress toward the Bogor target: A quantitative assessment of individual action plans. IAP Study Group of JANCPEC and APEC Study Center, Hitotsubashi University, Japan (September).

Zarsky, L. (1994). Lessons of liberalization in Asia: From structural adjustment to sustainable development. In *Regional Financing for the Environment.* Manila: Asian Development Bank.

Zarsky, L. (1998). *APEC, citizen groups, and the environment.* Working Paper No. 167, San Francisco: Nautilus Institute for Security and Sustainable Development.

Zarsky, L. and Drake-Brockman, J. (1994). *Trade, Environment, and APEC: Imperatives and Opportunities for Regional Cooperation.* San Francisco: Center for Asian Pacific Affairs, Asia Foundation.

Zarsky, L. and Hunter, J. (1995). *Environmental cooperation at APEC: The first five years.* Working Paper No. 48, Nautilus Institute for Security and Sustainable Development, San Francisco.

Chapter 8

Financial Resource Flows, the Exchange Rate, and Trade: Recent East Asian Experience

Glenville Rawlins
Chandana Chakraborty

INTRODUCTION

Less developed countries (LDCs) have for decades been shackled with the twin dilemmas of generous supplies of labor that possess varying degrees of attained skill levels, and a universal shortage of capital goods such as machinery, appropriate technology, and requisite managerial and entrepreneurial capabilities. Regarding the first dilemma, several indigenous organizations (especially nongovernmental organizations [NGOs]), as well as international agencies such as the United Nations Educational, Scientific, and Cultural Organization and the World Bank, have combined to upgrade literacy rates and provide a variety of technical training.

LDCs have experienced mixed results in dealing with the second dilemma. In the immediate postcolonial years, foreign aid, together with tax revenues from a few multinational companies, constituted the primary means of acquiring physical capital.

Prior to the 1980s, capital flows into developing economies were dominated by official funds from various multilateral agencies. Portfolio flows were nonexistent, and the relatively small quantities of foreign direct investment (FDI) were targeted at firms that produced raw materials. In the late 1970s, the need to invest the large supply of petrodollars led to a noticeable acceleration in the flows of private fi-

Globalization and East Asia: Opportunities and Challenges

doi:10.1300/5463_08

nancial resources to selected regions of the developing world, mainly to East Asia and Latin America.

While Latin American countries attracted the major share of foreign capital between 1975 and 1980, the early eighties debt crisis and the ensuing market-oriented reforms resulted in a higher level of volatility of capital flows in these countries during the 1980s. By contrast, the success stories of the East Asian tiger economies (Hong Kong, Singapore, South Korea, and Taiwan) over the same decade made their strongest appeal to investors abroad. Consequently, East Asia's share of net capital flows to all developing countries jumped to 40 percent by 1990. (Between 1990 and 1998, developing countries' share of global flows of FDI increased from under 25 percent to about 42 percent, with every country grouping from the developing world enjoying at least a tripling of FDI flow as a percentage of gross domestic product (GDP). This followed an annual decline of about 4 percent in overall resource flows during the 1980-1985 period.) The combination of the array of debt-reduction schemes and improved macroeconomic management precipitated a new surge in capital inflows into this region that lasted through the entire decade of the 1990s.

The explosive growth of net resource flows (especially its FDI component) to developing countries since 1990 stimulated a growing debate regarding its relationship with the macroeconomic environment of the recipient countries. The literature suggests that, in general, aggregate demand, the user cost of capital, and credit availability are all positively related to investment, both domestic and foreign. Thus FDI flows can be expected to depend on the investment environment of the host country and hence on the same set of factors that influence domestic investment. In this context, Fischer (1991) and Thirlwall and Sanna (1996) argue that macroeconomic policy-related variables play a significant role in determining domestic investment, and therefore are expected to affect FDI flows.

In a sample of selected developing countries, De Mello (1996) finds a weak impact of FDI on growth when instruments such as the terms of trade and foreign debt are incorporated into a model that seeks to capture overall macroeconomic instability, international credit constraints, and changes in international relative prices. In a similar study, De Gregorio (1992) argues that observed high FDI elasticities capture the effect of the availability of capital flows in developing countries, given that international credit constraints are highly correlated with FDI. Following a different line of argument, McCombie and Thirlwall (1994) and Fry (1995) show that FDI may be detrimental to growth in an open economy if it substitutes for domestic saving. With such substitution, FDI flows are expected to exacerbate balance-of-payment problems via foreign exchange remittances. Studying the Chinese economy, Chen et al. (1995) establish a positive impact of FDI on growth over the period 1968-1990. They find the impact of FDI on domestic saving to be negative but statistically insignificant.

Benefiting from the existing literature, this chapter differentiates itself by focusing first on the macroeconomic experiences of nations that have been the major recipients of resource flows (mainly FDI flows) over the period 1980 to 1999. With the selected group of countries in the East Asian region, the chapter explores the patterns and characteristics of the resource flows that are specific to the region of East Asia, as well as the influence of these resource flows on macroeconomic performance in the selected region. In addition, the chapter explores the link between the macro policy variables and resource flows by means of an empirical test of the relationship between exchange rate, trade, and FDI flows.

The selected East Asian panel in this chapter includes the following countries: China, Indonesia, South Korea, Malaysia, and Thailand. The choice of these countries is based on the fact that together they accounted for about 90 percent of the total resource flows to the region from 1990 to 1998. In 1996, these five countries received $114.3 billion of a total flow of $127 billion in the East Asian region (Table 8.1).

The study spans the years 1980 to 1997, although as the title suggests, the primary focus is on the period 1990 to 1997. The data set for the study has been prepared in the following manner. Aggregated resource flows of the five selected countries define the actual regional financial flow total for the region of East Asia. The major economic aggregates for this region have been calculated by following a share-weighted method in which the shares are the proportion of each country's FDI in the aggregated total for the entire region. The rationale for this approach is that it facilitates an uncomplicated investigation of the relationship between the flows and the economic indexes for the region.

After an initial examination of the varied pattern of financial flows in East Asia, this chapter sets out the relationship of these patterns to

TABLE 8.1. Foreign Direct Investment for Latin American and East Asian Countries: 1980-1998 (in Billions of US$)

Country	**1980**	**1981**	**1982**	**1983**	**1984**	**1985**	**1986**	**1987**	**1988**	**1989**
Argentina	0.678	0.837	0.227	0.185	0.268	0.919	0.574	–0.019	1.147	1.028
Brazil	1.910	2.520	2.910	1.560	1.598	1.348	0.320	1.225	2.969	1.267
Chile	0.213	0.383	0.401	0.135	0.078	0.114	0.116	0.230	0.141	1.289
Colombia	0.158	0.265	0.366	0.618	0.584	1.023	0.674	0.319	0.203	0.576
Mexico	2.161	2.835	1.655	0.461	0.390	0.491	1.523	3.246	2.594	3.037
China	–	0	0.430	0.636	1.258	1.659	1.875	2.314	3.194	3.393
Indonesia	0.180	0.133	0.225	0.292	0.222	0.310	0.258	0.385	0.576	0.682
Korea, Rep.	0.006	0.102	0.069	0.069	0.110	0.234	0.435	0.610	0.871	0.758
Malaysia	0.934	1.265	1.397	1.261	0.798	0.695	0.489	0.423	0.719	1.668
Thailand	0.1900	0.291	0.191	0.350	0.401	0.163	0.263	0.352	1.105	1.778

Country	1990	1991	1992	1993	1994	1995	1996	1997	1998
Argentina	1.840	2.439	4.384	2.763	3.432	5.279	6.513	8.094	6.150
Brazil	0.989	1.103	2.061	1.292	3.072	4.859	11.200	19.652	31.913
Chile	0.590	0.822	0.937	1.034	2.583	2.978	4.624	5.219	4.638
Colombia	0.050	0.457	0.729	0.959	1.445	0.969	3.123	5.703	3.038
Mexico	2.630	4.762	4.393	4.389	10.972	9.527	9.185	12.831	10.238
China	0.349	4.366	11.156	27.515	33.787	35.849	40.180	44.236	43.751
Indonesia	0.109	1.482	1.777	2.004	2.109	4.348	6.194	4.667	–0.356
Korea, Rep.	0.788	1.180	0.727	0.588	0.809	1.776	2.325	2.844	5.415
Malaysia	2.330	3.998	5.183	5.006	4.342	4.132	5.078	5.106	5.000
Thailand	2.440	2.014	2.113	1.804	1.366	2.068	2.336	3.746	6.941

Source: World Bank (1998, 1999).

various performance and policy macroeconomic variables in the region. Next, the importance of macro policy variables is highlighted by establishing the link between FDI, trade, and the exchange rate. Finally, a brief empirical test of this link is presented followed by a concluding summary.

THE NATURE OF CAPITAL FLOWS

Table 8.2 shows the 1990-1997 flows of net resources to East Asia together with its breakdown. An analysis of these data brings out sev-

TABLE 8.2. Financial Flows for East Asia: 1980-1997 (in Billions of US $)

Year	Net Resource Flow (NRF)	FDI	Portfolio Investment	FDI/NRF	NRF/GDP	FDI/GDP
1980	10.415	1.309	0	0.126	0.026	0.003
1981	12.433	1.790	0.053	0.145	0.030	0.004
1982	13.204	2.312	0	0.175	0.030	0.006
1983	15.862	2.607	0	0.164	0.034	0.006
1984	14.253	2.788	0.150	0.196	0.028	0.006
1985	12.991	3.06	0.138	0.236	0.023	0.006
1986	9.159	3.344	0.031	0.365	0.017	0.006
1987	3.962	4.090	0.318	1.032	0.007	0.007
1988	11.645	6.608	0.487	0.568	0.017	0.010
1989	18.415	8.636	1.820	0.469	0.024	0.011
1990	28.172	10.145	1.570	0.360	0.033	0.012
1991	31.192	13.04	1.039	0.418	0.033	0.014
1992	58.419	20.957	4.747	0.359	0.056	0.020
1993	72.091	36.917	19.116	0.512	0.065	0.033
1994	83.739	42.414	10.893	0.507	0.064	0.032
1995	87.937	48.172	15.692	0.548	0.054	0.030
1996	114.318	56.113	16.169	0.491	0.063	0.031
1997	118.716	60.617	9.215	0.511	0.066	0.033

Source: Authors' calculation from World Bank (1998, 1999).

eral interesting points. First, the steady growth of net resources, from $28 billion in 1990 to $119 billion in 1997, is apparent. More important though is the rise in net resource inflow as a percentage of the GDP; the ratio increased from 3.3 percent in 1990 to 6.6 percent in 1997. It is interesting to note that the growth in net resource flows increased with a higher percentage from 1987 onward, reflecting the improved macroeconomic environment created by the implementation of comprehensive economic reforms since the mid-1980s.

Second, of the two components of net resources flows that appear in Table 8.2, portfolio investment exhibits a decidedly higher degree of instability. From being almost nonexistent between 1980 and 1986, portfolio investment (which includes country funds, depository receipts, and direct share purchase by foreigners) rose to account for 5.3 percent of total flows in 1990, and peaked at 26.0 percent in 1995. However, the percentage declined to single digits in the following period with the onset of the Asian financial crisis in 1996-1997. The increasing numbers of mutual funds and pension funds in developed countries that invested in American Depository Receipts and the international bond issues of high-growth Asian countries supported the noted growth in portfolio investment. Interest in these instruments has ebbed and flowed based upon the risk tolerance of these fund managers, as well as the perceived degree to which economic events have reduced or heightened individual country risk.

Third, by way of contrast, FDI showed a steady growth through the study period. FDI share of net resource flows accounted for 36 percent in 1990 and 51 percent in 1997. Given that FDI represents the acquisition of at least 10 percent of the stock of a company, and that these acquisitions are longer-term decisions, flows corresponding to this component are expected to be more stable over the years.

Fourth, FDI and portfolio investment together account for an increasing share of total capital inflows over the period 1990-1997 (35 percent in 1990 and 59 percent by 1997). The reason for this development is that official flows and bank lending that are less market driven suffered a relative decline. An important observation in this context is that unlike Latin America, where Mexico and Brazil alternated their status as the primary net resource recipient over the decade of 1990, in East Asia, China alone remained the major recipient of net resource flows over the entire decade (Rawlins and Chakraborty, 2002). As is apparent from Table 8.1, net resource flows to China dwarfed those received by the rest of the region, accounting for at least 50 percent of the regional total from 1993 to 1998, and in fact topped 60 percent in 1995.

Fifth, the table brings out the resiliency of financial flows to East Asia in the face of the most severe crisis of the referred decade, the aforementioned Asian financial crisis. Portfolio flows in this region showed only a marginal fall from $9.1 billion in 1997 to $8.4 billion in 1998.

Finally, as indicated previously, official net transfers to East Asia have fallen consistently through the decade, from 24 percent of all flows in 1991 to about 4 percent in 1996. As a result of the Asian financial crisis, however, this percentage increased to 15 percent in 1997 and 20 percent in 1998, almost to levels seen prior to the beginning of the current surge. It may therefore be concluded that the role of official resource flows has evolved into that of being a shock absorber in times of crisis.

World Bank (1999) statistics indicate that for East Asia as a whole, the financial crisis of 1997 caused an overall 36 percent decline in net resource flows. Net resource flows fell from $120 billion in 1997 to $76 billion in 1998. Also, it is important to note that well over half of this decline was explained by the fall in long-term investment and not by portfolio investment.

THE IMPACT OF CAPITAL INFLOWS AND THE POLICY RESPONSE

The sharp increase in net capital flows brought about two broad results. First, the decline in U.S. interest rates in the first half of the 1990s prompted investors to assume greater risk levels as they searched for higher rates of return in developing countries, especially in the countries of Latin America and East Asia. Second, the simultaneous adoption of a broad range of economic liberalization policies in the developing countries drastically reduced the perceived risks of establishing new businesses in these countries and of investing in the equity offerings of existing firms.

Although we have shown the net resource flow to GDP ratio for the entire group of East Asian countries as high as 6.5 percent, for individual countries, the ratio has reached almost 10 percent. Edwards (1998) has shown that under the assumed elasticities for these countries, a ratio of 8 percent will generate a real exchange appreciation of 10 percent. This is so because in the 1990-1995 period, the high levels of capital inflows led to a surge in aggregate expenditures that resulted in the real exchange rate increase, possibly some expenditure switching between tradable and nontradable goods and, ultimately, a loss of international competitiveness. However, with their currencies mostly pegged to the U.S. dollar, the East Asian countries were expected to prevent the real exchange rate from rising significantly under such circumstances.

The explosion in the growth of capital flows gives rise to several questions. First, whether the significantly above average increase in private capital flows is sustainable over a long period. Second, in case the flows are not sustainable, whether the recipient countries would be able to adjust smoothly to a prolonged deceleration of the flows. Third, how would the macroeconomic aggregates, both policy and performance measures behave during this episode? The rest of this section directly addresses this third question with a view to illuminating the first two.

Several authors, including Ito (1999), Edwards (1998), and Sachs et al. (1996), have contended that the large inflows into developing countries in the early 1990s exerted upward pressure on their real exchange rate, especially those that operated on a de facto dollar peg. One manifestation of this process is the level of the current account. As indicated in Table 8.3, the East Asian group of countries ran up massive deficits relative to GDP in the early 1980s (as high as 4.5 percent in 1981) but settled down for the rest of the observed period until 1995. The rise in the deficit occurred again in the 1995-1996 period, immediately preceding the financial crisis. However, as reflected by Table 8.3, there was no pattern in the movement of international reserves in months of imports to validate the exchange rate misalignment.

With policymakers more conscious (in the 1990s than they were in the late 1970s) of the dangers of excessive increases in externally driven expenditure stimulus, monetary policy quickly moved into high gear. To avoid inflation these countries typically engaged in sterilized intervention (i.e., foreign exchange intervention coupled with domestic open-market operations). Since these open-market operations were done mostly in the short-term market, they forced short-term interest rates to increase, thus attracting new inflows in the form

TABLE 8.3. Macroeconomic Performance in East Asia: 1980-1997 (in Percentages)

Year	GDP Growth Rate	Inflation	Deposit Interest Rate	Savings (Percent of GDP)	Investment (Percent of GDP)
1980	6.297	9.412	18.887	32.615	32.941
1985	10.563	7.935	30.6647	32.047	34.440
1990	5.642	6.253	22.345	36.368	34.757
1991	9.059	7.087	24.918	36.367	35.095
1992	11.727	7.118	20.388	36.137	35.441
1993	11.383	11.596	16.664	39.039	40.303
1994	11.233	15.405	13.078	39.827	39.144
1995	9.910	11.063	14.052	39.674	39.294
1996	8.782	5.627	12.196	39.227	38.655
1997	7.394	2.581	12.644	39.837	36.799

Source: Authors' calculation from World Bank (1998, 1999).

of portfolio investment. (Note: Sterilization involves an attempt by the monetary authorities to prevent the capital inflow from affecting the overall supply of money. Since a capital inflow amounts to a net increase in the money supply, the central bank could simultaneously reduce the latter by an equal amount by perhaps selling treasury bills. This would assure that the capital inflow would not reduce domestic interest rates.)

However, since the surges in private inflows were in the form of FDI, and since the domestic intervention did little to affect the longer-term market, long-term interest rates could well decline, further stimulating FDI inflows. As it turned out, one measure of short-term interest rates, real deposit rates, remained high during the 1990s but then drifted down starting in 1995.

An alternative method of preempting inflationary pressure was the imposition of capital inflow restriction. In the early 1990s several countries, including Malaysia and Indonesia, experimented with a range of techniques. Among the most popular were raising the reserve requirements on bank deposits by foreigners and instituting withholding taxes on short-term instruments held by foreigners.

After the fact, many governments attempted to release pressure by implementing contractionary fiscal policies, which would leave them with smaller budget deficits. Although East Asia in general ran smaller budget deficits than Latin America in both the 1980s and 1990s (Rawlins and Chakraborty, 2002), it is important to note that there is no easily discernible pattern to East Asia's budget deficit for the period 1980-1997. (Compared to East Asia, Latin America's budget deficit has, in general, become smaller since the bottom of the debt-crisis-induced recession in the late 1980s.)

Despite these measures, it is clear that these massive capital inflows have brought about some overheating in these economies. As indicated in Table 8.4, inflation (as measured by the growth of the GDP deflator) in East Asia recorded its strongest advances from 1993 to 1995, before slowing appreciably in the crisis year of 1997.

TABLE 8.4. Macromanagement Indicators for East Asia: 1980-1997

Year	Overall Budget Deficit (Percent of GDP)	Current Account Balance (Percent of GDP)	TDS (Percent of XGS)[a]	Reserves in Months MGS[b]	International Tax Trade (Percent of Revenue)
1980	–0.992	–0.019	4.019	0.546	5.336
1985	–0.647	–0.029	14.729	4.062	4.074
1990	–1.171	–0.001	13.597	6.737	13.430
1991	–1.470	–0.011	12.942	7.795	14.872
1992	–1.439	–0.008	11.818	3.598	16.123
1993	–1.079	–0.019	12.695	3.295	20.034
1994	–0.866	–0.009	10.774	5.075	8.999
1995	–0.701	–0.021	11.284	5.290	8.631
1996	–0.749	–0.024	11.294	6.269	7.916
1997	NA	0.005	10.668	7.199	NA

Source: Authors' calculations from World Bank (1998, 1999).

[a]Total Debt Service as percentage of the Export of Goods and Services (the Debt Service Ratio)

[b]Import of Goods and Services

Further, this inflationary advance was accompanied by robust GDP growth rates in the 1990s after a relatively modest start to the decade. Given this fact, it is difficult to avoid the conclusion that strong rates of net capital flows (in some countries as high as 10 percent of GDP) stimulated a dangerously high level of aggregate demand.

While exports grew throughout the decade for East Asia, there was a noticeable pattern to the growth path. With an extraordinary surge in the first half of the decade, East Asia's export growth culminated in an annual rate of 25 percent in 1994 and 1995 before decelerating in 1996 and 1997. With East Asian currencies tied more firmly to the dollar, the appreciation of the yen in the early 1990s initially led to massive Japanese out-sourcing of labor-intensive processes to, and joint ventures with, East Asian-based firms. This in turn led to a general loss of competitiveness in contested third markets. The yen depreciation of 1996 to 1997 largely arrested both this devolution and the steep rise of East Asia's exports.

As seen in Table 8.3, for the period 1980-1997, gross domestic investment (GDI) as a percentage of GDP and gross domestic saving (GDS) as a percentage of GDP consistently made up almost the same percentage of GDP in the East Asian country group (slightly more than one-third during the 1990s). Second, both rates remained at consistently high levels (by world standards) over the referred period. The implication is that capital inflows have had less of a disruptive effect on the process of marshalling domestic savings and converting these savings into domestic investment allocations.

For the period 1980-1996, East Asia's taxes on international trade (a reflection of the degree of economic openness) were extremely volatile. This is especially true with the inclusion of China's figures starting from 1990 given the greater than 60 percent decline in China's ratio in 1994. Nevertheless, with the exception of 1994 a steady reduction in East Asia's international trade tax rate was observed.

Finally, a note of caution must be added. Doubtless a shift to more prudent economic policymaking played a crucial role in the increased share of global financial flows going to this regional group of countries. However, it must be pointed out that the start of these inflows also coincided with the end of the 1990-1991 recession and the commencement of the longest postwar economic boom that the United States had witnessed. In addition, it was during this recovery that so-called global "emerging market" funds in the United States achieved their fastest growth rate ever. Thus this note of caution emphasizes that in addition to the "pull" factors of improved macroeconomic management in the regional country group, the "push" factor of economic recovery accompanied by lower interest rates in the United States and the European Union combined to bring about these impressive financial flows.

CAUSAL LINK BETWEEN FDI, TRADE, AND EXCHANGE RATE

A significant accumulation of literature on the theoretical link between FDI and trade in developing countries (Goldberg and Klein, 1997). It is widely believed that what activates the link between FDI and trade is the movement in the bilateral real exchange rate. In this regard the literature documents two separate effects of the real exchange rates in developing countries. The direct effect measures the changes in trade caused by relative changes in the price of exports and imports. The indirect effect, on the other hand, reflects the impact of exchange rate movement on trade via changes in FDI. Increased flows of FDI can lead to an increase in imports of intermediate inputs in the host country if the investment is directed toward support of local affiliates of multinational corporations. By contrast, if the flows are channeled toward the creation of a domestic facility that produces goods that were formerly supplied by the source country, imports of final goods can be expected to decline. Thus the impact of FDI on the volume of host-country imports is ambiguous. The impact of FDI flows on host-country exports, however, is much more clear-cut. In the event that the host country is a member of a regional trading block, the host country will provide the source country with a production base for goods destined for member country markets.

The real exchange rate impact on FDI in the context of developing countries is often explained in the following manner. Real exchange rate depreciation reduces the relative cost of productive resources, especially labor, in the host country. Consequently, the return on capital in the host country rises through increased demand for and employment of labor. The expected rise in the return of capital then attracts an increased flow of FDI. Though of minor importance, a more indirect link between the real exchange rate depreciation and increased FDI flows is via the wealth effect on foreign investors (Froot and Stein, 1991).

It is interesting to note that a real exchange rate appreciation can also trigger an increase in FDI flows via the host country's efforts in balancing the income distribution effects of currency appreciation. More explicitly, a host country suffering from a persistent rise in inflation may experience an unintended real appreciation of domestic currency. Such appreciation, in turn, can bring about an inundation of imports of final goods. With the increase in imports, public opinion might gather strength and build pressure for the implementation of a protectionist regime in the host country. FDI flows, under these circumstances, may actually increase, in the belief that a real exchange rate appreciation will provide the perceived benefits of operating an affiliate behind the trade protection wall constructed by the host country. Although some ambiguity of the impact of the real exchange rate on FDI exists, the sign of exchange rate coefficient is expected to be negative.

EMPIRICAL ANALYSIS

This section explores the linkages between FDI, trade, and real exchange rate discussed earlier utilizing a panel regression model that depicts the relationship between a group of East Asian countries and their FDI sources. It is expected that such explorations will shed light on the probable channels through which specific exchange rate movements may yield a positive or negative impact on international flows of goods and investment in the selected group of countries.

The panel regression model includes three equations. The first equation defines FDI as a function of the bilateral exchange rate between the donor country and the individual country in the panel, the real GDP of the donor country, and the GDP of the host country of interest. The second equation models real exports of the host country as a function of the host and source countries' GDP (both contemporaneous and lagged), the lagged bilateral exchange rate between the host country and the donor country, and the real FDI flows. Similarly the third equation defines real imports of the host country as a function of the host and source countries' GDP, the bilateral exchange rate between the host country and the FDI donor, and real FDI flows.

The selected East Asian countries in the panel are China, Hong Kong, Indonesia, Korea, Malaysia, Singapore, and Thailand. The data set for our study consists of a cross-section, time-series panel of annual observations on bilateral real exchange rates, FDI flows, GDP, total exports, and total imports from all seven of the selected countries. The time period for the study spans 1982 through 1999. The variables of FDI, import, and export are measured in real dollars. All real exchange rates data in the panel, therefore, reflect bilateral rates measured as prices in the panel countries relative to prices in the United States. An increase in the real exchange rate in the panel represents a real appreciation of the currency of the country in the panel with respect to the U.S. dollar. Also, the data series on source-country GDP refers to the GDP in the United States. The International Financial Statistics database provided by the International Monetary Fund and the Bureau of Economic Analysis are the source of all the data series used in this analysis.

The three equations included in the panel regression model may now be expressed in the following specific forms:

$$\begin{aligned}\mathrm{FDI}_i = a_1\,\mathrm{REX}_{i(t-1)} + a_2\,\mathrm{HGDP}_i + a_3\,\mathrm{HGDP}_{i(t-1)} \\ + a_4\,\mathrm{USGDP} + a_5\,\mathrm{USGDP}_{t-1}\end{aligned} \tag{8.1}$$

$$\begin{aligned}M_i = b_1\,\mathrm{REX}_{i(t-1)} + b_2\,\mathrm{HGDP}_i + b_3\,\mathrm{HGDP}_{i(t-1)} \\ + b_4\,\mathrm{USGDP} + b_5\,\mathrm{USGDP}_{t-1} + b_6\mathrm{FDI}_i + b_7\mathrm{FDI}_{i(t-1)}\end{aligned} \tag{8.2}$$

$$\begin{aligned}X_i = c_1\,\mathrm{REX}_{i(t-1)} + c_2\,\mathrm{HGDP}_i + c_3\,\mathrm{HGDP}_{i(t-1)} \\ + c_4\,\mathrm{USGDP} + c_5\,\mathrm{USGDP}_{t-1} + c_6\mathrm{FDI}_i + c_7\mathrm{FDI}_{i(t-1)}\end{aligned} \tag{8.3}$$

where FDI defines real foreign direct investment flows; REX = real bilateral exchange rate; HGDP = host-country GDP; USGDP = GDP of the United States; M_i = host-country imports; and, X_i = home-country exports. Subscript i refers to the ith host country and t–1 refers to one period time lag.

The a priori theoretical expectations regarding the coefficients are the following.

$$a_1 < 0;\ a_2 > 0;\ a_3 > 0;\ a_4 > 0;\ a_5 > 0 \tag{8.4}$$

$$b_1 > 0;\ b_2 > 0;\ b_3 > 0;\ b_6 > 0;\ b_7 > 0 \tag{8.5}$$

$$c_1 > 0;\ c_4 > 0;\ c_5 > 0;\ c_6 > 0;\ c_7 > 0 \tag{8.6}$$

The actual estimates of the coefficients obtained from the results of the panel regression model are reported in Tables 8.5 through 8.7. The reported estimates of the FDI equation in Table 8.5 more or less meet the expectations outlined earlier. When the host country's currency depreciates with respect to the U.S. dollar, there is, as expected, a corresponding increase in FDI from the United States. Although the negative coefficient for REX is statistically significant, the effect of host-country GDP on FDI flows is statistically insignificant. In addition, the source-country GDP impacts positively on FDI flows.

As reported in Table 8.6, the real exchange rate appreciation has the expected positive effect on imports for the regional panel with the coefficient being highly significant. Also, direct investment has a positive and significant impact for the entire panel. This indicates that rising FDI induces trade in intermediate inputs from the source country. Although the lagged effect of U.S. GDP is positive and robust, that of host-country GDP is statistically insignificant. Host-country GDP does not appear to have much influence on import demand. It is likely that the fluctuation of the latter demand is in large part a function of the trade regime.

Table 8.7 presents results for regression of exports from the East Asian countries to the source countries. For the full panel of East Asian countries, the real exchange rate coefficients are robust and have the desired positive sign. This suggests that the local affiliates' exports to the MNCs in the source countries increase with increased

TABLE 8.5. Panel Regression Results: FDI Equation

	Estimates			
Coefficient	**All Developing Countries**		**Panel of EA Countries**	
REX (t – 1)	–0.006	(–2.158)	–0.003	(–2.384)
HGDP (t – 1)	5.26E-06	(2.099)	5.35E-06	(1.467)
USGDP	1.35E-06	(3.130)	1.02E-06	(2.128)
USGDP (t – 1)	1.91E-06	(3.513)	3.55E-06	(5.929)
R-squared	0.67		0.74	
No. of Observations	204		119	

Note: T-statistics are shown in parentheses.

Table 8.6. Panel Regression Results: Import Flows Equation

	Estimates			
Coefficient	**All Developing Countries**		**Panel of EA Countries**	
REX (t – 1)	9.101	(9.929)*	22.129	(2.528)*
HGDP	0.329	(8.166)*	0.158	(1.159)
HGDP (t – 1)	0.027	(0.674)	–0.044	(–0.307)
USGDP	0.008	(1.468)	0.001	(0.594)
USGDP (t – 1)	–0.0007	(–2.823)*	0.018	(7.739)*
FDI	11.868	(1.499)	1269.949	(3.336)*
FDI (t – 1)	105.141	(3.948)*	1418.493	(3.571)*
R-squared	0.90		0.98	
No. of Observations	153		102	

Note: T-statistics are shown in parentheses.

*Denotes significance at 1 percent level.

TABLE 8.7. Panel Regression Results: Export Flows Equation

	Estimates			
Coefficient	**All Developing Countries**		**Panel of EA Countries**	
REX (t – 1)	–8.547	(0.776)	–14.613	(–0.277)
HGDP	0.0832	(0.509)	–0.031	(–0.347)
HGDP (t – 1)	0.186	(1.069)	0.277	(1.881)**
USGDP	–0.0005	(–0.238)	–0.0007	(–0.734)
USGDP (t – 1)	0.0158	(6.604)*	0.0131	(10.544)
FDI	84.201	(2.31)*	563.219	(2.492)*
FDI (t – 1)	107.537	(2.62)*	375.453	(1.590)
R-squared	0.87		0.88	
No. of Observations	187		102	

Note: T-statistics are shown in parentheses.

*Denotes significance at 5 percent level.
**Denotes significance at 1 percent level.

flows of FDI to the countries in the panel. This effect, together with the effect of FDI on host-country imports noticed earlier, can be identified as the trade-promoting effect of FDI on the East Asian countries. In addition to FDI, the other important factor driving the demand for exports in the East Asian countries is the lagged U.S. GDP. The coefficient for the latter variable is positive and significant, indicating that export growth in the East Asian countries is stimulated by economic growth in the U.S. Real exchange rate movement does not seem to play any significant role in driving demand for exports in the East Asian countries.

A lack of comparable estimates in the literature makes it difficult to evaluate these findings. To overcome this problem, at least partially, the panel was broadened to include the developing world's top 15 FDI recipients. Equations 8.1, 8.2, and 8.3 were reestimated for the panel of all developing countries to obtain a set of coefficients comparable with the one obtained for the East Asian countries. The estimates for the full panel of all developing countries are listed together with those for the East Asian countries in Tables 8.5 through 8.7. As is apparent from the results, these estimates are similar to our regional estimates, and therefore, reinforce the conclusions reached earlier.

CONCLUSION

This chapter laid out and analyzed the various dimensions of net capital inflows into the five primary recipients in the East Asian region. An explosive growth of net resource inflows into the region occurred in the 1990s, with FDI showing a fairly steady growth rate and portfolio flows rising but exhibiting significant volatility. A quick comparison with the behavior of these flows in the 1980s brought out the fact that they are now dominated by private flows, and that official flows have come to be significant only in crisis years, as was the case during the Asian crisis of 1997-1998. Finally, the analysis illuminated the decreased volatility of financial flows in the face of the crisis.

This chapter pointed to two probable catalysts of this surge in capital flows: the decline in U.S. interest rates predisposing U.S. investors to assume greater risk in diversifying their investment to the East Asian countries, which offered higher rates of return but greater risk, and the pro-growth and risk-reduction impacts of the general economic liberalization packages that these countries adopted starting in the mid-1980s.

Given the demonstrated pattern of the financial flows, the chapter analyzed the differential impact of these inflows on key economic aggregates and how policymakers responded to the potentially high levels of economic stimulus. As revealed by the analysis, policymakers are now (compared with the 1980s) much more aware of, and ready to craft policy to respond to, the not-insignificant potential disturbances emanating from large and fluctuating net-capital inflows.

Finally, the chapter evaluated the strength of the reverse impact, specifically the impact of macroeconomic aggregates on resource flows by empirical estimation of the link between the exchange rate, trade, and FDI in the East Asian region. The results of the panel regression estimation model of seven selected Asian countries suggest that the depreciation of a developing country leads to an increase in FDI flows into the country. In addition, the results show that increased FDI flows contribute to trade promotion of the host country by increasing the demand for both imports and exports in the host country.

REFERENCES

Bureau of Economic Analysis (1999). National Economic Accounts. Washington, DC: U.S. Department of Commerce.

Chen, C., Chang, L., and Zhang, Y.M. (1995). The role of foreign direct investment in China: Post 1978 economic development. *World Development, 23,* 691-703.

De Gregorio, J. (1992). Economic growth in Latin America. *Journal of Development Economics, 39,* 59-84.

De Mello, L.R. (1996). *Foreign Direct Investment, International Knowledge Transfers, and Endogenous Growth: Time Series Evidence.* University of Kent, UK: Department of Economics, Mimeo.

De Mello, L.R. (1997). Foreign direct investment in developing countries and growth: A selective survey. *The Journal of Development Studies, 34*(1), 1-34.

Edwards, S. (1998). Capital inflows into Latin America: A stop-go story? National Bureau of Economic Research Working Paper Series, March. Cambridge, MA: NBER.

Edwards, S. (1999). On crisis prevention: Lessons from Mexico and East Asia. National Bureau of Economic Research Working Paper Series, July. Cambridge, MA: NBER.

Elias, V.J. (1990). *Sources of Growth: A Study of Seven Latin American Economies.* San Francisco, CA: ICS Press.

Fisher, S. (1991). Growth, macroeconomics, and development. In Blanchard, O. and Fischer, S. (Eds.), *National Bureau of Economic Research Macroeconomics Annual.* Cambridge, MA: MIT Press, pp. 330-364.

Froot, K. and Stein, J. (1991). Exchange rates and foreign direct investment: An imperfect capital markets approach. *Quarterly Journal of Economics, 106*(4), 1191-1217.

Fry, M. (1995). *Money, Interest, and Banking in Economic Development,* Second Edition, Baltimore, MD: John Hopkins University Press.

Goldberg, L. and Klein, M. (1997). Exchange rates and investment response in Latin America. In Cohen, B.J. (Ed.), *International Trade and Finance: New Frontiers for Research: Festschrift in Honor of Peter Kenen.* Cambridge, UK: Cambridge University Press.

International Monetary Fund (1999). *International Financial Statistics,* CD-ROM.

Ito, T. (1999). Capital flows in Asia. National Bureau of Economic Research Working Paper Series, May. Cambridge, MA: NBER.

McCombie, J.S.L. and Thirlwall, A.P. (1994). *Economic Growth and the Balance-of-Payments Constraint.* New York: St. Martin's Press.

Rawlins, G. and Chakraborty, C. (2002). Accounting for financial resource flows in Latin America and East Asia: A comparative study working paper. Montclair, NJ: Montclair State University.

Sachs, J., Tornell, A., and Velasco, A. (1996). Financial crisis in emerging markets: The lessons from 1995. National Bureau of Economic Research Working Paper Series, May. Cambridge, MA: NBER.

Thirlwall, A.P. and Sanna, G. (1996). The macro determinants of growth and "new" growth theories: An evaluation and further evidence. In Arestis, P. (Ed.), *Employment, Economic Growth, and the Tyranny of the Market: Essays in Honor of Paul Davidson.* Cheltenham, UK: Edward Elgar.

World Bank (1998). *World Development Indicators.* CD-ROM.

World Bank (1999). *World Development Indicators.* CD-ROM.

PART III: INTERNATIONAL FINANCE

Chapter 9

Emerging Trends in Asian Financial Markets: Evidences from Malaysia

Rajesh Mohnot
Wan Fadzilah Wan Yusoff

INTRODUCTION

A well-diversified and competitive financial market system is vital for long-term economic growth and development to ensure that risks in the economy are well distributed among the various subsectors. In the new millennium, the future of the financial market lies in its ability to create dynamic financial players who are able to support the domestic economy and, more important, are increasingly more efficient, competitive, sound, stable, and capable of facilitating the economic transformation process.

Needless to emphasize, well-functioning financial markets result in more and better projects getting financed, managers who are compelled to run companies in accordance with the interests of investors, higher rates of innovation, and individuals who are able to select their preferred time pattern of consumption and their preferred risk-return trade off.

The main functions of financial markets are to mobilize savings and to allocate those funds among potential users on the basis of expected risk-adjusted returns. Facilitating both the transfer of risk and the reduction of risk, financial markets help to monitor managers and exert corporate control. More important to point out, they also supply liquidity to investors by enabling them to sell their investments before maturity. As the wealth of a country increases, the financial markets lead to a successful transition from a nation of savers to a nation of investors (Kadir, 2001).

Globalization and East Asia: Opportunities and Challenges

doi:10.1300/5463_09

THE MALAYSIAN FINANCIAL SYSTEM STRUCTURE

The structure of the Malaysian financial system has always been unique and best suited to its internal application and viability, and is optimally flexible to capitalize on external opportunities. In the new environment, Malaysia is constantly endeavoring to ensure that its financial sector remains effective and responsive in the face of a more globalized, liberalized, and more complex domestic economy. The active involvement through institutional development and capacity building, competitive environment, and the continuous improvement in the existing payments and financial markets infrastructure was observed during the 1990s in the Malaysian financial system.

The Malaysian financial system has been largely confined to the banking institutions and its activities. During the initial period of the decade, the banking system was strong and stable, and core banking principles were already in place. Commercial banks, finance companies, and merchant banks geared up their assets and deposits well enough to boost the financial system of the country. Commercial banks' assets rose to RM 471.5 billion at the end of 1999 from RM 152 billion in 1991 while financial companies' assets were recorded at RM 115.9 billion in 1999, more than double from RM 49 billion in 1991. The deposits of these two institutions also showed remarkable growth of three times and two times respectively between 1991 and 1999 (Bank Negara Malaysia, 2000). Much of the financing was through banking and non-financial-institution systems because the risk associated with the cyclical downturn in the economy was focused on the banking system. The ratio of bank credit to GDP was as high as 149 percent in 1997 (Bank Negara Malaysia, 1999). After the crisis in particular, the banking institutions followed the minimum capital funds requirements in line with the overall objective to strengthen the resilience and to enhance the level of capitalization of the players in the domestic market. Given the rapid pace of development in the financial markets, it is crucial that banking institutions are strongly capitalized to better withstand challenges arising from a more competitive and liberalized economic environment, and undertake investment in information technology. In addition, the stronger capital position would place banking institutions in a better position to meet the demands of the new economy.

DEVELOPMENTS IN FINANCIAL MARKETS

Stock Markets

The 1990s witnessed almost all of the phases of economic development in most of the Asian regions financial and capital markets. Basically, the changes occurred due to major technological advances, market innovations, and financial liberalization in the face of globalization. The capital markets project quite a different picture if we look into the decade between the pre- and post-financial crisis period. During the 1990s, and particularly in the later period, almost all of the Asian capital markets plunged, as did the Malaysian capital markets. Investors lost confidence in the capital markets, market capitalization declined, and share prices consequently came down to their mean values.

The annual turnover in Malaysian government securities remarkably increased on Kuala Lumpur Stock Excange (KLSE) from RM 7.699 billion in 1991 to RM 18.808 billion in 1993, but then sharply fell down to RM 3.846 billion in 1995 and RM 2.786 billion in 1997. The annual turnover in respect to other commercial transactions on the KLSE recorded a constant growth from 1991 to 1994 but then faced a sharp and constant decrease.

Since the end of the financial crisis, the stock market has performed dynamically in the Malaysian economy. The successful privatizations of Telekom Malaysia Berhad and Tenaga Nasional Berhad have increased the market capitalization of the KLSE by more than 10 percent at the time of their respective initial offerings. This provides ample evidence of the receptiveness of domestic and foreign investors toward the quality of the Malaysian stock markets.

Liberalization and globalization have continued to increase market capitalization in the KLSE. As is evident from Table 9.1, market capitalization rose to RM 619.64 billion in 1993 from RM 161.39 billion in 1991, fell slightly to RM 508.7 billion in 1994 and began to recover in 1995 and 1996. The financial crisis clearly contributed to the reduced market capitalization after 1997. The KLSE composite index of share prices reflects investors' confidence in the stock market almost until 1996, but this confidence plummeted in 1997 and was not regained until recently.

Several major developments occurred in the Malaysian stock markets, particularly during the past decade. In 1990, efforts were made

TABLE 9.1. Market Capitalization and KLSE Composite Index

Year	KLSE CI of Share Prices	Market Capitalization (RM Billion)
1991	556.22	161.39
1992	643.96	245.82
1993	1275.32	619.64
1994	971.2	508.7
1995	995.17	565.63
1996	1237.96	806.77
1997	594.4	375.8
1998	586.1	374.5
1999	812.3	552.7
2000	679.6	494

Source: KLSE Directory, various issues.

to delist all Singapore-incorporated companies from the KLSE. The Central Depository System (CDS) and Fixed Delivery & Settlement System (FDSS) were introduced to improve the clearing and settlement system. To boost the private debt securities market, the Rating Agency Malaysia (RAM) was introduced. The government established a minimum paid-up capital of RM 20 million requirement for all stock-broking companies in order to ensure that these companies are better capitalized and financially strong enough to meet the needs of the growing securities industry.

In March 1993, the Securities Commission (SC) was established. To increase accessibility for investors, the share application forms for new public issues were made available in newspapers, and share transfer forms were printed on the reverse of share certificates.

In 1995, component stocks of the KLSE Composite Index were increased to 100 and call warrants were permitted for listing and trading on the KLSE. To improve the transparency of the market and regulatory framework, the ceiling limit of ten listed stockbroking companies was lifted, and the paid-up capital requirement for main and second-board companies was fixed at minimum of RM 50 million and RM 10 million respectively.

Marching on the globalization path, the Ministry of Finance approved the listing of foreign companies on the KLSE in 1996. Short-selling of 50 approved stocks was permitted but had to follow regulatory guidelines.

In an epic development in 1997, the Australian Securities Commission granted the status of an "approved foreign stock exchange" to the KLSE. The KLSE-RIIAM Information System was launched to make the security industry system unique, comprehensive, and consolidated. To stabilize the demand and supply of securities, companies were allowed to buy back their own shares under the amended section 67–A of the Companies Act.

In 1998, the exchange instituted incisive new measures to further enhance transparency in the stock market, specifically streamlining (1) an orderly and fair market in the trading of Malaysian securities and (2) overall market transparency in the Malaysian Capital Market. The exchange launched a new index to expand participation in the stock market from local and foreign investors and keen interest to invest in securities approved by the principles of Islamic law.

In 1999, the KLSE launched the Institutional Settlement Service, a program offered by SCANS to achieve delivery versus payment for institutional investors in securities settlements. The Securities Commission also launched its Capital Market Masterplan to chart the strategic positioning and future direction of the Malaysian Capital Market over a ten-year period. The six key objectives masterplan are

1. to be the preferred fund-raising center for Malaysian companies,
2. to promote an effective investment management industry and a more conducive environment for investors,
3. to enhance the competitive position and efficiency of market institutions,
4. to develop a strong and competitive environment for intermediation services,
5. to ensure a stronger and more facilitative regulatory regime, and
6. to establish Malaysia as an international Islamic capital market center.

Foreign Exchange Markets

In the initial years of the 1990s, the Malaysian ringgit was quite strong against the U.S. dollar. Due to strong economic indicators, the country's capital inflows were spectacular. The interest rate spread in favor of Malaysia was one of the factors that attracted short-term inflows, which increased ringgit deposits by foreign banks and non-bank foreign customers with Malaysian banks. However, the 1997 financial crisis degraded the ringgit exchange rate and a paniced down trend was observed. At the height of the crisis, the ringgit fell to a low of 4.88 against the U.S. dollar on January 9, 1998, which was about 48.8 percent lower than the average of about 2.50 in April 1997.

The fundamentals of Malaysia's foreign policy objectives and approaches are well established. Nevertheless, the task of implementing and managing a consistent and proactive foreign policy requires the managers of Malaysia's international relations to be alert and sensitive to the ever-changing international politics and environment. A primary objective of Malaysia's foreign policy is to promote peace and security, particularly in the Southeast Asian region.

The foreign exchange reserve showed a remarkable increase from US$10.421 billion in 1991 to US$26.156 billion in 1996, but then slipped to US$20.013 billion in 1997. It recorded an increase again in 1998 to US$24.7 billion, as shown in the following list (Bank Negara Malaysia).

Year	Billion US$
1991	10.4
1992	16.8
1993	26.8
1994	24.9
1995	22.9
1996	26.2
1997	20.0
1998	24.7
1999	30.6
2000	29.5

The currency turmoil of 1997 disrupted the foreign exchange markets of Malaysia, and resulted in decreased private external capital flows and negative net foreign-bank lending and portfolio equity investment. The government had to take measures to reduce the current account deficit primarily by cutting down on planned infrastructure expenditures and deferring other large investments. A package of austerity measures announced in December 1997 included an 18 percent reduction in government spending and the postponement of all megaprojects not yet started. In September 1998, the government imposed selective capital controls and fixed the ringgit-U.S. dollar exchange rate. These tough monetary controls gave the authorities sufficient flexibility to pursue expansionary fiscal and monetary policies that would stimulate domestic demand without precipitating capital flight. Using capital controls to accelerate corporate and financial sector reforms, and replacing the quantitative restrictions on repatriating portfolio investment with an exit levy also helped restore international confidence and reestablished portfolio capital inflows.

Labuan International Offshore Financial Centre

A spectacular milestone in Malaysian history was the designation of the Federal Territory of Labuan as an international offshore financial center (IOFC) on October 1, 1990. In view of the vast potential in this strategic location, and in line with the objective to enhance Malaysia's position as a regional financial center, the Labuan IOFC was established as one of the few "super markets" in Asia. The primary objective of the Labuan IOFC was to generate financial activities to complement Kuala Lumpur as the premier regional financial center in the Asia-Pacific region. The Labuan IOFC was also intended to strengthen the financial sector's contribution to the gross national product, much in congruence with the vision for Malaysia to obtain an industrialized status by the year 2020.

As of May 1996, more than 700 offshore companies and 13 trust companies had set up operations in Labuan. Of the total offshore companies, 51 are offshore banks, including 44 which were set up by international banks, while six are insurance and insurance-related companies. The offshore banks in Labuan are well represented from various countries in the world. Offshore banking activity has grown steadily over the years and is gaining momentum for further growth. Deposits amounted to US$2.5 billion, while outstanding loans and advances were close to US$9.0 billion as of March 1996.

DERIVATIVE MARKETS

The first Malaysian derivative exchange was established in 1980 as the Kuala Lumpur Commodity Exchange (KLCE), which introduced the crude palm oil (CPO) futures contract in 1980, followed by the rubber futures contract (RSS 1) in 1983, rubber futures contract (SMR 20) in 1986, tin futures contract in 1987, cocoa futures contract in 1988, palm olein futures contract in 1990, and the crude palm kernel futures contract in 1992. Of the seven commodity futures, the crude palm oil futures contract is the most popular.

The Kuala Lumpur Options and Financial Futures Exchange (KLOFFE) was established in 1993, but did not introduce its first product until December 1995. With the introduction of the Stock Index Futures Contract (based on the KLSE's, CI), the KLOFFE became the second Asian emerging market derivative exchange (after Hong Kong) to trade its own equity derivative (Obiyathulla, 2001).

On June 11, 2001, KLOFFE and the Commodity and Monetary Exchange of Malaysia merged and gave birth to a new exchange called the Malaysian Derivative Exchange (MDEX). The MDEX is a wholly owned entity of the Kuala Lumpur Stock Exchange (KLSE). The exchange products are: (1) KLSE CI Futures Contracts, (2) KLSE CI Options Contract, (3) Crude Palm Oil Futures Contract, and (4) Three-month KLIBOR Futures Contract. The products have further developed to Malaysian Government Securities Bonds Futures, Individual Shares Futures, Islamic Index Futures, US$-denominated CPO Futures, Capitalized Index Derivatives, Other Commodity Derivatives, Strategic Alliances, etc. All these derivative products have migrated from floor to screen-based trading since the end of 2001 (Sreekumar, 2002).

FINANCIAL MARKETS AND ECONOMIC IMPLICATIONS

The most spectacular development in the world economy in recent decades is the increasing globalization of financial markets and integration of economic activities. The capitalist system is gradually being understood as global rather than national in the wake of the globalization process. The integration of global financial markets, facilitated by regulatory changes and by technological innovations in the information economy, is one of the most important factors contributing to this globalization (Walter, 1989; O'Brien, 1992). In this era of globalization, it is pertinent to take note of the financial markets' role in developing and emerging economies, particularly in Asia.

The financial markets have definitely played an important part in boosting the Malaysian economy. In 1992, Malaysia's precrisis GDP was 8.9 percent, which was far better than the world's GDP of 2.0 percent. Malaysia recorded a robust growth rate of 9.2 percent in 1994, which was not only higher than the world's GDP of 3.7 percent but also Southeast Asia's GDP of 7.8 percent and even Asia's regional GDP average of 8.7 percent. The growth rally continued, registering the highest, ever growth rate, 10 percent, in 1996. Unfortunately, the financial crisis of 1997 derailed the economic growth, which worsened to –7.4 percent in 1998.

Foreign direct investments (FDI) have long been an important source of external finance in Malaysia. FDI growth was consistent from 1991 to 1997. Malaysia's FDI share in Southeast Asia's total FDI was 44.3 percent in 1993, but declined to a low of 26.3 percent in 1998.

FDI remained stable at the level of US$3.8 billion in 1999. It also proved to be much more stable than other forms of capital flows during the crisis period. In 1998 and 1999, net FDI flows into the five worst-hit countries—Indonesia, Korea, Malaysia, the Philippines, and Thailand, increased slightly from the 1997 level of US$17.5 billion (Asian Development Bank, 2000). To help rejuvenate distressed companies, the governments of Korea, Thailand, and Malaysia instituted some effective measures promoting FDI flows in the country. Thanks to the Investment Incentive Act of 1968, Malaysia, through a range of incentive and policy mechanisms, attracted many Fortune 500 companies to invest and establish manufacturing plants in that country (Ramasamy, 2001). Korea opened several sectors welcoming foreign investments, including property, securities dealings, and other financial businesses, while Malaysia suspended the restrictions on foreign holdings in new export-oriented manufacturing projects until 2000. Foreign ownership limits in Malaysia were also relaxed.

Malaysia's merchandise exports and imports consistently fared well until 1995. Sometimes the exports growth rate did better, while other times the import growth rate was higher than the export growth rate (Table 9.2). The years 1996, 1997, and 1998 were the most disappointing from an exports point of view. Of course, the balance of payments strengthened in 1998, 1999, and 2000 following a substantial

TABLE 9.2. Major Economic Indicators

Year	Merchandise Export Growth (percent)	Merchandise Import Growth (percent)	Debt-Service Ratio	Current Account Balance/GDP (percent)	Inflation Rate (Consumer Price Index) percent
1991	17.1	26.9	5.8	–8.8	4.3
1992	18.3	9.9	4.7	–3.7	4.7
1993	16.0	18.1	5.5	–4.8	3.5
1994	23.3	28.5	5.0	–7.8	3.7
1995	26.3	30.3	5.7	–9.9	3.4
1996	7.0	1.4	4.7	–4.9	3.5
1997	1.5	1.8	6.6	–5.5	2.7
1998	–7.8	–26.8	6.6	+12.9	5.3
1999	10.1	10.0	6.2	+14.0	2.8
2000	8.0	12.6	5.3	+11.3	3.3

Source: Economic Outlook, various issues, and Bank Negara Malaysia, various bulletins.

improvement in the trade surplus. The current account balance to GDP recorded a positive figure of 12.9 percent in 1998, which was driven mainly by import compression as imports declined by 26.8 percent. In 1999, however, the export and import growth rates expanded almost equally, which resulted in an improved higher trade surplus. Another important driving factor of export buoyancy was the real depreciation of the ringgit and stronger demand for electronic goods.

The debt-service ratio was also at comfortable levels throughout the 1990s. Because of higher repayments and less borrowing by the private sector, the external debt position improved consistently after the crisis. The lower incidence of debt and the improved export situation helped reduce the debt-service ratio to 6.2 percent in 1999 and 5.3 percent in the year 2000.

The consumer-price-inflation rate decreased consistently until 1997. In 1998, it increased to the decade's highest rate of 5.3 percent. However, continued excess capacity, greater exchange rate stability, and a slower increase in food prices helped reduce the rate to 2.8 percent 1999.

CONCLUSION

Malaysia's financial markets have been somewhat different from other crisis countries. Malaysia's markets have been stronger in the sense that they have been backed by well-structured and effectively instituted bankruptcy and foreclosures laws. Not only this, but they have been led by a well-capitalized banking sector as well. Malaysia is on track in developing and modernizing its security industry in order to promote long-term savings and investments in profitable industrial and infrastructure projects.

As discussed in the preceding paragraphs, Malaysia was the only Asian country to come out of the crisis quickly. The economic indicators in the later part of the decade are well reflected by the robust economic growth, low-inflation environment, and improved foreign direct investment in Malaysia. The economy has responded well to the expansionary fiscal and monetary policies pursued since 1998. Concurrent with the high growth, macroeconomic and financial stability has been restored.

Although Malaysia's financial markets are performing satisfactorily, a number of concerns pose some risks to the future outlook. These include the risk of hard lending in the United States, the uncertain direction of private foreign and domestic investments that may curtail economic activity and growth in future, and the sustainability of the demand for electronic and electrical products given the slowdown in the U.S. economy.

REFERENCES

Asian Development Bank (2000). *Asian Development Outlook 2000. New York:* Oxford University Press.

Bank Negara Malaysia (Reports), Various Issues.

Economic Outlook, Various Issues.

Eun, C.S. and Resnick, B.G. (2001). *International Financial Management.* Boston: Irwin McGraw-Hill.

Kadir, D.A.A. (2001). *Financial Planning in a Liberalized Market.* Second International Financial Planning Conference, Malaysia.

KLSE Directory, Various Issues.

O'Brien, R. (1992). *Global Financial Integration: The End of Geography.* London: Royal Institute of International Affairs.

Obiyathulla, I.B. (2001). *Financial Derivatives: Markets and Application in Malaysia.* University Putra Malaysia.

Ramasamy, B. (2001). Gear up for globalization: Practical guidelines for managers. *Accountant Nasional,* January, 19.

Sreekumar, K. (2002). Malaysia Derivative Exchange: Growth and Future of the Derivative Markets. Paper presented at a talk organized by University Tenaga National in February.

Walter, N. (1989). Implications of EC financial integration. *Business Economics.*

Chapter 10

The Impact of Globalization on Economic Transition in China

Joanna K. Poznanska

ECONOMIC PERFORMANCE

China symbolizes the latest example of an economic miracle in the modern era. In fact, no country in modern history has shown such strong economic growth as China during the past two decades. It has outperformed even the most successful postwar leaders in economic growth from among the Far Eastern economies, including Japan and South Korea. China has outperformed all these countries not only in terms of the rate of growth but also in terms of the duration of this phenomenal spurt, one that seems to have no quick end in sight.

Macroeconomic Picture

Another appropriate point of reference for measuring the growth performance of China is to compare it with other countries that, as with China, have been in transition from state-socialism to market-capitalism. Among those other countries, Russia seems more suitable for such a comparison, since unlike China, with these reforms initiated, the country into an instant major recession. Although almost all other transition countries also entered into recession, although bit earlier, mainly in 1990 when their reforms started, recession in those other countries lasted two to three years. In Russia, however, positive growth did not resumed until 1998.

With such contrasting economic performance, China quickly surpassed Russia's GDP and then left Russia trailing far behind. Mea-

Globalization and East Asia: Opportunities and Challenges

doi:10.1300/5463_10

sured in dollar terms, Russia's GDP initially declined by almost half, but then, as a result of the 1998 crisis (in which the ruble plummeted), GDP decreased to one-third of the initial figure. At the same time, China's GDP increased threefold with no interruption. Precisely speaking, Russia's GDP in 1991 was $466 billion, but in 1999 GDP was at $167 billion. China's GDP on the other hand, increased from $262 billion in 1991 to more than $974 billion in 1999. Thus, while China's GDP represented 70 percent of Russia's GDP in 1991, it was almost 600 percent of Russia's in 1999 (see Table 10.1).

If one splits national production into the public (state) and private sectors, then it becomes clear that the entire collapse in Russia's GDP came from the former state sector, while the newly established private "entries" showed a steady expansion. These newly formed private businesses were very dynamic in the early years, but later they lost much of their momentum. In China, on the other hand, the non-state sector

TABLE 10.1. Foreign Trade Sector Indicators, China, 1990-2005 (in Billion $)

Year	GDP	GDP/Capita	Exports	Imports	Balance	Foreign Reserves
1990	224.8	197.5	62.0	53.3	8.7	29.6
1991	261.9	227.2	71.8	63.7	8.0	34.7
1992	320.9	275.5	84.9	80.5	4.3	20.6
1993	417.2	354.1	91.7	103.9	−12.2	22.4
1994	516.7	471.3	121.0	115.6	5.4	41.2
1995	700.7	580.8	148.7	132.0	16.7	71.4
1996	808.3	674	151.0	138.8	12.2	83.7
1997	884.4	732	182.7	142.3	40.4	116.0
1998	930.0	762	183.7	140.2	43.4	142.8
1999	974.3	791	194.4	165.7	29.2	154.7
2000	1066.3	855	249.2	225.0	24.1	160.1
2001	1160.3	925	266.6	244.9	21.7	182.0
2002	1270.8	994	327.0	295.9	21.1	292.0
2003	1430.0	1100	438.7	413.1	25.6	409.0
2004	–	1269	593.4	561.4	32.0	610.0
2005	2250.0	–	752.2	631.8	110.4	659.1

Source: Calculated from *China Statistical Yearbook* (various years).

that provided most of the economic expansion, though the state sector has turned out to contribute to the overall growth as well. The state sector of China has grown only at one half of the growth rate of the non-state sector, which has been quite respectable and higher than right before 1978, when the first market reforms where instituted.

The main contrast between Russia and China is that the former eliminated its state sector to stimulate growth (but failed to do so), whereas the latter's economy has surged while retaining its state sector almost intact. Not even for one moment has the state sector in China experienced any growth regression, and, more important, the growth of this sector has not been simply a function of adding resources. Forced to compete for resources with the private sector, the Chinese state sector has had to rely also on increasing productivity of resources. Although lower than in the private sector, productivity gains by state entities have been quite remarkable. One study (Chen et al., 1988) established, for instance, that these gains were in the range of 4 to 5 percent per year after 1978, whereas earlier productivity rates were stagnant.

Sectoral Picture

China's industry grew much faster than the overall economy, around 20 percent a year during 1990-1995, and then experienced a relative slowdown to an average of 10 percent for 1996-2000. At this speed, China's industry almost tripled its capacity, so that its share in national product increased (see Table 10.2). Almost all industries in China show equally dramatic increases, though not at the same rate, suggesting that a great deal of restructuring has occurred. This may be called a sort of "creative destruction," in which old makes room for new, or, as some would prefer to say, "unwanted" makes room for "wanted." Most economists would probably agree, that "creative destruction," which is efficiency maximizing, is more likely to occur, or at least less costly, when the economy is expanding.

Beginning with industrial equipment, one finds that the production of pumps in China increased from 4209 thousand to 6746 thousand units between 1990 and 1998. In the area of transformers > 5 KVA, China managed to increase its output from 99311 thousand KVA to 149896 thousand KVA. Turning to consumer goods, China multiplied its output at the same time to 42 million units in 1999. Telephone production increased several times, namely from 8800 thousand to

TABLE 10.2. Basic Economic Indicators for China, 1990-2005

Year	Real GDP Percent	Consumer Prices Percent	Agricultural Output Percent	Industrial Production Percent	Electricity Generation Percent
1990	3.8	3.1	7.6	7.6	6.2
1991	8.2	3.4	3.7	14.8	9.0
1992	13.1	6.4	6.4	27.5	11.3
1993	13.7	14.7	7.8	28.0	11.3
1994	11.5	24.1	8.6	26.1	10.5
1995	8.9	12.1	10.9	12.9	8.6
1996	10.2	8.9	9.4	13.1	7.2
1997	9.4	2.8	6.7	12.1	5.0
1998	8.2	–0.1	6.0	18.6	2.9
1999	7.1	–1.4	4.7	17.6	6.3
2000	7.3	0.7	4.1	16.4	9.4
2001	7.5	0.7	4.2	15.8	8.9
2002	8.3	–0.8	4.9	15.3	11.5
2003	9.3	1.2	3.9	14.6	16.5
2004	9.5	3.9	–	–	–
2005	9.8	1.9	–	27.7	–

Source: Bucknall, 1997, for 1990-1994; *China Statistical Yearbook* (various years) for 1995-2000.

65205 thousand. Production of irons increased from 14056 thousand to 17017 thousand. Output of sewing machines grew from 7610 thousand in 1992 to 8612 thousand in 1994.

Sharp increases in output were also reported in the production of agricultural inputs and in food production. China registered an increase in the production of tractors from 39400 to 67800, or 185 percent of the initial figure. Another important input to agriculture is nitrogen fertilizers, which in China increased from 14636 thousand metric tons to 22257 thousand metric tons. With the rapid growth in agricultural inputs came a sharp rise in agricultural outputs, as in the case of pork production which increased from 22 million tons to 39 million.

It is evident that agriculture in China has in many ways shown particularly strong performance, which, given the dominant share of farming in the national product, greatly helped to accelerate the overall growth of the economy. It has often been said that the transition in China came easier than it did in the other former socialist countries, particularly because it did not require large economic sacrifices. Apparently, it should be easier to reform China, since farming, dominated by small-scale operations, poses fewer problems than dominated by large-scale entities industry does. However, for this argument to be true, one would have to demonstrate that no other factor could have had a more important role to play, to include policy choices.

Among transition economies, the greatest contrast is with the pattern found in China, as well as in Vietnam, where reforms were followed by an increase in both output and productivity. Russia stands out as another special case, where market reforms have been followed by an agricultural downturn both in total output and labor productivity (Macours and Swinnen, 2002). This same pattern can be found only among certain former member republics of the Soviet Union, such as Ukraine, Belarus, Kazakhstan, and Kyrgyzstan. A different pattern, with agricultural output declining but with labor productivity increasing, can be found among central European transition economies, among them the Czech Republic, Hungary, Poland, and Slovakia.

If one examines the first five postreform years in China, starting in 1978, one will see that output increases reached 20 percent, whereas productivity gains in the same sector reached 30 percent. However the numerical picture shows that Russia allowed its agricultural output to fall by 40 percent during the first five years after the reform of 1992, with productivity simultaneously collapsing by the same 40 percent. In eastern Europe (specifically in Czech Republic, Hungary and Slovakia combined), the output of the agricultural sector decreased by about 25 percent during the first five post-reform years, whereas productivity showed an increase of about 45 percent.

Reforming agriculture is much easier than reforming industry. However, in the case of eastern Europe, both sectors collapsed. This would imply both sectors had to be faced with a common adversity that made these structural differences largely irrelevant. One possible explanation is that in Russia, as well as in eastern Europe, agriculture collapsed mainly for policy reasons. Everywhere the health of agriculture depends on state policies, various financial supports that favorably change its cost and profit structure. To test this theory, one would have to look at the levels of state support received in those economies and China respectively, including one key indicator, namely the so-called terms of trade, or the ratio of agricultural outputs and prices for industrial inputs to agriculture.

If one takes the prereform price ratio as a basis, or as 100, then in most cases in the former Soviet Union and in eastern Europe, one finds a major deterioration. In Russia, but also in Ukraine, largely due to the elimination of state subsidies (e.g., favorable energy prices, preferential credits for machinery purchases, above market-level output prices) this ratio fell to one-quarter of the prereform level. In countries such as Czech Republic, Poland, and Romania, this ratio fell to one-half, and in Hungary and Slovakia it fell by one-third. Although agriculture faced unfavorable, profit-reducing changes in national price structure in all these countries, the terms of trade improved for agriculture by one-half in China. In fact, a very strong correlation exists between changes in price ratio and agricultural output.

Economic Prospects

China has its measure of economic problems, but they are not of the nature that they would easily upset the expansion of the economy. If anything, political problems, such as those related to the widening income gap, particularly between the urban and rural populations, might interfere with economic expansion. However, if the past is a good indicator of the efficiency of state agency, one would guess that proper measures would be taken in time to avert political backlash. Already there are signs that the state is trying to assist the poorest members of the population, as in the case of the recent campaign to force lower taxes in rural areas or bring to those areas some state projects.

The true test of China's resilience was the financial crisis in the Far East, which started with the speculative panic in Thailand in 1997. Almost no Far Eastern economy was spared the crisis, though some areas, such as Taiwan and Hong Kong experienced limited change. But it is China which showed almost no negative effects of the crisis. So that while local currencies were sharply devaluated, stock markets plummeted, and production went down almost everywhere, nothing of this nature happened in China. China's economic growth continued, and no steps were taken to devalue its currency to compensate for the devaluation that its Far Eastern competitors were faced with.

One major economic problem for China is its inefficient state sector, which suddenly stopped showing strong positive gains in productivity, and after years of declining profits, the bulk of state-owned companies have become unprofitable. This has forced the state to use its bank to issue credit to bail these companies out, leaving the bank with a mounting pile of so-called bad debt and a growing prospect of the collapse of the outdated banking system. In 2002, bad debt accounted for 43 percent of China's GDP. On the other hand, the leadership of China has shown great skills in fixing some major problems without losing control over the economy and letting it to go under. Accordingly, the state recapitalized major banks in 2004-2005, and when they were eventually floated investors showed strong interest in their stocks.

Whatever the level of its inefficiency, the existing banking system of China has proven sufficiently effective to support the phenomenal growth of its economy, and it has done so without any signs of inflation. This sector has more or less kept up with the expanding size of real economy, so that the level of the so-called monetization of China's economy is quite impressive, surely by the standards of medium-developed economies. In 1998, the overall supply of money in the Chinese economy, including credit and equity, was close to the value of GDP, which indeed was very high by international standards.

Critical for the future is, of course, capital formation, since all economies need capital expansion to grow, and, regardless of the influx of foreign funds, it is domestic savings that always constitute the major source of funding needed for capital expansion. For most of the years since 1994, saving rates in China were above the average for countries at this level of development. This was typical of a socialist economy, with direct taxation of largely state-owned companies and strict control over wages. In 1991, similar to the pattern from the previous decade, this rate was at 36 percent. Since then, however, the savings rate increased to 42 percent in 1995. The investment rate in turn increased from 36 percent in 1991 to 43.6 percent in 2005.

LIBERALIZATION PROCESS

Certainly the sudden acceleration of China's development has to be attributed to its reforms, or more specifically to the specific choice of state measures, including the type of their implementation. By this we mean the pace of respective reform programs, namely how gradual or how radical they have been, at least in such key areas as trade opening. There is also the question of sequencing of reforms, or what aspects are tackled first or what sectors are reformed first, something that often is not given proper attention in transition analysis. The key questions regarding sequencing involve whether priority should be given to economic or political reforms, as well as whether reforming agriculture should precede industry reforms.

Different Pathways

Although the Chinese economy appears similar in some ways to other emerging economies, and is certainly similar to the transition economies, the country's exceptional performance may have something to do with the special way in which it has approached building and expanding its markets. Indeed, some striking differences exist in the approaches used by China and those countries whose economies were once state run. Clearly, China's vision of a capitalistic economy establishes it as a separate case from those other countries. The principal difference between reform strategies lies in the fact that of the transitional economies only China (and to a lesser degree Vietnam) has adopted the so-called gradual approach with slow or measured reforms. Further, Chinese reforms have been more focused on economic issues than political ones, leaving in place a strong state to supervise reform activities. In contrast, as further evidence of a more radical approach, Eastern Europe has opted for practical reforms, both political and economic. In China, due to the cautious outlook of its reformers, reforms started in agriculture and a decade later were shifted to industry, whereas in Eastern Europe both sectors were targeted for reform at the same time (Naughton, 1995).

For instance, in Eastern Europe, as well as in Russia, the choice was made at the outset to emulate the kind of capitalism operated in western Europe, whereas in China it is Far East that provided such a model. Although both models have proven very successful, at least for most of the postwar period, they differ quite considerably, particularly in the role of state. This role has been much more pronounced in the case of the Far Eastern economies, where even today state ownership holdings are larger than in western Europe, most notably in the banking sector (e.g., in Taiwan, where the state share of banking assets exceeds 40 percent; see Poznanska and Poznanski, 2001).

China took on a reform task that was less difficult, but, more important, the country chose a slower pace of reaching its respective end-goal model of capitalism. This has a lot to do with politics, namely with the fact that China, unlike other nations, cured itself of the radicalism of the socialist period. There we have a real paradox, since under socialism these other countries were more restrained than China; certainly the other countries avoided during their communist period as ultraradical a shift as China's Cultural Revolution. It is quite possible, however, that because of this special experience, China has learned to stay away from any such experiments.

It is not just the lesson of its quite recent ultraradicalism of the Cultural Revolution that made China more cautious, but also the fact that it has retained its communist leadership. To hold onto its power, the reform-minded elements within the Chinese leadership has had to act in a very measured way. Gradualism in China resulted from political constraints on policymakers, namely the presence of conservatives within the communist party (Fukasaku, 1996). In this China resembles the pattern once present in socialist Hungary, where similar split led to both endless reforms and reform restraint.

Capital Ownership

Historically speaking, China has allowed for more of a strong presence of private, or more broadly, non-state ownership, than most of the other socialist countries. In 1976, when the overall process of reforming the communist system had begun, China's leadership decided to abandon the state-based collective system of farming—or communes—for family-based farming. Although for a number of years land continued to be exclusively state-owned, the use right was turned then to families. Eventually families were allowed some, though still limited, rights to transfer land. Since farming accounts for more than 70 percent of Chinese production, this was by all means a radical systemic change.

The seriousness of China's property reforms has often been questioned on the grounds that what is classified there as private often is not. This is because China has developed some unusual forms of ownership, which are difficult to classify, including a very popular version of the so-called town ownership. Nominally, companies in this category belong to local authorities, but are often run by narrow groups or individuals though, as documented on numerous occasions, those who run these businesses seriously take local needs into considerations.

China's special forms of ownership further suggest that the transition from communism to capitalism is a unique process. In other words, the rejection of public ownership does not lead, at least immediately, to the emergence of some well-known forms of property rights found in advanced capitalist economies. What takes place is the formation of some hybrid forms of ownership that fuse old and new elements, but there is no proof that such hybrids cannot perform their functions properly, at least under the conditions that are typical for transition economies.

Keeping in mind the fact that in most transition countries the actual nature of the non-state sector is somewhat unclear, it would appear that after more than 20 years of reforming property rights the non-state sector in China is almost as advanced as in most of the other former socialist economies. In China, the share of the non-state sector was reported to exceed 65 percent in 2001, while for Russia this share was 80 to 85 percent in the same year. With this 65 percent of non-state ownership, China clearly belongs, with countries such as Russia or Poland, to the category of transition economies.

In almost all countries of eastern Europe the choice was made to privatize through sales of state assets to foreigners, while in Russia the choice was made to allow for privatization by the citizens, mainly management (see Blasi et al., 1997). These insider deals have become almost the sole vehicle for changing Russia's ownership structure, particularly since the formation of new private businesses, although the so-called "entries" have never really picked up the pace. This is completely different from the Chinese model, where until recently privatization has not been tried at all, so that most of the state assets have remained in state hands.

The fact that China did not allow for large-scale privatization does not mean that its ownership structure has not been changed at all. For example, many state companies, have been listed on the local stock market, and cross-ownership in which state-owned companies own stock in one another, has been permitted as well. Although the Chinese state sector has not been subjected to privatization, very favorable conditions were created for non-state "entries" from the very beginning of economic reforms. Most have taken the form of some sort of collective ownership at the township level, thus typically called "township companies." They are collective in the sense that they formally represent the ownership of township citizens, presumably to benefit the whole community (Whiting, 2001).

Given the fact that China has practically not allowed for privatization of its state sector, its progress in reforming ownership relations has been quite remarkable. Looking at China's industry, in 1980 the share of the non-state sector in total output was around 26 percent, but in 1990 it jumped to 45 percent. With the subsequent expansion of the non-state sector at rates higher than those reported by the state sector, the respective share increased to 67 percent in 1995 and then passed 70 percent by 1999. It took two decades for China to reach this level, whereas Russia reached a higher level in less than two years.

Where China really trails is banking, since its banking system is very much the same as it was under the traditional central-planning regime. Banking is almost exclusively in the state hands with a small group of five banks dominating the credit market. In contrast, outside of China banking is almost all in private hands, as in Russia where most of the banks formed in the frenzy that followed the 1992 collapse of the communist party. In eastern Europe very few new private banks have been formed, and most of the new setups quickly went out of business. Still, almost all banking in eastern Europe is now in private hands, with most of the private sector formed through asset sales by the state.

Although permitting foreign ownership has helped eastern Europe to quickly privatize its economy, this has not come without a price, since now most of the assets are foreign owned and thus claims on most of the profits and dividends were removed abroad. The model that has emerged is that most often 50 to 60 percent of industry has been turned over to foreigners, or as much as 75 percent in the case of Hungary. An even greater concentration of foreign ownership can be found in banking, since the pattern that emerges is that 75 to 80 percent of banking (as well as insurance) has fallen under foreign control, as in Croatia, Hungary, and Poland.

China initially allowed foreign banks to deal only with foreign currency primarily to assist foreign investors operating in China. In 1997 the first few foreign banks were licensed to enter domestic currency operations, but all under very tight restrictions. They were allowed to carry such transactions only to the extent that they were no higher than 50 percent of their relatively small foreign-currency operations. In the insurance sector only 2 percent of all assets are foreign, and only 1.3 of all premiums—largely due to the 50 percent upper limit of foreign ownership in place (Lardy, 2002).

With its accession to the world Trade Organization (WTO), China has been gradually relaxing its restrictions on foreign ownership in the financial sector, as well as in other sectors of its economy. In a sign of substantial liberalization China's government allowed to float a few major banks with up to 10 percent of stocks made available to foreign investors (e.g., Bank of China). It is difficult to say to what degree China will open its economy to foreign ownership, but if it sticks to the Far Eastern practice, with legal barriers or without, it is not likely to invite any strong presence (e.g., in South Korea, a long-standing member fo the WTO, only 2 percent of banking is foreign owned).

Trade Protection

Similar to privatization, China's liberalization, or the opening of foreign trade, started in 1978. As it began revamping its agricultural system, China began reforms in its trading system, both with respect to exports and imports. In essence, China's reformers engaged in systematic elimination of various state interventions in trade typical of the communist-type system, such as currency allocations, import-export targets, and price-setting. For most of the period, reforms were rather slow, and only after 1995 did China make some really major changes to finally open up its economy.

China's dismantling of the old system first concentrated on the reduction of mandatory targets, i.e., numerical targets on quantities that companies were supposed to ship or receive from abroad. As part of national planning, this dismantling of state targets proceeded quite rapidly, so that while in 1970 about 100 percent of exports were subject to mandatory targets, in 1978 the respective share was 45 percent, but in 1992 it was only 15 percent. On the import side the change was somewhat slower, with 100 percent of imports subject to central targets in 1970, 40 percent in 1984, and 20 percent in 1993 (Fukasaku, 1996). That China has retained the domination of state ownership in its banking is consistent with the state's decision to keep state-owned industry. It is the state-owned industry that receives most of the credit allocated through state banks. According to Garg (1997), non-state-sector industry accounted for 33.3 percent of total investment in 1985, which then increased to 45.6 percent in 1995. However, in 1995 only 12.6 percent of the total bank credit was issued for non-state industry, compared with 18 percent in 1985. In 2004 more than 50 percent of bank credit went to the state-owned sector.

With the state withdrawing from direct control over trade operations the whole organization of foreign trade was changed as well. The traditional system of organization was based on few state-trading companies, hierarchically set up from the national down to the provincial level, each specializing in certain broad categories of goods. From 1978 on, the reformers decided to decentralize the system by allowing lower-level units to act in an autonomous way to serve local needs. In 1978, 12 such trading companies were authorized to facilitate exports and imports. In 1985, however, there were already 800 such companies, 12,000 in 1995, and in 2001 there were as many as 35,000 of such entities (Lardy, 2002).

With its 1978 reform China had introduced a tariff system as well, but it had also adopted some quantitative restrictions or quotas. It decided to ensure that the protection once offered by state-set targets would be provided now by relatively high tariffs. In China, for instance, as late as in 1994, the average tariff for industrial goods was at the level of 32 percent, whereas it was 4.5 percent in the Czech Republic, 7 percent in Romania, 9.2 percent in Poland (plus a 6 percent import surcharge), and 13 percent in Hungary (plus an 8 percent import surcharge). With its high tariff China was in line with the majority of other developing countries (e.g., Thailand at 35 percent and India at 54 percent), while eastern Europeans followed the pattern of countries much more developed them themselves (e.g., Western Europe at 5 percent, Japan at 9 percent, and the United States at 5.4 percent).

Though from a higher starting level, China has also engaged in tariff reduction, so that by 2000 the average tariff was 15 percent, and with the recently acquired WTO membership further cuts in tariff protection were expected. More important, while in 1985 only 16 percent of imports were fully free of tariff, in 2000 as much as 40 of imports were subject to no duty payments at all (largely in the category of raw materials and intermediate goods). This was not only the result of steady cuts in the statutory tariff rates applied to imports, but a reflection of the fact that the state had provided foreign investors with many incentives, one of which was that they were exempt from import duties on their supplies.

Past experience also suggests that China may continue to more frequently apply non-tariff barriers, such as quantitative restrictions.

Another important tool against imports in China is trading rights, namely state permission to engage in the distribution of imports of specific goods. Although it is true that foreign companies do not have to use special trading companies for their business-related transactions, they cannot import other goods for resale. Very few companies have the right of distribution, though it is easy for other companies—much more numerous—to use them for helping with their business. For some products, these rights are restricted to only one company (e.g., fertilizers, cotton, crude oil), though the share of import goods subject to trading requirements is down from 90 percent in 1980 to 40 percent in 1988, and 11 percent in 1998.

China started from an economic system in which planners routinely subsidized various sectors of production or even companies. Consequently, many of their exports will continue to be subsidized, though not with the intention of promoting exports, since under communist rule they will follow the traditional import substitution. China did not move out of export subsidization with the advent of market-type reforms, but rather chose to be more selective. However, the level of export support by the Chinese state clearly exceeds such support found in the European Union, but this is not much different from the practice of many Far Eastern economies.

GLOBALIZATION IMPACT

The preceding analysis has shown the extent to which China globalized its economies in terms of institutional infrastructure, or making its institutions fit the open-market concept. However, removing barriers to external contacts does not guarantee that a given economy will automatically be integrated into intense contacts with the external world. Even if an economy becomes integrated it does not follow that intense contacts with the outside world will ensure that a given country will enjoy some visible economic benefits. It is also the type of external relations that matters, since some contacts are helpful and others are not.

Capital Mobility

One important indicator of an economy becoming globalized is the extent to which it participates in the international capital mobility, including foreign direct investment. It is this dimension of world economy that represents the real essence of globalization, since it is the growth of the stock of foreign investment that has shown recent acceleration way above the expansion of trade volume. With this more intense flow of capital, the world stock of capital can be allocated more rationally. In particular, it is expected that with liberalization capital will move from capital-rich to capital-poor countries, since yield is higher where capital is more scarce.

China began allowing foreign investment in 1985, which is the turning point for its economy, marking the mentioned transition from import-substitution to export-promotion. Consequently, while the cumulative value of foreign capital stock in China reached $61.8 billion in 1993, the stock reached $219 billion in 1997 (Table 10.3). These figures give the impression that China is by far more attractive for foreign investors than many other semi-industrialized nations. However, in per capita terms (or per unit of the national product, or total investment) the amount of foreign investment is not exceptional at all.

China has continuously experienced considerable outflows in recent years, though their exact sizes are difficult to quantify. Such quantification is important for determining the degree of globalization of these economies, since the extent of moving capital out of a country is as important an indicator of openness as moving it in. It is true that a tendency exists to measure globalization in terms of how much foreign capital enters a given economy, but it is hard to find a rationale other than the inertia of a once accepted analytical convention.

Looking at the numbers in Table 10.3, China started larger exports of capital in 1990, when it invested $0.8 billion with a total stock of $2.4 billion. In 1995, China's annual investment abroad was $3.5 bil-

TABLE 10.3. Levels of Foreign Capital Inflows into China (in Billion $)

Year	Annual	Stock
1990	3.5	18.9
1991	4.3	23.3
1992	11.0	34.3
1993	27.5	61.8
1994	33.7	95.6
1995	37.5	133.1
1996	41.7	174.8
1997	45.0	219.1
1998	40.7	–
1999	43.3	–
2000	45.4	346.6
2001	–	–
2002	–	–
2003	–	–
2004	64.0	563.8
2005	43.0	–

Source: Congressional Research Service, 2005.

lion with a cumulative value of $15.8 billion. However, this picture is based on officially reported outflows—the possibly exists of much larger outflow of capital in the way of capital flight. Estimates are that this was, unofficially, something like $10.2 billion invested in 1990 and $24.5 billion in 1992, an outflow that continued in the following years. If true, these annual figures would give a cumulative value of the stock of such capital at around $100 billion during 1990-1994.

Based on this analysis one could reasonably argue that China offers a fast-growing economy that still sends major capital flows abroad with a trade surplus. This raises the question of the extent to which the inflow of capital is nothing more than the recycling of outward capital flows, such that it does not represent a loss of capital for the local economy. Of course, the extent to which capital is sent abroad only to be returned changes the whole balance of capital flows. Specifically, the larger the extent of such recycling in a given country the lower the actual dependence on external supplies of capital is.

Capital flight typically takes place when internal problems in a given economy raise the level of uncertainty above the norm, but also when burdens on capital, such as taxation or/and regulations, are perceived to be excessive. Conditions in China are such that investors may be induced to take their capital abroad, but without an intention to actually spend it there. Because China's overall conditions are favorable, local investors may want to take their capital abroad and invest it in China from outside the country, taking advantage of various incentives the country offers exclusively to foreign investors.

Imports Exposure

Along with other reforms, China decided to engage in more intense imports, but the initial focus of China's policy after 1978 was on internal development. According to this policy, China provided heavy protection for its import-substituting sectors within industry as well as in agriculture. China changed its course after about ten years of reforming the economy, shifting around 1988 from an import-substitution strategy to an export-promotion strategy.

Even with this shift China has not allowed for major import penetration, except for the raw material sector, which is simply not self-sufficient. The most obvious area is crude oil, but even here China has tried to expand its own drilling to make sure that its dependence is not too high. China is not only largely dependent on crude oil imports, but large chunks of domestic demand on oil-related goods, or petrochemicals, are also satisfied with foreign supplies. Thus, major imports in China do not pose a major threat to domestic production.

This is surely the case with agricultural products, where China's dependence on imports is nominal, except for wheat. With the rapid expansion of farming China has been able to remain mainly self-sufficient and aims to eliminate wheat dependence in the coming years. It is difficult to compile proper indicators for all of the important consumer goods, but it appears that in most cases durable consumer goods imports account for small shares of domestic production, which is not much different from what is reportedly taking place in the consumption of agricultural goods.

For instance, this level of penetration is found in washing machines, microwave ovens, and refrigerators, goods for which there is very little importation in China. To be more specific, in the area of televisions, the ratio of imports to production is 2 percent, for apparel the respective ratio is 4 percent. Medications are an exception in China, since imports account for 10 to 15 percent of domestic output (Table 10.4). Although China is trying to make wide use of imported investment goods, one still finds low levels of import penetration within the Chinese market. A good example is farming equipment, where China almost exclusively depends on its own industry. Machine tools are an area where China is more dependent, with imports representing 7 percent of domestic production.

It seems that China is liberalizing its imports in a very methodic way, not only to its their domestic import-substitution sectors to mod-

TABLE 10.4. Market Penetration (Ratio of Imports to Domestic Production) in China, 1999 (in Percentages)

Products	
Industrial equipment	
Machine tools	7
Trucks	20
Synthetic fiber	14
Chemical pesticide	1
Chemical fertilizers	24
Coal	0
Crude oil	23
Rolled steel	39
Consumer products	
Sugar	5
Pharmaceuticals	10-15
Apparel	4
Furniture	3
Television sets	2
Passenger cars	1

Sources: Calculated from *China Statistical Yearbook 2001* (2002).

ernize—enlisting if necessary foreign investors—before accepting any major influx of imports, but also to make sure that imports do not prevent China from building export specialties. There is at least some preliminary proof that with her policy China has shown improvement in terms of building trade specializations. China has concentrated on very few industries, including such an area as textiles. Filling the gap created by the withdrawing Far Eastern economies, China has taken over much of the world market for textiles (i.e., about 15 percent of the total in 2000, and far above 30 percent in 2005).

China has not tried to build specialization in textiles by first exposing it to unrestrained import competition but instead by protecting it first, while encouraging producers to sell to the world economy. The strategy of China in this area, but also in others, has been to build export specialization with the help of foreign investors. In most of cases foreign investors will be invited to invest, but will not be allowed outright ownership of companies. The prevailing form in such cases is therefore a joint venture, and in those joint ventures China has insisted on great autonomy, making it impossible for foreign investors even to gain managerial control. Moreover, China will insist on numerous privileges (e.g., the ability to run parallel arrangements in a given domestic company with more than one foreign investor).

Careful liberalization in China refers not only to areas with a potential for becoming exports, but also to areas in which China is not seeking an immediate export specialization, as in the automotive industry. In such areas, China the automotive industry is trying to postpone import liberalization until domestic producers are prepared to face external competition. In 1985, when China made about 5,000 passenger cars the duty on imports was 260 percent, making it virtually impossible for foreign companies to enter the market. With the eventual lowering of tariffs on cars, imports increased rapidly, reaching a peak in 1985, when China spent $3 billion to import 350,000 vehicles. These numbers should be compared to the 41,000 vehicles of total domestic production in China in the same year (Harwit, 2001).

The above situation was unsustainable, unless China was ready to give up having its own strong motor vehicle sector. When the decision was made in 1983 to replace imports with domestic production, China started assembling foreign-designed cars. A limit of 50 percent was imposed on foreign ownership, and foreigners were expected to ensure that each car was constructed from 40 percent local content. In addition, many incentives were offered to attract foreign investors, including import-duty reductions or exemptions on equipment and parts or components. Various restrictions were also put in place to prevent imports, so that the 1985 boom in imported cars was quickly extinguished, leaving room for the newly established companies.

With the help of all these measures, China's total car production in 1995 reached about 325,000 vehicles, and in 1998 the total reached 508,000 units. Already in 1995, companies with foreign participation reached 85 percent local content, mainly by bringing into China other foreign companies to start production of parts and components. With this progress China reduced tariffs during 1994-1996 from 150 to 100 percent on small cars, and from 220 to 180 on large cars. In 2001, the respective duty rates were further lowered to 70 and 80 percent. The second wave of imports occurred in 1992-1995, but by then imports had sharply declined so that the total in 2000 reached 37,000 foreign vehicles (this occurred largely through a ban on state-sector and official purchases and quotas enforced though license import requirement).

CONCLUSIONS

The lessons learned from market reforms in China are multiple. One important lesson is that a gradual approach to restructuring economic institutions offers substantial advantages. As reforms are initiated by the state to ensure proper execution, the state has to take on changes that it can handle given its limited capabilities. What is essential is that the state is fully committed to the end goal of creating a strong market system. Slowing the pace of reform or reversing its course on a temporary basis might be helpful in making sure that reforms produce (1) steady economic growth and (2) a distribution of expanding wealth that helps to establish or maintain strong support for reforms among the population.

Such a gradual approach is also essential for ensuring that with the opening of an economy such as China's, nationals retain control over local assets, banking, and industry. A country may choose to transfer majority ownership to foreign investors as eastern Europe did. Such an approach clearly helped these countries phase in a market system faster than China did. It appears from China's example that by ensuring a slow pace of reform the state allowed sufficient time for the local investor class to develop and thus a pool of talent exists to take assets away from the state as the time of full-scale privatization—which seems to be coming in the next few years—approaches.

REFERENCES

Blasi, J., Kroumova, M., and Kruse, D. (1997). *Kremlin Capitalism: Privatizing the Russian Economy.* Ithaca, NY: Cornell University Press.

Bucknall, K. (1997). Why China has done better than Russia since 1989. *International Journal of Social Economics, 24*(7/8/9), 1023-1037.

Chen, K. et al. (1988). New estimates of fixed investment and capital stock or Chinese state industry, *China Quarterly,* 113, 77-93.

Congressional Research Service (2005). Washington, DC: The Library of Congress. January 7.

Fukasaku, K. (1996). *Economic Transition and Trade Policy Reform: Lessons from China.* Paris: OECD.

Harwit, E. (2001). The impact of WTO membership on automobile industry in China. *The China Quarterly,* 167, 655-670.

Lardy, N. (2002). *Integrating China into the Global Economy.* Washington, DC: Brookings Institution Press.

Macours, K. and Swinnen, J. (2002). Patterns of agrarian transition, economic development, and cultural change. *Economic Development and Cultural Change, 50*(2), 365-394.

Naughton, B. (1995). *Growing Out of the Plan: Chinese Economic Reform, 1978-1993.* Cambridge: Cambridge University Press.

Poznanska, J. and Poznanski, K. (2001). Foreign direct investment and ownership structure in Austria, Hungary, and Poland. *EMERGO Journal of Transforming Economies and Societies, 8*(4).

Whiting, S. (2001). *Power and Wealth in Rural China: The Political Economy of Institutional Change.* New York: Cambridge University Press.

Chapter 11

The Exchange Rate of Chinese Yuan: Before and After WTO Entry

Robin H. Luo
Yunhua Liu

INTRODUCTION

The prereform exchange system of China was characterized by strict control of foreign exchange transactions and rigidity of the exchange rate of the Chinese yuan. It neither responded flexibly to the change of price parities between China and the rest of the world, nor made prompt adjustment according to the changing supply and demand of foreign exchange. The official exchange rate was pegged to the U.S. dollar since 1986. In 1991, the exchange policy was altered to accept small-scale, more frequent adjustments in the official rate. One notable step in the foreign exchange rate reform was the unification of the swap rate and the official rate, which allowed the exchange rate to float freely in a limited band beginning in 1994. Since then the nominal exchange rate of the yuan has remained stable.

The Chinese government's de facto peg to the appreciating U.S. dollar in the late 1990s is said to have stabilized financial flows in the Asia-Pacific region during the Asian financial crisis. However, the peg did lead to substantial nominal and real appreciations against most of Asian export competitors. Although the suitability of the

A previous version of this chapter was presented at the 12th International Trade and Finance Association International Conference, Thailand, May 2002. We thank Professor Murray C. Kemp for useful discussions on the topic of this paper. All remaining errors that have evaded our attention are exclusively our responsibility.

Globalization and East Asia: Opportunities and Challenges

doi:10.1300/5463_11

de facto peg has increasingly been questioned, the associated fluctuations in China's real exchange rate (RER) highlight the need to identify the equilibrium real exchange rate (ERER) and misalignment of RER.

Little research has been made on measuring the ERER of the Chinese yuan. One early estimation of Chinese yuan RER was made by Yi and Fan (1997). They presented several methods related to the determination of the RER of the Chinese yuan, including purchasing power parity, interest rate parity, and the balance of payments. The PPP exchange rate they estimated was 4.2 yuan to 1 U.S. dollar. But this parity, as they mentioned in the article, was very crude because they took only 100 goods and services in both countries from 1993 to 1995 for their observations. They also calculated the parity of tradables. The results were 7, 7.3, and 7.5 yuan per U.S. dollar at the end of 1993, 1994, and 1995, respectively. Another estimation of ERER of Chinese yuan was made by Chou and Shih (1998), who used two approaches to estimate the equilibrium RER, the PPP model, and the shadow price of foreign exchange (SPFE) model. Long-run PPP was examined by using an augmented Dickey-Fuller (ADF) test upon the quarterly data consisting of 68 observations from Q1 1978 to Q4 1994. Their result supported a long-run PPP relationship, and their estimated PPP exchange rates indicated that the yuan was overvalued between 1978 and 1989 and undervalued in the early 1990s. However, on the basis of the SPFEs, Chou and Shih concluded that the official exchange rates of yuan were overvalued throughout the entire sample period rather than undervalued from 1990 to 1994 as suggested by the PPP rates. They took SPFE as a more creditable model than PPP because the SPFE model reflects the social value of foreign exchange for the Chinese economy, which has been characterized by extensive trade restrictions and factor price distortions.

In addition to the previous two approaches, another approach may be used to study ERER determination and RER misalignment, i.e., the fundamental equilibrium real exchange rate (FEER) approach (Williamson, 1985).* FEER is the relative price of tradables to nontradables that, for given equilibrium values of other relevant variables—such as taxes, international prices, and technology—results

*Where Williamson (1985, 1994) referred it to FEER, and Edwards (1988) and Elbadawi (1994) wrote of ERER (equilibrium real exchange rate). They all mean the same thing but have not attempted to force a standardization of terminology. In this chapter we follow Williamson's terminology.

in the simultaneous attainment of internal and external equilibrium. Internal equilibrium means the nontradable goods market clears in the current period, and is expected to be in equilibrium in future periods. In this definition it is implicit that equilibrium is achieved with unemployment at the natural level. External equilibrium, on the other hand, is attained when the discounted sum of a country's current account equals zero. In other words, external equilibrium means that the current account balances are compatible with long-run sustainable capital flows (Edwards, 1988).

This chapter measures the ERER of the Chinese yuan through all three approaches: PPP, SPFE, and FEER. First, this chapter tests the PPP hypothesis between the Chinese yuan and the U.S. dollar by using the ADF unit root test and the Engle-Granger and Johansen cointegration tests. Although adopting relatively long period time series and high-frequency quarterly data, Q1 1980 to Q4 2001, the test results significantly reject the long-run PPP relationship between the United States and China. For this reason the PPP exchange rate of the Chinese yuan would not be treated as the ERER. Second, this chapter estimates the SPFE based on Chao and Yu's (1995) model. Third, this chapter follows the single-equation econometric model described by Edwards (1988), and constructs a time series for the RER. This is then regressed against the terms of trade, domestic interest rate, productivity, and the exchange and trade controls and fitted values extracted as the FEER of the Chinese yuan. After measuring two types of misalignment of the yuan based on SPFE and FEER approaches, the relationship between the trade balance of China and those two misalignments is examined.

The two special features of this chapter are: (1) the attempt to measure the ERER and RER misalignment of the Chinese yuan through three different approaches and pre-WTO data, and forecast the ERER for the post-WTO period, and (2) the attempt to arrive at a better understanding of the relationship between RER misalignment and trade balance through a comparison of the misalignments using vector autoregression (VAR) tests.

The remainder of this chapter is organized as follows. The second section examines the PPP between China and the United States by using unit root tests and the Engle-Granger and Johansen cointegration tests. Then, two types of ERERs are measured through SPFE approach and FEER approach respectively. The third section measures two types of misalignment of the Chinese yuan based on SPFE and FEER approaches, and tests the relationship between China's trade balance and two types of misalignment of the yuan using VAR methods. The fourth section provides a summary by way of concluding the chapter.

APPROACHES TO MEASURING EQUILIBRIUM REAL EXCHANGE RATE (ERER)

The real exchange rate is defined as the relative price of tradable to nontradable goods,

$$RER = NER \frac{WPI^F}{CPI} \tag{11.1}$$

where *RER* is the real exchange rate, *NER* is the nominal exchange rate in terms of domestic currency per unit of foreign currency, WPI^F is the wholesale price index in the foreign country and is used as a proxy for the foreign price of tradables, and *CPI* is the domestic consumer price index and is used as a proxy for the domestic price of nontradables. In Hinkle and Montiel (1999), this ratio is called the two-good internal real exchange rate for tradables and nontradables. Note that a decline in the real exchange rate denotes appreciation, whereas an increase in the RER indicates depreciation.

PPP Approach

Empirical tests for the long-run PPP are based on the following equation:

$$s_t = \alpha + \beta_1 p_t + \beta_2 p_t^F + \mu_t \tag{11.2}$$

where s_t is the logarithm of the nominal exchange rate, defined as the domestic price of foreign currency; p_t and p_t^F are the logarithms of the domestic and foreign prices; α, β_1, and β_2 are parameters; and μ_t is the error term. The symmetry and proportionality restrictions commonly imposed on the parameters are $\alpha = 0$, $\beta_1 = 1$, and $\beta_2 = 1$.

With these restrictions, the error term μ_t becomes a measure of the real exchange rate r_t,

$$r_r - s_t - p_t + p_t^F \tag{11.3}$$

If PPP holds, the long-run movement of s_t, p_t, and p_t^F cancel out, that is, (s_t, p_t, p_t^F) are cointegrated. The Engle-Granger (1987) cointegration test examines whether μ_t or r_t follows a stationary process, whereas the Johansen (1988) cointegration test investigates whether there exists a cointegration vector in the (s_t, p_t, p_t^F) space with (1, –1, 1) as the expected coefficients for the cointegrating vector.

The nominal exchange rates between the Chinese yuan and the U.S. dollar, the wholesale price index (WPI), and the consumer price index (CPI) were taken from the International Monetary Fund, International Financial Statistics (IFS) CD-ROM (2002), and the Thomson Datastream database on a quarterly basis from Q1 1980 to Q4 2001.*

The time series were first examined for stationarity. The results of the augmented Dickey-Fuller (1979) test for a single-unit root are reported under I(0) in Table 11.1. Based on the models chosen by Akaike Information Criterion (AIC), the unit root hypothesis is not rejected for nominal exchange rates of yuan, U.S. WPI, and CPI of China. The acceptance of the unit root hypothesis for all series requires a test for a second unit root. The results are reported under I(1) in Table 11.1. Clearly, the hypothesis of a second unit root is rejected for all series. The conclusion is that all series are nonstationary in the log of levels and stationary in first differences.

TABLE 11.1. Testing for Stationarity

	Level [I(0)]	**First-Difference [I(1)]**
e	2.0200 (2)	–5.8077 (2)
CPICN	1.2533 (4)	–2.9150 (4)
WPIUS	1.4231 (3)	–3.7796 (3)

Note: (a) All variables are in the log-form. (b) Numbers in the parentheses capture the number of lags based on the Akaike Information Criteria (AIC). (c) The MacKinnon critical values for rejection of hypothesis of a unit root at 10 percent, 5 percent, and 1 percent levels of significance are, respectively, –1.62, –1.94, –2.59.

*The codes in the parentheses correspond to the series in the IFS CD-ROM and Datastream database.

To perform the Engle-Granger (1987) cointegration test, Equation 11.2 was first estimated using ordinary least squares (OLS) to obtain the estimated residuals that were then analyzed for stationarity using the ADF test. RER was calculated from Equation 11.3 and also applied to the ADF test. The results of the ADF test for the real exchange rate and the residuals are reported in Table 11.2. In Table 11.2, the ADF test shows that the unit root hypothesis must be accepted for the real exchange rate. The nonstationary real exchange rate suggests that the long-run PPP between the United States and China should be rejected.

The result of the OLS estimation of Equation 11.1 is:

$$s_t = 11.514 + 2.203 cpi_t^{cn} + 0.719 wpi_t^{us} \qquad (11.4)$$
$$(-10.02) \qquad (9.434) \qquad (1.536)$$

where the numbers in the parentheses are the values of the t-statistic, adjusted $R^2 = 0.946$, and Durbin-Watson stat = 0.23. The estimate of wpi_t^{us} in Equation 11.4 does not carry the correct sign and is statistically insignificant. The value of the Durbin-Watson test is very low. The result of the OLS estimation indicates that the U.S. and Chinese price indices did not explain the nominal exchange rate between the U.S. dollar and the Chinese yuan well.

In applying the Johansen (1988) cointegration test, one must first decide the deterministic components and the order of the lagged endogenous variables to be included in the test. If PPP holds, the long-run movements of the exchange rate and the U.S. and Chinese price indices should cancel out over time. The inclusion of a deterministic

TABLE 11.2. Results of the Engle-Granger Cointegration Test

	Real Exchange Rate		**Residuals**	
	Test statistics in level	Test statistics in 1st difference	Test statistics in level	Test statistics in 1st difference
ADF	1.7731 (2)	–6.4822 (2)	–2.6042 (2)	–5.2823 (2)

Note: (a) The test for the stationarity of the real exchange rate is based on Equation 11.2, and the test for the stationarity of the estimated residuals is based on Equation 11.1. (b) Numbers in parentheses capture the number of lags based on the Akaike Information Criteria (AIC). (c) The MacKinnon critical values for rejection of hypothesis of a unit root at 10 percent, 5 percent, and 1 percent levels of significance are, respectively, –1.62, –1.94, –2.59.

trend in the long-run equilibrium relationship means that one variable is drifting away from the others, which is inconsistent with the long-run PPP. Hence, only a constant but not a deterministic trend is included in the cointegrating equations. The order of lagged endogenous variables for the cointegration test was selected based on AIC. Four lagged endogenous variables were selected for the VAR.

The results of the Johansen cointegration test are reported in Table 11.3. The likelihood-ratio tests cannot reject the hypothesis of no cointegration (H_0:$r = 0$) in favor of cointegration at the 5 percent significance level. The hypotheses of no more than one cointegrating vector (H_0:$r \leq 1$) and no more than two cointegrating vectors (H_0:$r \leq 2$) are also accepted. The result of the Johansen cointegration test suggests that the long-run PPP between the United States and China does not exist.

SPFE Approach

The second approach to calculating equilibrium exchange rates is based on the shadow price of foreign exchange. As described by Chao and Yu (1995), the official exchange rate in developing economies does not reflect the social value of foreign exchange because

TABLE 11.3. Results of the Johansen Cointegration Test

H_0:r	Likelihood-ratio	Cointegration Coefficients		
= 0	30.85	e	CPICN	WPIUS
≤ 1	16.86	1.000	0.295	–0.296
≤ 2	7.39		(2.72)	(3.51)

Note: (a) Under the first column H_0:r is the hypothesized number of cointegration vectors, or the rank r. The values under L-ratio are the computer values of the likelihood ratio for Johansen's cointegration test. The numbers under cointegration coefficients are the values of the normalized cointegration coefficients with their corresponding standard errors in the parentheses. (b) The critical values at 5 percent (1 percent) level of significance are 34.91 (41.07) for $r = 0$, 19.96 (24.60) for $r \leq 1$, and 9.24 (12.97) for $r \leq 2$, under the assumption that there is a linear deterministic trend in the data but not in the cointegrating equations. The statistic is significant at the 5 percent level. (c) The likelihood-ratio test rejects one cointegrating equation at the 5 percent significance level.

of the existence of widespread trade restrictions. Accordingly, the SPFE is calculated for project evaluations and other developmental projects. In this chapter, the model of Chao and Yu (1995) is employed to estimate the SPFE. This SPFE model was also used by Chou and Shih (1998). Chao and Yu demonstrated that, in a developing dual economy with trade restrictions and labor market distortions, the SPFE is greater than the official exchange in the presence of tariffs.

$$SPFE = \frac{e}{1 - mt(1+t)} \tag{11.5}$$

where e is the actual official exchange rate, m is the marginal propensity to spend ($0 < m < 1$), and t is the tariff rate.

The principal exchange rate of yuan was obtained from the IFS CD-ROM consisting of 88 observations from Q1 1980 to Q4 2001. The tariff rate t is computed as the ratio of tariff revenues to imports, where the data of China's tariff revenues and imports were compiled from *China Statistical Yearbook* (1980-2000). To estimate the unknown m, this chapter employs a simple consumption function. The consumption function is specified as:

$$C_t = \alpha_0 + \alpha_1 Y_t + \alpha_2 C_{t-1} \tag{11.6}$$

where C_t is the per capita household consumption, Y_t is the per capita GDP, and C_{t-1} is the lagged consumption. The annual data for consumption and GDP for the period 1978-1999 were taken from *China Statistical Yearbook,* (2002) in domestic currency. OLS is employed to estimate the consumption function with these 22 annual observations. The regression result is

$$\begin{aligned} C_t &= 19.80375 + 0.373286 Y_t + 0.22169 C_{t-1} \\ &\quad (2.438) \qquad\qquad (20.024) \qquad (5.066) \end{aligned} \tag{11.7}$$

where t-ratios are in parentheses, adjusted $R^2 = 0.9994$, and the Durbin-Watson stat = 1.82. The estimate of Y_t is 0.373286, used as a proxy for m. The estimated SPFE and actual RER are shown in Figure 11.1.

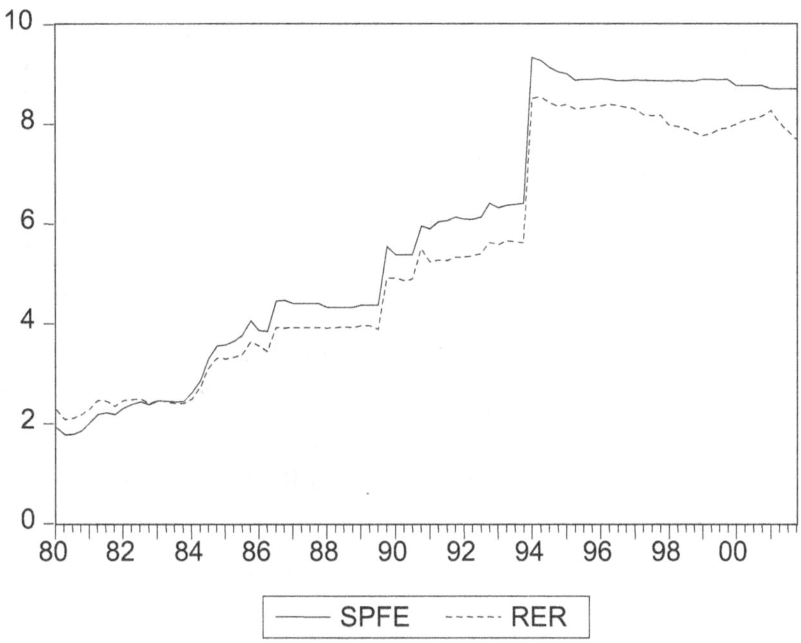

FIGURE 11.1. SPFE and RER (Yuan per U.S. Dollar)

FEER Approach

The FEER approach begins with the assumption that there is a vector of fundamentals that determines an economy's FEER (Edwards, 1994). The most important fundamentals in determining the behavior of equilibrium RERs are

1. external terms of trade *(TOT),*
2. domestic interest rate *(ROR),*
3. productivity *(PROD),* and
4. exchange and trade controls *(EXCHCONTROLS).*

The simplest possible way of writing down the FEER is:

$$FEER_t = f(TOT_t, R_t, PROD_t, EXCHCONTROLS_t) \qquad (11.8)$$

Before actually estimating the FEER equation, a number of issues related to the data have to be resolved. One of the more serious obstacles encountered refers to data availability. In fact, the only fundamentals for which we have reliable time-series data are the external terms of trade *(TOT)* and the interest rate *(R)*. This means that in the estimation of the FEER equation the other fundamentals have to be proxied by other time-series data. Productivity was proxied by the real GDP per capita of China. This type of proxy has been used in a number of empirical investigations. With respect to exchange and trade controls *(EXCHCONTROLS)*, import tariff was used as proxy. This proxy, however, has a number of limitations. First, it is only available for a few years; and second, it ignores the role of nontariff barriers. For this reason the ratio of tariff revenues to imports is computed to compose a continuous time series.

Since the ERER is not observable, FEER approach estimates the following set of equations*:

$$rer_t = \beta_1 tot_t + \beta_2 r_t + \beta_3 prod_t + \beta_4 exchcontrols_{t-1} + \beta_5 rer_{t-1} + \varepsilon_t \qquad (11.9)$$

The small letters represent natural logs. Equation (11.9) seeks the best fit of the RER on the economy's relevant economic fundamentals.

A brief highlight is given to show the expected prior signs of the coefficients based on the theoretical literature. An improvement in the terms of trade *(tot)* will cause a capital inflow into the tradable sector, creating a real appreciation, that is, *rer* decreases, $\beta_1 < 0$. Assuming that the foreign interest rate is exogenous, an increase in the domestic interest rate will lead to an increase in domestic savings, and the demand for foreign capital will be lower. In the middle term, the capital inflow under the capital account will decrease and the trade surplus will fall as well. Increasing RER is needed to devalue foreign exchange to keep the external equilibrium when the interest rate increases, i.e., $\beta_2 > 0$. An increase in productivity *(prod)* is expected to appreciate the domestic currency via the Balassa-Samuelson condition, i.e., $\beta_3 < 0$. A relaxation of the extent of impediments to international trade will result in equilibrium real exchange rate depreciation, i.e., $\beta_4 < 0$. In light of the time-series properties of RERs, the coefficients of lagged RER should be positive, i.e., $\beta_5 > 0$.

*Such single equation econometric models are commonly used in the literature on the determination of equilibrium real exchange rates (Edwards and Savastano, 1999).

The data sources used in this chapter are presented as following. RER is the same as that calculated in the PPP approach. *TOT*, described as the unit price of export over unit price of import, was obtained from the Datastream database. Principle deposit rate of China was taken from the IFS CD-ROM (2002). Per capita GDP was calculated from China's total GDP and the population of China, which was also taken from the IFS CD-ROM (2002). The tariff rate calculated in the SPFE approach was used as the proxy of exchange and trade controls.

Two stages of sequential tests will be conducted. The first will be the unit root test. If the variables are all found to be integrated of order 1 ($I(1)$), the Johansen cointegration test will be applied to check for existence of cointegration relationships among all variables in Equation 11.9. The ADF test reveals all the variables to be integrated of $I(1)$ (Table 11.4). The Akaike Information Criteria test determines the appropriate number of lag periods.

Given all variables are $I(1)$, the Johansen cointegration test procedures are conducted on the single equation model. The trace statistics (likelihood-ratio) indicate that one cointegrating relationship (significant at 5 percent level) exists in the single equation model (Table 11.5).

$$\begin{aligned} rer_t = {} & -0.2176 tot_t + 0.0693 r_t + 0.1836 prod_t \\ & \quad (-4.199) \qquad (3.776) \qquad (4.286) \\ & -0.0695 exchcontrols_t + 0.7156 rer_{t-1} \\ & \quad (-2.073) \qquad\qquad (9.302) \end{aligned} \tag{11.10}$$

where t-ratios are in parentheses, adjusted R^2 = 0.9865, and the Durbin-Watson stat = 1.8447.

The estimated result shows that the fundamentals have influence on the RER behavior in China. The coefficient of the log of the terms of trade is negative and significant. This negative sign supports popular views that suggest that improvements in the terms of trade and an increase in *tot* will result in an equilibrium real appreciation. The positive sign of the interest rate coefficient also supports our assumption. The coefficient of productivity, however, turned out to be positive in the regression and significant. To the extent that GDP per capita is taken to be a proxy of productivity, this result

TABLE 11. 4. ADF Unit-Root Test

	Level [I(0)]	First-Difference [I(1)]
rer	1.7573 (1)	–6.4803 (1)
tot	–2.0479 (2)	–5.1962 (2)
r	–0.7667 (2)	–3.7838 (2)
prod	1.0857 (4)	–6.4420 (4)
excncontrols	1.1669 (4)	–3.3969 (4)

Note: (a) All variables are in the log-form. (b) Numbers in the parentheses capture the number of lags based on the Akaike Information Criteria (AIC). (c) The MacKinnon critical values for rejection of hypothesis of a unit root at 10 percent, 5 percent, and 1 percent levels of significance are, respectively, –1.62, –1.94, –2.59.

TABLE 11.5. Cointegration Test Results for FEER (Observation Period: Q1 1980 - Q4 2001)

Eigenvalue	Likelihood-Ratio	1 Percent Critical value	Hypothesized No. of CE(s)
0.4458	95.17	76.07	None
0.2190	46.19	54.46	At most 1
0.1845	25.67	35.65	At most 2
0.0799	8.74	20.04	At most 3
0.0217	1.82	6.65	At most 4

Note: The likelihood-ratio test indicates one cointegrating equation at the 1 percent significance level.

seems to contradict the Balassa-Samuelson hypothesis. A number of reasons, however, could explain why this estimated coefficient may not be negative as suggested in our assumption. First, GDP per capita is admittedly not a very good proxy for productivity; and second, whether the Balassa-Samuelson hypothesis is valid in China needs further study. The fact that coefficient of exchange and trade controls is significantly negative indicates that a relaxation of the extent of impediments to international trade resulted in ERER depreciation. The coefficient of lagged RER has a positive sign, as expected, and is quite high in the regression. From an economic perspective this high value for the coefficient implies that in the absence of other intervention, actual RER converges very slowly toward its long-run equilibrium level.

The FEER of the Chinese yuan is determined using the coefficient estimates obtained from regressing Equation 11.10. The estimated FEER and actual RER are shown in Figure 11.2.

MISALIGNMENT OF CHINESE YUAN AND CHINA'S TRADE BALANCE

Estimation of Misalignment of Chinese Yuan

This chapter is expressly interested in the question of whether any misalignment occurred in the yuan's SPFE and FEER during the period 1980 to 2001, just prior to China's WTO entry. The degree of

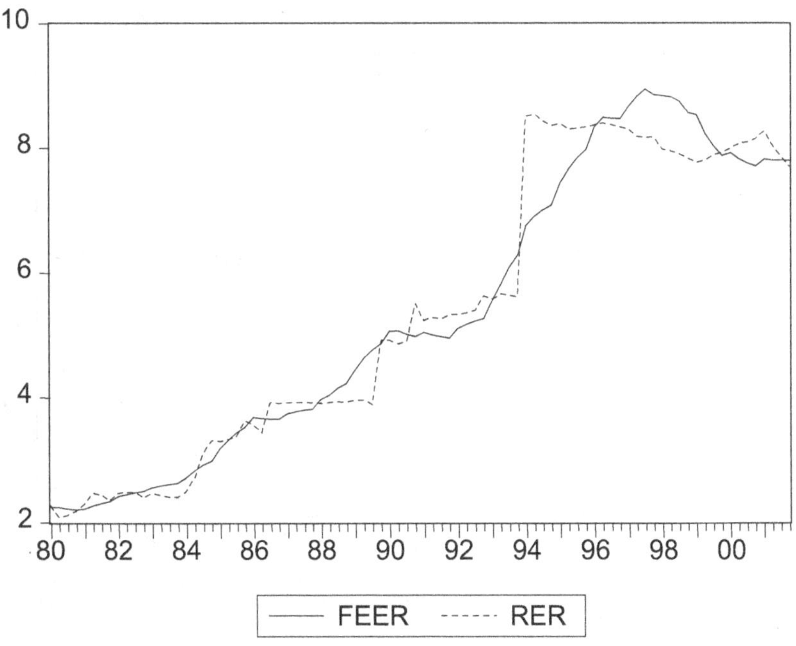

FIGURE 11.2. FEER and RER (Yuan per U.S. Dollar)

misalignment is computed as the difference between the equilibrium and the actual RER.

$$MIS1 = SPFE_t - RER_t \qquad (11.11)$$

$$MIS2 = FEER_1 - RER_t \qquad (11.12)$$

If SPFE or FEER is greater than actual RER, the model would suggest that the currency is overvalued; conversely, if SPFE or FEER is less than the actual RER, the model would indicate that the domestic currency is undervalued. The two types of misalignment are calculated based on SPFE and FEER respectively. Figure 11.3 plots the MIS1 and MIS2.

A comparison of the actual RER and the estimates of SPFE displayed in Figure 11.1 indicates that the RER of the Chinese yuan were overvalued throughout the entire sample period, except the period before 1983. The result is consistent with Chou and Shih's (1998) study.

Figures 11.2 and 11.3 display a more interesting pattern of misalignment in China. The actual RER fluctuated closely around the

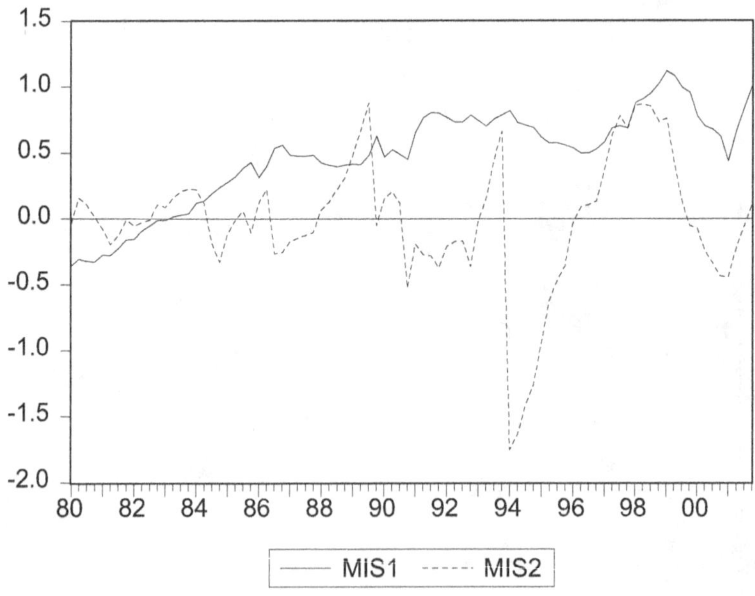

FIGURE 11.3. Misalignment of Chinese Yuan (Yuan per U.S. Dollar)

FEER before 1994. Periods of overvaluation occurred briefly in 1983 to 1984, 1988 to 1990, and 1993 to 1994. These periods of overvaluation were short-lived and the magnitude was generally smaller than that in the following Asia crisis period, that is, from 1996 to 1999. In fact, the Chinese yuan was undervalued six times during the pre-WTO period from 1980 to 2001, and in five of these occurrences the RER was close to the equilibrium. Regarding exchange rate reform, Figures 11.1 and 11.2 display a pronounced jump or devaluation in the actual RER in 1994 when the government announced that it was adopting a managed floating-rate regime based on a uniformed rate, coupled with a move to partial convertibility on current account. After that time, the RER of yuan moved away from the equilibrium rate in a period that included several nominal devaluations.

Impact of Yuan Misalignment on China's Trade Balance

The trade balance is important since it affects the confidence of the exchange rate regime. What were the economic consequences of the yuan's misalignment on China's trade balance?

To further evaluate the impact of real exchange rate misalignments as a factor in variations of China's bilateral trade balance with the United States (Figure 11.4), an unrestricted vector autoregressive impulse-response test is conducted for the pre-WTO period (1980-2001). A one standard deviation shock to the MIS1 leads to a larger and more persistent impact than does the MIS2 on the total trade balance. Throughout all 16 quarters, the impacts of the MIS1 on China's overall trade balance (TB) are larger than those of the MIS2 (Figures 11.5 and 11.6). Nevertheless, these two types of misalignment would not affect the trade balance of China much on the whole.

An unrestricted VAR variance decomposition test for the same period reveals that more than 6 percent of the variance in the trade balance variable can be explained by the variance of the misalignment in the RER of yuan measured by SPFE within four years (or 16 quarters) (Table 11.6). The misalignment in the RER measured by FEER contributes to less than 1 percent of the variance in the trade balance variable (Table 11.7). Equally insignificant, the results indicate that the share of the variance of MIS2 and the share of variance of MIS1 were relatively stable during the 16 lags. Consistent with the impulse-response-test results, the variance-decomposition test un-

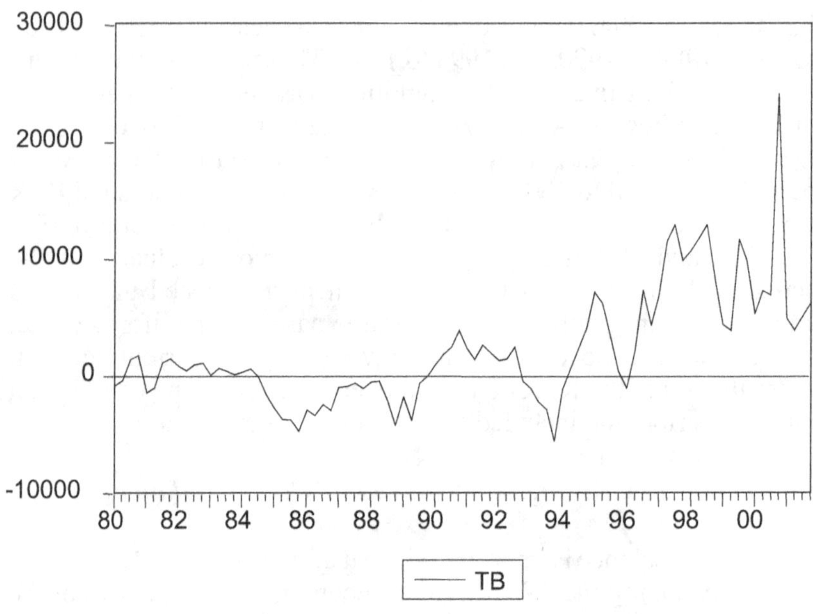

FIGURE 11.4. Total Trade Balance (in Millions of U.S. Dollars)

derscores that the misalignment level of the Chinese yuan is at a safe level. The impact of the misalignment on trade performance is very limited.

FORECAST AND CONCLUSION

Forecast

After measuring the ERER and misalignment of the Chinese yuan, it is meaningful to forecast SPFE and FEER for the post-WTO period. The forecast period is from 2002 to 2005, the first four years after China entered the WTO.

For SPFE, this chapter focuses on the change of tariff rate, which is considered to be the representative variable of the impact of WTO entry. Nominal exchange rate and marginal propensity to spend are assumed unchanged for the post-WTO period. Average tariff rate was 12 percent in 2002 and 10 percent in 2005 as reported by China Cus-

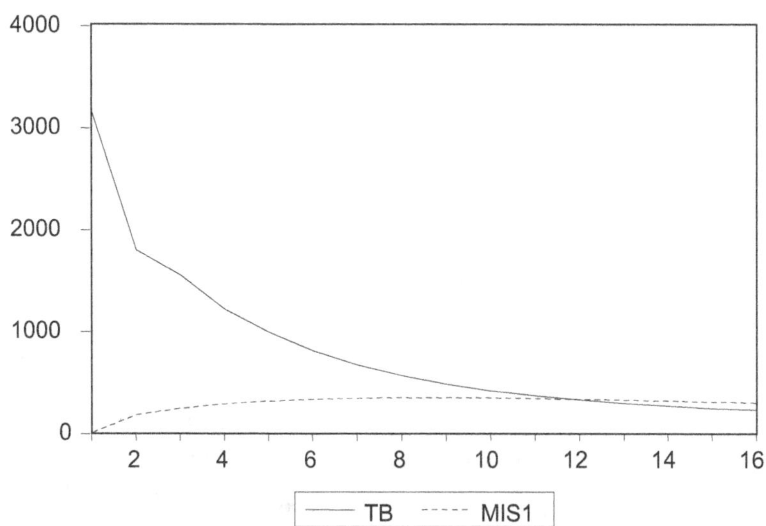

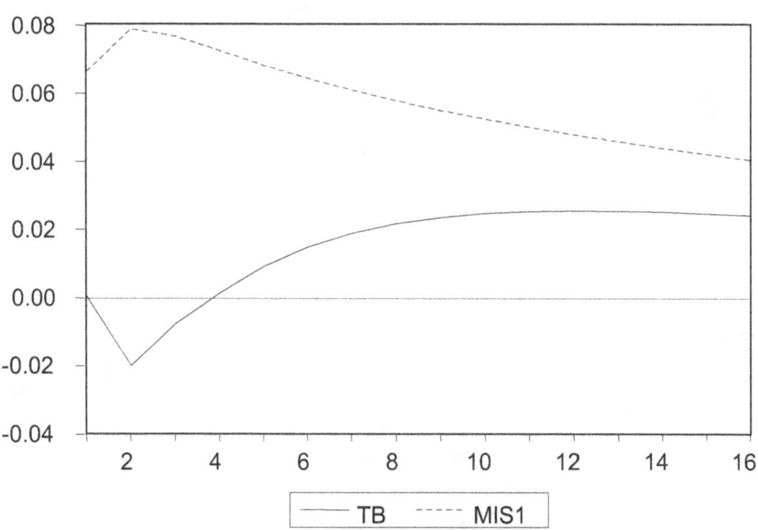

FIGURE 11.5. Impulse Response Test for Trade Balance and MIS1 (*Note:* TB = Trade Balance [total export – total import] of China. MIS1 = misalignment of the real exchange rate of the Chinese yuan measured by SPFE approach.)

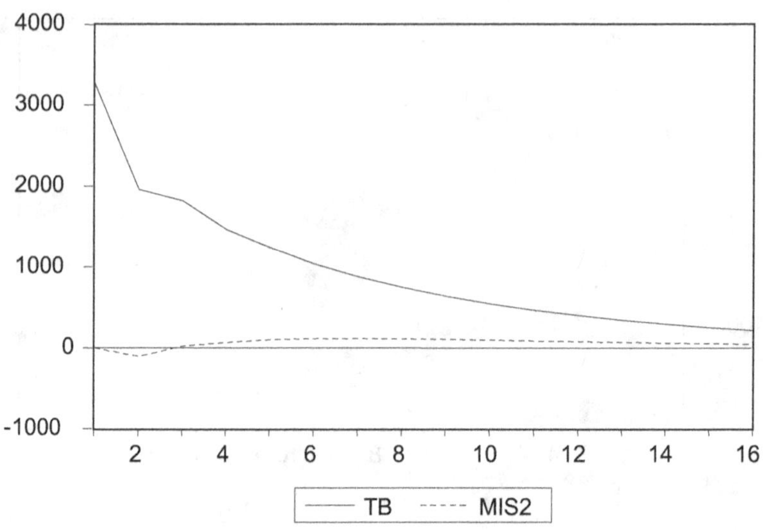

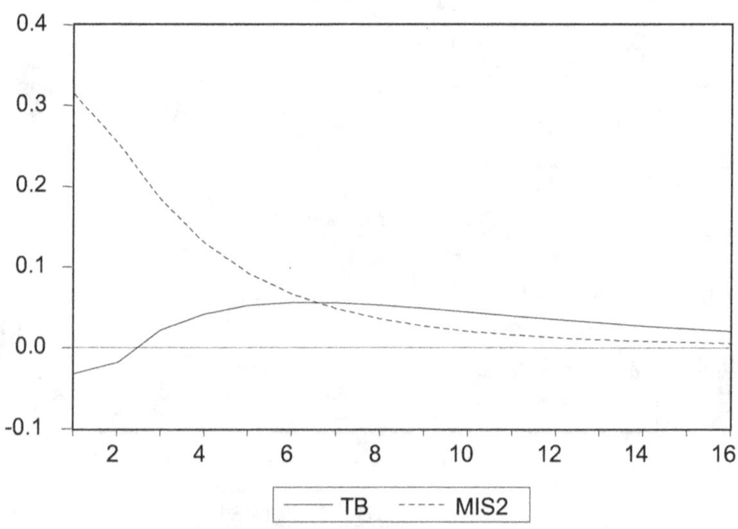

FIGURE 11.6. Impulse Response Test for Trade Balance and MIS2 (*Note:* TB = Trade Balance [total export – total import] of China. MIS2 = misalignment of the real exchange rate of the Chinese yuan measured by FEER approach.)

TABLE 11.6. Variance Decomposition of the Trade Balance and MIS1, Q1 1980-Q4 2001 (Percent) (VAR ordering: [Trade Balance, MIS1])

Period	**S.E.**	**Trade Balance**	**MIS1**
1	3140.537	100	0
2	3621.318	99.77	0.23
3	3944.14	99.45	0.55
4	4135.48	99.04	0.96
5	4262.53	98.57	1.43
6	4350.47	98.06	1.94
7	4414.56	97.53	2.47
8	4463.39	97.00	3.00
9	4502.08	96.47	3.53
10	4533.79	95.96	4.04
11	4560.50	95.47	4.53
12	4583.48	95.01	4.99
13	4603.60	94.58	5.42
14	4621.42	94.17	5.83
15	4637.37	93.79	6.21
16	4651.74	93.44	6.56

Note: Based on the knowledge that SPFE reflects the social value of foreign exchange under trade restrictions, the MIS1 (based on SPFE) should therefore be a more dominant force than the MIS2 (based on FEER) in explaining the trade imbalance of China.

toms (www.customs.gov.cn). For FEER, the actual real exchange rate and nominal interest rate is assumed changeless. The tariff rate setting is the same with that of SPFE. An autoregression method is used to forecast the term of trade and productivity after 2001.

SPFE and FEER for the post-WTO period are forecast based on previous assumption and are shown in Figure 11.7. It is easy to find that both SPFE and FEER will converge to a zone of 8.50-8.80, although FEER has taken on a more volatile movement since China's WTO entry.

TABLE 11.7 Variance Decomposition of the Trade Balance and MIS2, Q1 1980-Q4 2001 (Percent) (VAR ordering: [Trade Balance, MIS2])

Period	S.E.	Trade Balance	MIS2
1	3271.68	100	0
2	3814.57	99.92	0.08
3	4226.76	99.93	0.07
4	4473.85	99.92	0.08
5	4643.73	99.88	0.12
6	4760.46	99.83	0.17
7	4842.90	99.78	0.22
8	4901.75	99.73	0.27
9	4944.18	99.69	0.31
10	4975.00	99.66	0.34
11	4997.47	99.63	0.37
12	5013.94	99.61	0.39
13	5026.03	99.59	0.41
14	5034.93	99.58	0.42
15	5041.49	99.57	0.43
16	5046.33	99.57	0.43

Note: Based on the knowledge that SPFE reflects the social value of foreign exchange under trade restrictions, the MIS1 (based on SPFE) should therefore be a more dominant force than the MIS2 (based on FEER) in explaining the trade imbalance of China.

Conclusion

Based on the economic theory of ERER, this chapter estimated the long-run equilibrium path for the RER in China using three different approaches: PPP, SPFE, and FEER. A short summary and policy implications are provided as follows according to the estimated results.

First, the authors failed to find empirical support for the long-run PPP relationship between China and the United States. Thus the PPP exchange rate is an improper rate to measure the ERER of the Chinese yuan. The PPP hypothes needs to be revised when it is used to analyze China's case because in the take-off period the rise in price of nontradables, such as housing and service, is larger than that of

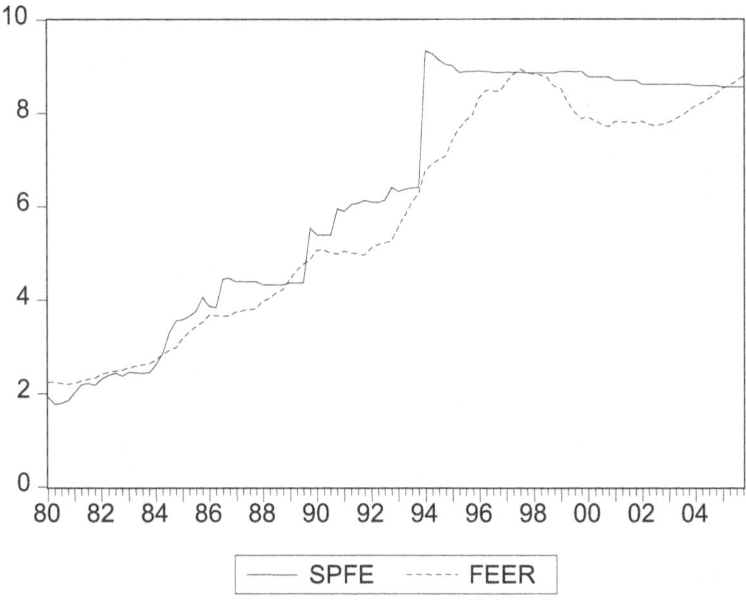

FIGURE 11.7. Forecasted SPFE and FEER (Yuan per U.S. Dollar)

tradables. In the take-off period the increase rate of tradables productivity is higher in developing countries, such as China, than that in the industrial countries.

Second, a comparison of the actual RER and the estimates of SPFE (Figure 11.1) indicated that the RER of the Chinese yuan was overvalued throughout the whole sample period except the period before 1983. This result is consistent with Chou and Shih's (1998) study. Throughout all the lags, the impacts of the misalignment based on SPFE on China's overall trade balance were larger than those of the misalignment based on FEER. However, SPFE did not reflect the exchange rate reform in China from 1980 to 2001.

Third, in the FEER approach, the systematic relationship between the actual RER and economic fundamentals was used as the basic equilibrium concept. Cointegration analysis indicated that the term of trade, domestic interest rate, productivity, and tariffs are long-run determinants of the equilibrium RER in China. Misalignment in China was estimated by using the unique cointegrating vector to derive the

FEER. By these means the authors reached two main conclusions using the data from Q1 1980 to Q4 2001 one was that during much of the 1980s the real exchange rate of the yuan coincided with the ERER (which can explain partially the rapid increase of export and import and China's GDP and other was that during most of the sample period overvaluation and undervaluation appeared alternately. The largest undervaluation, in 1994, reflected the exchange rate reform of unification of the official and swap rates. A following overvaluation, which persisted from 1996 to 1999, showed the impact of the Asia financial crisis.

Finally, the FEER approach produced more appropriate estimates than the PPP and SPFE approaches when studying the ERER of the Chinese yuan. Although SPFE reflects the social value of foreign exchange for the economy of China, FEER is a more creditable rate because it considers both internal and external equilibrium, and the estimated results reflect the impact of exchange rate reform of China and Asia crisis accurately. These results indicate that China now has an effective exchange rate policy that employs the nominal exchange rate a policy tool, varied either frequently or occasionally, to attain either targets in the real sector or a real exchange rate target.

REFERENCES

Chao, C.C. and Yu, E.S.H. (1995). The shadow price of foreign exchange in a dual economy. *Journal of Development Economics, 46*(1), 195-202.

China Statistical Yearbook (1980-2002). Beijing: State Statistical Bureau of the People's Republic of China.

Chou, W.L. and Shih, Y.C.E. (1998). The equilibrium exchange rate of the Chinese renminbi. *Journal of Comparative Economics, 26*(1), 165-174.

Dickey, D.A. and Fuller, W.A. (1979). Distribution of the estimators for autoregressive time series with a unit root. *Journal of the American Statistical Association, 74*(June), 427-431.

Edwards, S. (1988). *Exchange Rate Misalignment in Developing Countries*. Washington, DC: The World Bank.

Edwards, S. (1994). Real and monetary determinants of real exchange rate behavior: Theory and evidence from developing countries. In Williamson, J. (Ed.), *Estimating Equilibrium Exchange Rates.* Washington, DC: Institute for International Economics, pp. 61-92.

Elbadawi, I.A. (1994). Estimating long-run equilibrium real exchange rate. In Williamson, J. (Ed.), *Estimating Equilibrium Exchange Rates.* Washington, DC: Institute for International Economics, pp. 93-132.

Engle, R.F. and Granger, C.W.J. (1987). Co-integration and error correction: Representation, estimation, and testing. *Econometrica, 55*(2), 251-276.

Hinkle, L.E. and Montiel, P.J. (Eds.) (1999). *Exchange Rate Misalignment: Concepts and Measurement for Developing Countries.* Oxford: Oxford University Press.

Johansen, S. (1988). Statistical analysis of cointegration vectors. *Journal of Economic Dynamics and Control, 12*(2-3), 231-254.

Thomson Datastream. Online database. Available at http://extranet.datastream.com/.

Williamson, J. (1985). *The Exchange Rate System.* Washington, DC: Institute for International Economics.

Williamson, J. (Ed.) (1994). *Estimating Equilibrium Exchange Rates.* Washington, DC: Institute for International Economics.

Yi, G. and Fan, M. (1997). The determinative factor and trend analysis of the exchange rate of renminbi. *Economic Research (Jingji Yanjiu), 10*(1), 26-35, in Chinese.

Chapter 12

Trade Elasticities of the Export-Oriented Household Electrical Appliances Industry of Hong Kong

To-Ming Ho

INTRODUCTION

The household electrical appliances industry was first established in Hong Kong in the 1950s. In 1955, only three factories produced electric fans, heaters, electric hair-dressing apparatus, kitchen appliances, and irons. The number of workers in the industry increased from 111 in 1955 to a peak of 21,200 in 1987, and the output of the industry jumped from HK$5 million in 1955 to a maximum of HK$7.558 billion in 1987. More than 90 percent of the electrical appliances produced are for export.

Although the household electrical appliances industry has been operating in Hong Kong for a long time, no economic research exists on this industry. The objective of this chapter is to estimate the trade functions and elasticities of this export-oriented industry during the period 1976-1989. Since the industry assembles the imported electrical components into electrical consumer products that are then exported to foreign countries, the dual-production-theory approach (Diewert and Morrison, 1988) is used to model the industry as a competitive producer in the international economy combining imported components with domestic labor into electrical goods for export. This approach derives the import demand (components) and export supply (appliances) functions of the industry from the variable profit function (McFadden, 1978), a dual representation of production technol-

Globalization and East Asia: Opportunities and Challenges

doi:10.1300/5463_12

ogy, and estimates the trade functions as a system of equations using the seemingly unrelated regressions estimation (SURE) method. Based on the estimated trade functions, various trade elasticities can be derived, which yield useful insights into the responsiveness of Hong Kong's electrical appliances outputs (exports) and inputs (imports) of electrical components to changes in export (electrical appliances) prices, import (electrical components) prices, etc., and enhances our understanding of the interrelationships between the electrical component imports and the electrical appliances exports of Hong Kong.

Following the introduction, the next section models the Hong Kong electrical appliances manufacturing sector as a competitive producer in the world economy using the dual-production-theory approach. A variable profit function is specified for the industry, and a set of export supply and import demand functions is derived from the profit function by Hotelling's lemma. In the third section, the set of export supply and import demand functions is estimated as a system of seemingly unrelated regressions using Zellner's SURE. Based on these estimated trade functions, various trade elasticities can be obtained. The fourth section interprets the export supply and import demand elasticities of the electrical appliances industry. The fifth and final section summarizes and concludes the chapter.

THE MODEL

Assuming perfect competition in both the input and output markets of the Hong Kong electrical appliances industry, a profit-maximizing firm in the international economy, the variable profit function of the industry is defined as

$$\text{Profit}(p,z) \equiv \max_x \{p \cdot x \colon (x,z) \,\varepsilon\, T\} \qquad (12.1)$$

where p is an $n1$ dimensional vector of positive prices for variable inputs and outputs, x is an $n1$ dimensional vector of variable net outputs ($x_i > 0$ if good i is an output, $x_i < 0$ if good i is an input). The term $p \cdot x$ is the inner product of vectors p and x. z is an $(N - n1)$ dimensional vector of fixed inputs. T is the producer's production possibilities set, $T \equiv \{x, z\} \subset R^N$ (Euclidean N-space). The variable profit function (Equation 12.1) is (positively) linearly homogeneous and convex in p for each z.

For estimation purposes, a (normalized) biquadratic flexible functional form (Diewert, 1986) is postulated for the variable profit function (Equation 12.1):

$$\begin{aligned}\text{Profit}(p,z,t) = {} & \Sigma^{n1}{}_{n=1}a_n p_n + (1/2)\Sigma^{n1-1}{}_{n=1}\Sigma^{n1-1}{}_{i=1}b_{ni}(p_n p_i/p_{n1}) \\ & + \Sigma^{n1}{}_{n=1}\Sigma^{N-n1}{}_{m=1}c_{nm}p_n z_m \\ & + 1/2(\Sigma^{n1}{}_{n=1}B_n p_n)(\Sigma^{N-n1}{}_{m=1}\Sigma^{N-n1}{}_{j=1}d_{mj}z_m z_j) \quad (12.2) \\ & + \Sigma^{n1}{}_{n=1}a_{nt}tp_n \\ & + (\Sigma^{n1}{}_{n=1}G_n p_n)(\Sigma^{N-n1}{}_{m=1}c_{mt}tz_m + (1/2)b_{tt}t^2)\end{aligned}$$

where t represents a time trend that takes into account of the existence of technical progress. a_n, b_{ni}, c_{nm}, d_{mj}, a_{nt}, c_{mt}, and b_{tt} are unknown parameters to be estimated. The parameters b_{ni} and d_{mj} satisfy the following symmetry conditions: $b_{ni} = b_{in}$ for $1 \leq n < i \leq n1$, and $d_{mj} = d_{jm}$ for $1 \leq m < j \leq N - n1$. The parameters B's and G's in Equation 12.2 are known non-negative numbers not all equal to zero, and they take the following values (Diewert, 1986): $B_n \equiv 1/p^1{}_n$ for $n = 1,...,n1-1$. $p^1{}_n$ is the price of variable output/input n in period 1. $B_{n1} \equiv 0$, $G_n = B_n$, for $n = 1,...,n1$.

By Hotelling's lemma, the variable output supply and input demand functions can be obtained by differentiating the variable profit function (Equation 12.2) with respect to the output and input prices p. Assume that the variable inputs of the Hong Kong electrical appliances industry consist of domestic labor and imported components, and that the outputs comprise the total quantity of electrical appliances produced by the industry (since more than 90 percent of locally produced appliances are for export, export and output are synonymous). Capital is assumed to be a fixed input. The set of output supply (domestic exports of household electrical appliances) and input demand functions (labor, components) is given as follows.

Demand function (domestic labor):

$$\begin{aligned}x_1 = {} & a_1 + \Sigma^2{}_{i=1}b_{1i}(p_i/p_3) + c_{11}z_1 + 1/2B_1 d_{11}z_1{}^2 + a_{1t}t \\ & + G_1(c_{1t}tz_1 + (1/2)b_{tt}t^2) + u_1 \qquad (12.3)\end{aligned}$$

Demand function (imported components):

$$x_2 = a_2 + \Sigma^2{}_{i=1} b_{2i}(p_i/p_3) + c_{21}z_1 + 1/2B_2 d_{11}z_1{}^2 + a_{2t}t + G_2(c_{1t}tz_1 + (1/2)b_{tt}t^2) + u_2 \quad (12.4)$$

Output supply function (domestic exports of household electrical appliances):

$$x_3 = a_3 - (1/2)\Sigma^2{}_{n=1}\Sigma^2{}_{i=1} b_{ni}(p_n p_i/p_3{}^2) + c_{31}z_1 + (1/2)B_3 d_{11}z_1{}^2 + a_{3t}t + G_3(c_{1t}tz_1 + (1/2)b_{tt}t^2) + u_3 \quad (12.5)$$

Variables x_1, x_2, and x_3 are quantities of labor, components, and outputs (domestic exports) respectively (Table 12.1). The stochastic disturbances u_i ($i = 1,...,3$) are assumed to be independently distributed with a multivariate normal distribution with zero means and covariance matrix Ω.

TABLE 12.1. Variable Descriptions and Data Sources, 1976-1989

Variable	Description	Data Source
p_1	Nominal wage index of workers in the electrical appliances industry (1981=100)	Source (1)
p_2	Unit value index of imported electrical parts and components (1981=100)	Source (3)
p_3	Unit value index of domestic exports of electrical appliances (1981=100)	Source (3)
x_1	Quantity of labor in the electrical appliances industry (1981 HK dollars)	Source (2)
x_2	Quantity of imported electrical parts and components (1981 HK dollars)	Source (3)
x_3	Quantity of domestic exports of electrical appliances (1981 HK dollars)	Source (3)
z_1	Capital stock of the electrical appliances industry (1981 HK dollars)	Source (2)

Sources: Hong Kong Monthly Digest of Statistics, selected issues; *Survey of Industrial Production,* selected issues; *Hong Kong Review of Overseas Trade,* selected issues.

ESTIMATION AND RESULTS

The system of export supply and import demand in Equations 12.3, 12.4, and 12.5 is estimated as a system of seemingly unrelated regressions using Zellner's SURE. The maximum likelihood estimates for the unknown parameters can be obtained using the iterative Zellner SYSTEM command in version 7 of the SHAZAM econometrics software (White, 1978). Annual observations for the period 1976-1989 on prices and quantities of outputs, labor, components, and capital stock are used (Table 12.1). The parameter estimates are shown in the second column of Table 12.2. The estimated symmetric matrix $B \equiv [b_{ni}]$ is positive semidefinite, and hence the estimated biquadratic profit function satisfies the required convexity property. The runs test (Geary, 1970) shows that the residuals are random (Table 12.3).

TRADE ELASTICITIES AND INTERPRETATION

Table 12.4 gives the estimated price elasticities of output (export) supply and input (import) demands. These elasticities measure the responsiveness of export supply and import demands of the household electrical appliances industry to the prices of domestic exports, domestic labor, and imported components. The interpretations of these elasticities are as follows.

Own-Price Elasticities of Inputs (Imports) and Outputs (Exports)

The signs are correct a priori. The high export supply elasticity estimate (+2.93) indicates that manufacturers' ability to respond to changes in prices of household electrical appliances is high. This may be attributable to the fact that the imported components (inputs) are readily available (the demand elasticity of imported components is –3.71). Actually, electrical parts and components for electric fans, heaters, electric hair-dressing apparatus, kitchen appliances, irons, etc., are low-end technology devices, and technology information is

TABLE 12.2. Parameter Estimates of Export Supply and Input/Import Demand Functions of the Hong Kong Household Electrical Appliances Industry

Coefficient	Estimate	T-ratio
a_1	–489.3	–4.9
a_2	–7073.1	–6.1
a_3	3258.4	3.5
c_{11}	1.7	3.9
c_{21}	–3.6	–1.0
c_{31}	7.7	1.4
d_{11}	-0.1×10^{-1}	–13.9
a_{1t}	–112.2	–12.4
a_{2t}	–388.3	–5.6
a_{3t}	557.8	5.3
c_{1t}	0.2	18.5
b_{tt}	0.8	3.5
b_{11}	186.3	3.4
b_{12}	234.5	5.1
b_{22}	6963.0	6.1

Note: Log-Likelihood Value = –236.808.

well disseminated, hence many suppliers, viz. Japan, Korea, Taiwan, the United States, exist. Furthermore, since only a small amount of technical know-how is required in the manufacturing process, workers can efficiently assemble the components into electrical appliances. All in all, as manufacturers have an adequate supply of electrical components and a skillful labor force, they can quickly adapt to changes in prices of household electrical products in the international markets.

Effect of Wage on Inputs/Outputs

Comparing the different columns (inputs/outputs) in Table 12.4, the level of labor wages has only a minor effect on the input demands and output supplies. This may be due to fact that the proportion of labor input (cost) in the total input portfolio (costs) is small.

TABLE 12.3. Runs Test

Equation	Runs Test
	6 runs
Labor Demand	$N_1 = 7 +$
	$N_2 = 7 -$
	(3, 13)
	6 runs
Components Demand	$N_1 = 8 +$
	$N_2 = 6 -$
	(3, 12)
	6 runs
Export Supply	$N_1 = 7 +$
	$N_2 = 7 -$
	(3, 13)

Note: Figures in parentheses (lower critical value, upper critical value) are critical values of runs at the 0.05 level of significance for values of N_1 (number of "+" symbols, i.e., [+] residuals) and N_2 (number of "–" symbols, i.e. [–] residuals).

TABLE 12.4. Price Elasticities of Export Supply and Input/Import Demand Functions of the Hong Kong Household Electrical Appliances Industry

		Price		
		Domestic Labor	**Imported Components**	**Output (Export)**
	Domestic Labor	–0.73	–0.78	1.52
Quantity	Imported Components	–0.15	–3.71	3.86
	Output (Export)	–0.20	–2.73	2.93

Note: Each figure represents the elasticity of demand (supply) for the input (output) in that row with respect to the price of input (output) in that column.

Complementarity of Inputs

When the labor wage decreases by 1 percent, the quantity demanded for imports of electrical components increases by 0.15 percent. Similarly, when the price of components decreases by 1 percent, the quantity demanded for labor increases by 0.78 percent. This means that labor and components are complements in the production process. This empirical finding matches the assembly-oriented nature of the industry.

Effect of Input (Import) Prices on Outputs (Exports)

When the price of imported components drops by 1 percent, the quantity supplied of household electrical appliances exports rises by 2.73 percent. Similarly, when the labor wage decreases by 1 percent, the quantity supplied of exports increases by 0.2 percent. In other words, any decrease (increase) in the price of labor and components will lead to a higher (lower) usage of these two inputs, and hence a higher (lower) volume of exports.

Effect of the Output (Export) Price on Inputs (Imports)

When the export price increases by 1 percent, the quantity supplied of outputs (domestic exports) increases by 2.93 percent, and the quantity demanded for inputs (domestic labor, imported components) increases by 1.52 percent and 3.86 percent respectively. This clearly reveals the importing and exporting characteristic of the Hong Kong household electrical appliances sector, and illuminates the distinctive role of the industry in the international economy, that is, as a producer that assembles the (imported) electrical components of electrical appliances using domestic labor and exports the outputs to overseas markets.

SUMMARY AND CONCLUSION

The variable-profit-function approach simplifies the derivation of the input (import) demand and output (export) supply functions of the export-oriented Hong Kong household electrical appliances industry. The price elasticities yield useful insights into the complementarity of inputs/imports, the effects of the export prices on input/import demands, and the effects of the input/import prices on export supplies. This enhances our understanding of the interrelationships between the inputs/imports and the exports of Hong Kong's domestic electrical appliances manufacturing. All in all, this research methodology can be applied to the study of many industries in the newly industrialized countries (NICs) that are export-oriented in nature, and the elasticity estimates obtained in this chapter will be of value to the policymakers of Hong Kong and other NICs exporting similar products.

REFERENCES

Diewert, W.E. (1986). *The Measurement of the Economic Benefits of Infrastructure Services.* Heidelberg: Springer-Verlag.

Diewert, W.E. and Morrison, C.J. (1988). Export supply and import demand functions: A production theory approach. In Feenstra, R.C. (Ed.), *Empirical Methods for International Trade.* Cambridge, MA: MIT Press, pp. 207-222.

Geary, R.C. (1970). Relative efficiency of count of sign changes for assessing residual autoregression in least squares regression. *Biometrika,* Vol. 57, 123-127.

Hong Kong Monthly Digest of Statistics. Census and Statistics Department, Hong Kong Government, January 1976-December 1989.

Hong Kong Review of Overseas Trade. Census and Statistics Department, Hong Kong Government, 1976-1989.

McFadden, D. (1978). Cost, revenue, and profit functions. In Fuss, M. and McFadden, D. (Eds.), *Production Economics: A Dual Approach to Theory and Applications,* Vol. 1. Netherlands: North-Holland Publishing Company, pp. 3-109.

Survey of Industrial Production. Census and Statistics Department, Hong Kong Government, 1976-1989.

White, K.J. (1978). A general computer program for econometric methods—SHAZAM. *Econometrica,* Vol. 46, 239-240.

Chapter 13

A Multifactor Stock Valuation Model: An Empirical Application to the Thai Telecommunications Sector

Sethapong Watanapalachaikul
Sardar M. N. Islam
Nicholas Billington

INTRODUCTION

Many different emerging and enduring financial issues are present in the financial sectors of developing countries (Islam and Watanapalachaikul, 2004). However, one important issue is valuation, which is the process of converting financial forecast into an estimate of the value of the stock or firm. In practice, a wide variety of valuation methods and models are employed. Among the available methods are the discounted cash flows model (DCFM), the capital asset pricing model (CAPM), and the arbitrage pricing model (APM). Limitations of the existing models are based on the concept of market equilibrium and the existence of a perfect market. In many developing countries, market imperfections and other market characteristics exist for which the existing models may not be suitable. Therefore, a suitable approach to the valuation of stocks in developing countries needs to be developed.

The objectives of this chapter are to determine the principles and estimate the models valuation of stocks in a developing economy. The Thai telecommunications sector is used as a case study to determine the valuation principle of telecommunications stocks in developing countries. The chapter is structured as follows. The second sec-

Globalization and East Asia: Opportunities and Challenges

doi:10.1300/5463_13

tion reviews general valuation models, and the third section presents characteristics of the financial market in developing countries to analyze these characteristics and determine whether the valuation models can be applied to these economies. The fourth section presents financial characteristics of the financial market in developing countries. The fifth section critically reviews the shortcomings of existing models in their application to the Thai telecommunications sector and introduces a new multifactor model for the valuation of Thai telecommunications stocks. The sixth section shows the data gathered for the empirical analysis, and the seventh section presents empirical evidence of the test on the new valuation model. The eighth section shows implications of the result for valuation of stock. The ninth section shows the need for other approaches to the equity valuation problem in the Thai telecommunications industry, and the tenth section contains the conclusions of this study.

STOCK VALUATION

The traditional stock valuation models, such as the DCFM, CAPM, and APM, are commonly used in empirical studies of the valuation of stocks. The DCFM is a widely accepted basic valuation model for a security that is expected to generate cash payments. The value of a particular stock is defined as

$$V_0 = \sum_{n=1}^{\infty} \frac{CF_n}{(1+k)^n} \tag{13.1}$$

where, V_0 = present value of the anticipated cash flows from the security; CF_n = cash flows expected to be received; and k = discount rate or the required rate of return.

Chen et al. (1986) use CAPM to explain the relationship between interest rates macroeconomic activity, and stock returns. CAPM is interpreted as a model of *equilibrium asset return.* It is one of the economic models relevant to business valuation in which businesses and business interests are a subset of the investment opportunities available in the total capital market. It predicts a trade-off between expected return under specific conditions and systematic risk β (Cuthbertson, 1996). Thus, the determination of prices of stocks theoretically should be subject to the same economic forces and relationships that determine the prices or values of other investment assets (Peirson et al., 2000). According to Sharpe (1964), CAPM is defined as

$$E(R_i) = R_f + \beta\,(E(R_m) - R_i) \tag{13.2}$$

where $E(R_i)$ = expected return on investment; R_f = risk-free rate of return; β = investment's systemic risk; and $E(R_m) - R_i$ = expected risk premium in the market.

The arbitrage pricing model could be seen as an alternative to the CAPM to determine the expected rate of return on particular stocks and on the portfolios of stocks. In the CAPM only one factor influences expected return, which is the covariance between the return on the stock and the return on the market portfolio. However, the APM allows a larger number of factors that affect the rate of return on a particular stock. Empirical evidence suggests that the APM explains expected returns better than the single-factor CAPM (Cuthbertson, 1996). The APM is defined as

$$R_{it} = R^e_{it} + u_{it} \tag{13.3}$$

where R_{it} = actual rate of return on the ith stock; R^e_{it} = the expected rate on the ith stock; u_{it} = unexpected, surprise and news element.

CHARACTERISTICS OF THE FINANCIAL MARKET IN DEVELOPING COUNTRIES

Economic Crisis

The economic and financial crisis, market instability, and high volatility in the stock market have become worldwide phenomena in recent years. In early 1997, macroeconomic conditions had seriously deteriorated in most Asian countries. The crisis affected the trade, investment, and financial linkages between many developing countries, especially Asian countries, and the rest of the world (CSES, 1998; Mishkin, 1997).

Thailand was the first to experience the effects of the crisis. The Thai government was forced to implement a devaluation policy, moving from a fixed to a managed float currency system in July 1997.

Many finance companies, 56 out of 91, were closed in December 1997. The crisis caused sudden and unprecedented collapse in asset prices, corporate and financial fragility, and a drastic economic slowdown in the East Asian markets. In just over 12 months, the region's stock markets shrunk by as much as 85 percent in U.S. dollars. At the same time, East Asian currencies depreciated sharply beyond the levels needed to maintain export competitiveness, whereas the credit rating of government bonds fell from AA+ to AA– and unemployment jumped to 1.31 million people (International Financial Risk Institute, 2001; Bank of Thailand, 2000; Leightner, 1999).

Foreign Capital Flows

Foreign capital has played an important role in developing economies by filling the gap when domestic savings were insufficient to finance the country's investment activities (Akrasanee et al., 1993). Foreign capital flows comprise direct foreign investment, portfolio investment, foreign loans, and short-term foreign loans. Since 1990, international capital flows to developing countries have become an important phenomenon, and many developing countries have implemented financial liberalization and globalization to attract these flows. However, in most cases the capital flows went into financial and portfolio investments rather than real investments and consumptions (Siamwalla et al., 1999).

Exchange Rate and Interest Rate in an Open Economy

Exchange rates are important for macroeconomic policy in an open economy for a number of reasons. First, the exchange rate is used as a transmission mechanism of monetary and fiscal policy, affecting real income and domestic price levels. Second, it can be viewed as a filter to external shocks that could disrupt the domestic economy. In most cases in developing economies, financial shocks are concerned with the level of interest rates in the international capital market that would directly impact on the level domestic interest rate, the level of foreign capital flows, and domestic investment. Finally, the short-run dynamics of exchange-rate adjustment is used in formulating and implementing aggregate demand policies (Akrasanee et al., 1993).

Market Imperfection

The sudden crises in Asia and Mexico revealed the shortcomings of traditional open-economy models, which assume efficient global financial markets. Financial market imperfection could be seen as a product of asymmetric information, adverse selection, moral hazards, and incomplete markets. Information asymmetry can severely restrict financial market transactions. Adverse selection would create unequal or inefficient exchange on the market caused by information asymmetry between the two parties. Moral hazard is the risk resulting from misleading information about a company's assets, liabilities, or credit capacity, or by an incentive to take unusual risks in a desperate attempt to earn a profit before the contract settles. These imperfections harm long-term development and account for many characteristics of the recent crisis (Dixon, 1995).

FINANCIAL CHARACTERISTICS IN THE THAI TELECOMMUNICATIONS SECTOR

Capital Investment

There are many options in modernizing telecommunications infrastructure and service. One of the common ways uses state intervention. However, in developing countries government bureaucracy and corruption can pose serious threats to flexibility and innovation and can create inefficiency. Government direct investment could be a problem. Other forms of investment options could be seen as bank loans, loans from multilateral lending institutions, and foreign investment (Mody et al.,1995).

Liberalization and Privatization

In 1993, the Thai government employed a liberalization policy to encourage investment in the Thai telecommunications sector by establishing the Bangkok International Banking Facility (BIBF). The BIBF lured foreign funds by providing tax incentives. In 1996, the BIBF's lending to domestic sectors amounted to 1.8 times the size of the monetary base (Leightner, 1999). Liberalization opened the telecommunications sector to competition by private firms. For years, nearly all Thai telecommunications were government owned and operated, however, by the late 1990s, movements were underway to liberalize, reregulate, and privatize the sector (Rattananubal and Somboontanon, 2001; Mody et al., 1995).

Telecom privatization is a means of overcoming the effects of government failure under public ownership. Thailand accepted the 2006 telecommunications industry liberalization deadline proposed by the World Trade Organization (WTO). Beginning in 1999, two state-owned telecoms, the Telephone Organization of Thailand (TOT) and the Communications Authority of Thailand (CAT), were gradually privatized and liberalized by 2005 (Chinvanthananond, 1999).

Globalization

Globalization has affected the Thai telecommunication sector. The Thai government has enshrined the market-liberalizing moves in the context of the WTO's basic telecommunications regional and multilateral agreements. Major telecommunications companies have operations in other countries and develop new global services. These services include cellular roaming, global satellite systems, calling cards, and third-generation mobile services (International Telecommunication Union, 2002).

In the next section, we discuss whether and how the characteristics of the Thai financial sector and the telecommunications industry can be relevant for determining the applicability of the standard valuation models to the Thai telecommunications sector.

A NEW MODEL FOR VALUATION OF STOCKS

Traditional valuation theories are formulated in the framework of developed countries, and not all of these models are relevant for the valuation of stocks in developing countries. It is necessary to determine how far the traditional theory can be applied in exploring the valuation process of financial stock in developing countries. To accomplish this task, the equity market of the Thai telecommunications sector is taken as a case study in this chapter.

Shortcomings of Existing Models

The discounted cash flow and capital asset pricing models do not reflect all important factors for valuating stocks, for example, changes in telecommunication policy and technology are not accounted for. In general, DCFM measures the stock value by estimating the earnings. The earning history of most telecommunication stocks has fluctuated in recent years. Existing valuation models are based on the concept of market equilibrium and the existence of a perfect market. In many developing countries, there are market imperfections and other market characteristics for which the existing models may not be suitable.

In this section, we argue that the standard valuation models of CAPM and APM cannot be applied to the Thai telecommunications sector due to the characteristics of the financial market and the Thai telecommunications sector discussed earlier. Principally, these models are based on a perfect financial market, and there are imperfections in the Thai financial market. A multifactor model can overcome the limitations of the equilibrium models, therefore this approach is adopted.

The development of this valuation model makes a valuable contribution to our understanding of the effects of internal and external factors that influence share prices, return, and volatility. Mathematically, a multiple factor model can be expressed as follows:

$$R_{it} = \alpha_i + (\beta_1)_i (F_1)_t + (\beta_2)_i (F_2)_t + \ldots + (\beta_n)_i (F_n)_t + \varepsilon_{it} \quad (13.4)$$

where R_{it} = the return of stock i in period t; α_i = the expect value if each factor as a value of zero; $(F_1)_t$ and $(F_2)_t$ = the values of factors 1 and 2 with pervasive influence in period t; $(F_n)_t$ = the value of factor n; $(\beta_1)_i$ and $(\beta_2)_i$ = the price of factor 1 and 2 (the risk premium) for stock i; $(\beta_n)_I$ = the price of factor n (the risk premium) for stock i; and ε_{it} = the stock-specific return.

The multiple regression technique is used to identify the significant factors/variables that influence the value of the stock. Hypothesis testing is conducted to find a basis for determining the significance of various factors in valuation of the telecommunications stocks.

Several advantages exist in using a multiple-factor model over CAPM and DCFM. First, since economic logic is used in the development of multiple-factor models and selecting the appropriate factors, these models are not dependent purely on historical relationships. Second, multiple-factor models allow for a more thorough understanding of a portfolio's exposure to different factors or variables. Third, multiple-factor models allow for analyses that are more precise and lead to better-informed investment decisions.

In this research, the sector return is calculated from the price of the telecommunication companies listed in the Stock Exchange of Thailand (SET). The return of the sector (R_t) is calculated from the following equation:

$$R_t = \frac{P_t - P_{t-1}}{P_t} \qquad (13.5)$$

where P_t is the price of an asset at date t and assumes that this asset pays no dividends. The simple net return, R_t, is on the asset between dates t-1 and t.

DATA

The Thai telecommunications companies considered in this chapter are Advanced Info Service Public Company Limited (ADVANC), The International Engineering Public Company Limited (IEC), Jasmine International Public Company Limited (JASMIN), Samart Corporation Public Company Limited (SAMART), Samart Telecom Public Company Limited (SAMTEL), Shinawatra Satellite Public Company Limited (SATTEL), SHIN Corporations Public Company Limited (SHIN), Telecomasia Corporations Public Company Limited (TA), Thai Telephone & Telecommunication Public Company Limited (TT&T), and United Communication Industry Public Company Limited (UCOM).

Three sets of economic factors will be analyzed for the years 1997-2000, i.e., economic, fiscal, and monetary and financial factors. *Economic indicators* include statistical data of the SET index, consumer price index (CPI), foreign direct investment (FDI), manufacturing production index (MPI), export (X), import (M), and balance of payment (BOP); *fiscal indicators* include government revenue (GREV) and government expenditure (GEXP); and *monetary and financial indicators* include bank deposits (BDEP), bank credits (BCR), nonperforming loans (NPL), total debt restructuring (TDR), foreign assets

(FA), foreign liability (FL), interest rate (IR), exchange rate (Exchange), and M1, M2, and M3.

RESULTS

According to Islam and Oh (2003), the factors need to be tested to determine their relevance. This can be done by examining the correlation coefficient of each factor with the return on each company's stock (see Table 13.1).

Table 13.1 shows the correlation coefficient of individual telecommunications stocks as well as the Thai telecommunications sector. The next step is to create a generic six-factor model, in which the factors are selected from the statistically significant results in Table 13.1, for the Thai telecommunications sector. Named the Thai Telecommunication Multifactor Model (TTMM), this model is described as follows:

$$R_t = 31.7 - 0.24CPI + 0.03EX - 0.003FL - 0.0002BCR + 0.0000003GREV + 0.001SET + \varepsilon_t \tag{13.6}$$

where CPI = the value of the factor: consumer price index; EX = the value of the factor exchange rate; FL = the value of the factor foreign liability; BCR = the value of the factor bank credit; $GREV$ = the value of the factor government revenue; SET = the value of the factor Stock Exchange of Thailand index.

All six factors in the estimated equation are the highest factors, which are significant at the 5 percent significance level. The systematic risk measured by the CPI, EX, FL, BCR, GREV, and SET explains only 40 percent of the Thai telecommunications sector.

IMPLICATIONS OF THE RESULTS FOR STOCK VALUATION

Table 13.2 reports the regression analysis. Data show a weak to moderate long-run relationship among stock returns and consumer price index, exchange rate, foreign liability, bank credit, government revenue, and the Stock Exchange of Thailand index. The variables

TABLE 13.1. Correlation Coefficient (Percentage)

	ADVANC	IEC	JASMIN	SAMART	SAMTEL	SATTEL
SET	–5.11	17.65	11.56	34.02	22.08	3.63
CPI	–34.90	–38.85	–44.48	–47.52	–48.90	–44.54
FDI	9.49	–8.76	5.98	–5.42	–10.75	–10.57
MPI	–6.36	–8.84	–6.02	4.24	1.46	–15.12
X	–12.73	–14.06	–11.61	–12.62	–7.37	–22.49
M	–9.27	–11.28	–14.90	–8.07	–8.78	–18.31
BOP	4.12	7.94	17.02	17.37	10.88	7.57
GREV	8.37	26.56	29.48	18.33	17.76	14.16
GEXP	12.32	0.48	3.64	–21.48	0.27	2.03
BDEP	–5.96	–1.36	–3.21	1.93	–10.82	–24.94
BCR	29.36	17.24	25.03	15.90	28.34	40.67
NPL	–5.06	8.59	5.06	15.02	–0.31	–12.19
TDR	–11.81	–10.91	–12.37	–3.24	–6.37	–23.41
FA	20.35	1.84	10.23	8.15	13.68	5.85
FL	35.04	20.13	25.32	13.65	28.73	46.08
IR	9.62	1.60	9.84	–2.49	10.30	26.27
EX	48.58	18.71	35.82	14.01	41.26	56.31
M1	5.07	–5.15	–0.86	7.40	11.56	7.29
M2	–6.06	–4.78	–6.13	1.67	–9.47	–21.68
M3	–9.24	–7.47	–11.20	–2.19	–13.42	–24.18
SECTOR	77.03	86.63	72.45	83.39	84.24	85.06

	SHIN	TA	TT&T	UCOM	SECTOR
SET	18.48	–4.63	11.66	5.61	15.49
CPI	–41.65	–42.82	–43.34	–32.86	–49.79
FDI	–16.52	–7.52	–12.69	–17.02	–9.02
MPI	0.24	–6.89	–7.64	–4.43	–5.42
X	–5.47	–25.39	–16.11	–10.43	–16.04
M	–1.45	–25.65	–14.76	–7.63	–13.90
BOP	31.34	11.53	10.89	0.91	14.45
GREV	14.14	4.05	14.06	0.74	18.53
GEXP	7.05	–1.24	–4.10	–4.33	–1.92
BDEP	–10.92	–4.56	–7.15	–5.33	–7.45
BCR	22.74	34.30	25.72	20.32	29.28
NPL	–6.10	18.54	3.82	–4.92	3.92
TDR	–7.72	–17.75	–13.34	–8.33	–12.96
FA	11.18	–0.23	4.03	7.10	9.11
FL	27.11	31.18	27.60	24.10	31.27
IR	10.54	3.69	6.82	4.02	8.29
EX	38.98	30.52	32.66	35.45	39.09
M1	13.14	1.88	2.92	11.79	5.97
M2	–7.95	–4.12	–7.41	–2.84	–7.33
M3	–10.39	–10.69	–10.73	–4.50	–11.49
SECTOR	89.68	84.75	96.87	84.89	100.00

Source: Bank of Thailand, Authors' calculations.

TABLE 13.2. Regression Statistics

Multiple R	0.635291
R Square	0.403594
Adjusted R Square	0.2802
Standard Error	0.228778
	Coefficients
Intercept	31.70693
CPI	–0.2379
EX	0.032259
FL	–0.0003
BCR	–0.00029
GREV	3.91E-06
SET	–0.00132

Source: Authors' calculations.

explain only 40 percent of the stock return. According to the empirical tests, a multifactor model measured by macroeconomic factors cannot be used as a single method in valuating the Thai telecommunications stocks. Unsystematic risks such as political influence and other behavior finance issues discussed previously, are present.

THE NEED FOR OTHER APPROACHES FOR VALUATION

The low R-square could be explained by the high level of unsystematic risk elements. As mentioned ealier in this paper, the unsystematic risk elements are asymmetric information, adverse selection, moral hazards, and incomplete market. It is suggested that the Thai telecommunications industry could be dealing with idiosyncratic factors instead of general macroeconomics factors. Further econometrics studies could be developed by using more focused factors or microeconomic factors at the sector level. Political influences could be one of the relevant areas to determine stock prices of the telecommunications sector. It may also be useful to undertake fundamental and technical analysis.

CONCLUSION

Tentative results in this chapter suggest that no standard models can be applied to determine the value of stocks in a developing country such as Thailand. An approach is needed in which a combination of modeling and fundamental, technical economic analysis and behavioral finance can be undertaken for this empirical study.

REFERENCES

Akrasanee, N., Jansen, K., and Pongpisanupichit, J. (1993). *International Capital Flows and Economic Adjustment in Thailand.* Bangkok: Thailand Development Research Institute.

Bank of Thailand (2000). *Economic Conditions.* Monetary Policy Group, November 2.

Center for Strategic Economic Studies (1998). Crisis in East Asia: Global watershed or passing storm? Conference Report, Victoria University, Melbourne.

Chen, N.F., Roll, R., and Ross, S. (1986). Economic forces and the stock market. *Journal of Business,* July, 383-403.

Chinvanthananond, S. (1999). Telecommunication Industry: Thailand, U.S., & Foreign Commercial Service. Available at http://www.tradeport.org/ts/countries/thailand/isa/isar0011.html.

Cuthbertson, K. (1996). *Quantitative Financial Economics: Stocks, Bonds, and Foreign Exchange.* London: John Wiley & Sons.

Dixon, H.D. (1995). *The New Macroeconomics: Imperfect Markets and Policy Effectiveness.* New York: Cambridge University Press.

International Financial Risk Institute (2001). Background to the Financial and Economic Turbulence of 1997-1998. Available at http://newrisk.ifci.ch/145900.htm.

International Telecommunication Union (2002). World Telecommunication Development Report: Reinventing Telecoms, Executive Summary. Available at http://www.itu.int/ITU-D/ict/publications.

Islam, S. and Oh, K.B. (2003). *Applied Financial Econometrics in E-commerce.* Amsterdam: North Holland Publishing.

Islam, S. and Watanapalachaikul, S. (2004). *Empirical Finance: Modeling and Analysis of Emerging Financial and Stock Markets.* Heidelberg: Springer-Verlag.

Leightner, J.E. (1999). Globalization and Thailand's financial crisis. *Journal of Economic Issues, 33,* 367-373.

Lintner, J. (1965). The valuation of risky assets and the selection of risky investments in stock portfolios and capital budgeting. *Review of Economics and Statistics,* No. 47, 13-37.

Mishkin, F.S. (1997). *Understanding Financial Crises: A Developing Country Perspective.* Washington, DC: The World Bank.

Mody, B., Bauer, J.M., and Straubhaar, J.D. (1995). *Telecommunications Politics: Ownership and Control of the Information Highway in Developing Countries.* Mahwah, NJ: Lawrence Erlbaum Associates.

Peirson, G., et al., (2000). *Business Finance,* Seventh Edition. Sydney: McGraw-Hill.

Rattananubal, R. and Somboontanon, A. (2001). *Thai Telecommunications.* Bangkok: Monetary Policy Group, Bank of Thailand.

Sharpe, R.F. (1964). Capital asset prices: A theory of market equilibrium under conditions of risk. *Journal of Finance,* No. 19, 425-442.

Siamwalla, A., Vajragupta, Y., and Vichyanond, P. (1999). *Foreign Capital Flows to Thailand: Determinants and Impact.* Bangkok: Thailand Development Research Institute.

PART IV: INDUSTRY-SPECIFIC STUDIES AND FUTURE RESEARCH

Chapter 14

Implications for the Vietnamese Textile and Apparel Industry in Light of Abolishing the Multifiber Arrangement and the U.S.-Vietnam Bilateral Investment Treaty

Joseph Pelzman

INTRODUCTION

An important feature of the Uruguay Round agreement was the agreement to abolish the Multifiber Arrangement system of quotas that regulated exports of textile and apparel products from developing countries for close to four decades. While enormously welcome, the abolition of these quotas will not necessarily generate automatic benefits to individual countries. The abolition of the quotas will create opportunities for developing countries, but will also expose them to additional competition from other, formerly restrained, exporters. The outcome for any individual country will depend heavily on its policy response. Countries that take the opportunity to streamline their policies and improve their competitiveness are likely to increase their gains from quota abolition.

The objective of this chapter is to evaluate the export potential of the Vietnamese textile and apparel industry in light of the changed circumstances in its access to the world market. The chapter is organized as follows: the second section will review the local market trends in the domestic Vietnamese textile and apparel industry, whereas the third section presents the current state of the U.S.-Vietnam textile

Globalization and East Asia: Opportunities and Challenges

doi:10.1300/5463_14

agreement debate in the context of their new normalization. Concluding remarks are presented in the fourth section.

THE VIETNAMESE TEXTILE AND APPAREL INDUSTRY

Trends in Production and Trade

The development of the textile and apparel (T&A) sector in Vietnam in the 1980s was closely associated with the bilateral cooperation programs between Vietnam and the former Soviet Union (FSU) and Eastern European countries (FEE). Under these bilateral agreements Vietnam's T&A industry was primarily a subassembly operation. All machines and inputs were provided by the FSU and FEE with the corresponding charge off for assembly fees. These barter arrangements led to distortionary trade patterns, input costs, and final goods prices. Moreover, the quality of the fabrics inputs used and the resulting end products originating from Vietnam were substandard as compared to Western quality expectations.

With the collapse of COMECON/CMEA (Council for Mutual Economic Assistance) in the late 1980s, and the restructuring of most of the FSU and FEE, Vietnam's T&A sector took a major hit. The share of textile output in gross domestic product (GDP) declined substantially, leading to a drop of the share of the total T&A industry in Vietnam's GDP. During the 1990s the apparel sector improved its output while the performance of the textile sector continued to be more modest.

The success of the apparel sector is, to a large extent, attributable to the negotiated opening of access to "quota-regulated" foreign markets in the early 1990s. With the signing of a trade agreement with the European Union (EU) in 1992, Vietnam's apparel export benefited from preferential access to the large EU market. Following the EU agreement, Norway and Canada allocated quota rights to Vietnam's textile and apparel sector. These quota-regulated markets have played an important role for Vietnam with its share out of total T&A export increasing from 22 percent in 1993 to 35 percent in 1999.

Since late 1998, Vietnam's apparel exporters have focused on nonquota markets, most notably Japan, South Korea, Taiwan, and ASEAN (Association of Southeast Asian Nations). Exports to these nonquota markets are a function of foreign subsidiaries who have located facilities in Vietnam primarily to export back to their home countries. This is similar to U.S. offshore assembly operations with the exception that much of the products are reexported to the EU or U.S. markets. Over the past few years, some Vietnamese firms have attempted to bypass these operations by directly exporting to the Japanese market with some limited success.

The apparel industry was hit hard by the Asian financial crisis and the slowdown of the Japanese economy. The share of apparel export to these markets declined to 40 percent from 60 percent in the mid-1990s. As compared to 1997, the volume of apparel exports to these markets declined by 22 percent and 11 percent in 1998 and 1999 respectively. The decline in export growth of the apparel sector in recent years (–3.5 percent in 1998, and 4 to 5 percent in 2000—preliminary estimate) may indicate a loss of competitiveness in the face of fierce international competition. The two primary subcategories with double-digit growth over the 1996-1999 period were knitting wool and assembled apparel.

It is widely believed that the poor export performance of Vietnam's textile industry is due mainly to the obsolescence of the technology present in most of its firms and resulting low quality of the outputs, and consequently the lack of the industry's competitiveness in the world market. Despite the fact that there has been substantial government support of this industry, that support is still far from sufficient to help the T&A state-owned enterprises (SOEs) improve technology to meet the quality requirements of the market.

The Ownership Structure of Vietnam's Textile and Apparel Industry

The ownership structure of Vietnam's T&A industry reflects the overall fluid nature of an economy in transition. A diversity of ownership forms are present, including SOEs, private firms, and foreign invested firms. With the fall of the FSU came a change in the fundamental ownership structure of the Vietnamese textile and apparel sector. The share of the state sector shrank while the shares of both the domestic private sector and the foreign sector increased. Since the mid-1990s the shares of state and formal domestic private sectors have been stabilized at 40 percent and 3.5 percent, respectively. Over the same period, shares of household and mixed sectors declined, while the share of the foreign sector increased from 6.3 percent in 1995 to 11.7 percent in 1999.

Although the share of the state sector has been decreasing, the textile sector is among those industries in which the state sector takes the major share of total output, at around 53 percent on average in the late 1990s. Most textile output originating from the state sector has been produced by central SOEs (80 percent on average) and this share has been rising in recent years, as compared to local SOEs, which are facing difficulties due to the capital shortage.

Although it is true that the transition to a market economy has resulted in a reduction of SOEs by at least 50 percent, the government of Vietnam has created a major loophole by setting up general corporations that appear to be SOE conglomerates. It is still not fully clear how efficient these corporations are, but the dominant role of these large corporations in the respective markets makes it difficult for nonstate enterprises to grow. In the textile and apparel industry, the majority of state firms have become members of a T&A corporation named VINATEX. At present, VINATEX has 52 member-enterprises, and takes a large share of this industry. It is estimated that VINATEX produces 80 percent of total fiber, 65 percent of fabrics, and 45 percent of apparel products, and represents 40 percent of the total export value of this industry. Although the member enterprises of VINATEX can work independently, VINATEX plays an important role in export quota allocation and allocation of state and bank credits to its member enterprises.

Overall, private enterprises in Vietnam appeared to have had an initial inducement in the early period of market reforms. Their share of total GDP increased to 3.5 percent by the mid-1990s. Despite this increase continued development of the private sector declined in the late 1990s, given a general decline in reforms.

Similarly, in the textile industry, the private sector grew quite rapidly until 1996, but has slowed since then. Even in the years of high growth, the share of the formal private sector in the textile industry was modest with peaks of 2.1 percent in 1996 and 1997. In general, GDP share of the private sector in the textile industry is smaller than its share in the whole industry (2.1 percent versus 3.38 percent), but both indicate that the private sector is underdeveloped.

The late 1990s witnessed a large reduction of output shares of both textiles and apparel. The household and collective (cooperative) sectors normally produce traditional products targeting low-income consumers. These sectors face fierce competition from large-scale enterprises and foreign-made goods. Cooperatives are a legacy of the centralized economy, and although they were important in the past, they are now almost nonexistent with the share of total industry output shrinking from 2 percent in 1995 to about 1 percent in 1998.

The decline of the collective sector is due to the withdrawal of government assistance, which was common in the past, and to poor economic management, which was largely due to the low motivation of managers caused by an improperly designed incentive system. The share of household enterprises declined also, but the decline was smaller as compared to the collective sector. The sector's output share in the industry dropped significantly from 22 percent in 1995 to 15 percent in 1999. The decline of the household sector in relative terms is mainly explained by the expansion of the formal sector, and to a lesser extent, reduction of the sector in absolute terms as evidenced by a reduction of total employment of this sector from 552,000 people in 1993 to 539,000 people in 1998.

The foreign "invested" sector (which includes joint ventures and firms with 100 percent foreign capital) in the textile industry has become more important in the past few years. It has surpassed the household sector in terms of output share since 1997 and become the second largest ownership sector in the textile industry (30.5 percent in 1999).

Overall, the textile and apparel industry is considered a major player by the Vietnamese government, which has directed special benefits to it. It therefore enjoys preferential treatment in numerous forms including tax reduction and a high level of protection from foreign competition with tariffs on imported consumer goods ranging from 40 percent to 50 percent. Vietnam's low labor costs help attract foreign investors. Other Asian countries, including Korea, Taiwan, Malaysia, and Indonesia, top the list with about 85 percent of total foreign investment in the industry.

In the textile industry, the most popular form of mixed ownership firms is the joint venture between SOEs and foreign firms. Foreign investors prefer these joint ventures as compared to 100 percent ownership because the former has several advantages over the latter in terms of access to land, workers rights, and authority. Although the share of joint ventures has been increasing in recent years, this subsector has been growing slower than firms with 100 percent foreign capital.

The apparel subsector has had the same ownership experience as the textile industry. The state sector is still the most important but its role in the industry is declining. The shares of mixed and foreign-invested sectors have been rising. The private sector is still under-developed with the share reaching a peak in 1997 and declining afterward. The collective sector is almost nonexistent, whereas the share of the household sector has been shrinking quite sharply.

As compared to the textile industry, the state sector has a smaller output share (33 percent versus 53 percent on average for the period 1995-1999) within the apparel subsector, and that share has been declining. The reduction is more substantial for local SOEs than central SOEs. The former have had their shares shrunk by 5 percent over the period from 1995 to 1999. The poorer performance of local SOEs may be partly explained by their less favorable conditions in terms of connections with policymaking bodies, access to quotas and credit, etc., as compared to those of central SOEs.

Although the relative importance of local SOEs is declining, they still produce more output than central SOEs. As compared to the textile industry, the output share of local SOEs is much higher. This is partly explained by the government's efforts to distribute quotas more evenly across localities to encourage local apparel SOEs to develop and thus increase local employment.

The role of the non-state sector in the apparel industry, as in the textile sector, is still very modest. One reasons is the capital shortage experienced by non-state firms. A more important reason is the lack of favorable environment for non-state firms to flourish. Private firms often complain about the complicated registration procedures,[1] difficult access to land, credit, and quota. The unfavorable business environment has had its negative impact not only on private firms, but also on cooperatives and household enterprises. As a consequence, these sectors have declined over the past few years. The relatively smaller scale of production of non-state firms is also widely perceived as a cause of their poor performance and their disadvantage vis-à-vis SOEs and foreign-invested firms. Also, as the economy develops and household's income increases, apparel consumption favors ready-made clothing that, in Vietnam, is normally better produced in larger enterprises.

The share of the foreign-invested sector predominately increased in the apparel industry in the late 1990s. (The foreign-invested sector is broadly defined to include the mixed sector consisting of mainly joint ventures between SOEs and foreign investors with the dominance of the latter.) The majority of foreign investors came from Asian countries. Although these foreign firms do not have access to export quotas, they benefit considerably from cheap labor employed to produce goods to be exported to their home countries, or to do transit trade, i.e., reexporting to other regions such as the EU or the United States. The value of total transit trade of textile or apparel products is estimated at 20 percent of total Vietnam T&A exports.

The data for 1997 show that in the textile sector, there were 19 joint venture enterprises and 40 enterprises with 100 percent foreign capital and an output share of 20 percent. In the apparel sector there were 29 joint venture enterprises and 53 enterprises with 100 percent foreign capital and an output share that was almost the same as foreign textile enterprises. The actual foreign capital invested in the textile sector was more than US$500 million (40 projects) employing about 36,000 workers. Data for 1998 showed that the foreign sector share was 17 percent of employment and 16.7 percent of establishments in the textile sector, and 24 percent of employment and 19 percent of establishments in the apparel sector.

The Labor Market in Vietnam's Textile and Apparel Industry

The employment data by industry in Vietnam are poorly recorded and inconsistent. Different sources quote different data and it is therefore difficult to obtain a consistent picture of employment in the T&A industry. The only reliable source is the Living Standards Surveys, which were conducted in 1992/1993 and 1997/1998. Based on this survey one should not be surprised to find that this industry is very labor intensive and therefore creates the largest number of jobs among the manufacturing industries.

In 1992/1993 total employment in the T&A industry (both formal and informal sectors) was 1.04 million people, and the figure for 1997/1998 was 1.17 million. The annual growth rate for the period 1992/1993 to 1997/1998 was 2.37 percent. A special feature of the T&A industry is that formal employment (wage employment) has increased in both absolute and relative terms. Total wage employment in the T&A industry was 491.6 thousand people and 538.9 thousand in 1992/1993 and 1997/1998 respectively. Its share out of total industry employment increased from 47 percent to 54.1 percent between 1992/1993 and 1997/1998.

It is noteworthy that the share of both wage employment and self-employment in urban areas has declined. This indicates a tendency of moving T&A industry toward rural areas to exploit cheap labor costs there. This tendency is likely to be for the apparel industry only, which requires much lower relocation costs than the textile industry. Furthermore, it is easier for the apparel industry to absorb low-skilled rural labor as compared to the textile industry.

The domestic non-state sector makes up the majority of total employment in both the textile and apparel industry, followed by the state sector. The foreign sector generates the smallest number of jobs. Household enterprises, which dominate the domestic non-state sector, are very small in size, and are much smaller than SOEs and foreign-invested firms. In terms of employment per establishment, SOE is the largest, with its size being 2.6 times and 2.2 times larger than the average foreign firm in the textile and apparel industries, respectively. However, foreign firms have the highest labor productivity with output per employee being 1.4 times and 1.6 times higher than SOEs in the textile and apparel subsectors, respectively.

The Production Structure of Vietnam's Textile and Apparel Industry

Although the fabric sector is more capital intensive than the apparel sector, it is still fairly labor intensive. The fiber production is essentially capital intensive. Vietnam is unlikely to have a comparative advantage in the upstream and some midstream sectors, since these sectors are relatively capital intensive and capital is a scarce factor in Vietnam. In fact, those sectors that produce fibers or fabric of high quality are almost nonexistent in Vietnam, and the country is still heavily reliant on imported fabrics.

A distinctive feature of the Vietnamese textile industry is that while the vertical linkage between up- and downstreams is weak, mixed production is relatively common in which textile firms produce both textile and apparel items. The primary reason behind this downstream production is labor availability. An additional factor is the possibility to export these apparel products.

It is difficult to get accurate estimates of the production capacity of the apparel industry. However, the rapid growth of this sector in recent years may imply that the capacity of the industry has increased. Ready-made-cloth items have grown rapidly in physical units at an average growth rate of 24 percent per year during the 1990s.

Despite these positive signs, the production capacity of this industry cannot meet the diversity of demand. The industry primarily focuses on production of unsophisticated products such as shirts, jackets, coats, home dressings, and the like. This is a primary reason why Vietnam's apparel industry can fill only a portion of categories under the EU-granted quota arrangement. For example, among 106 items under the EU quota, only a small portion of the quotas were filled in 1992. Under the 1995 framework agreement, the number of quota items was reduced to 54, and was then reduced further to 29 in 1998. It is not clear whether Vietnam's apparel industry can participate in the international market in more sophisticated downstream products without direct technology transfers from foreign sources.

The Geographic Location of Vietnam's Textile and Apparel Industry

In general, textile and apparel firms are located primarily in two poles of the country: the north and the south. The south takes the largest share (50 percent) of the output followed by the north (40 percent) and the center (10 percent). The main reason for central Vietnam's small share is the absence of adequate infrastructure such as seaports, airports, roads, and the like. In the north and south, the distribution of these two industries is uneven with the majority of firms being located in big cities such as Hanoi, Hai Phong, Nam Dinh, Ho Chi Minh City, and to a lesser extent, provincial capital cities. In recent years, Vietnam's government has made great efforts to promote these industries in remote areas in order to reduce the income gap between urban and rural areas. Quota allocation and financial assistance are major forms of promotion, but this policy does not seem to work well due to poor infrastructure, which does not allow local firms to easily access foreign markets and/or brokers.

The uneven distribution of the T&A industries is clearest in the case of foreign-invested firms. Foreign investors in these industries prefer the south to the north. For example, up to 1997, foreign investment in the textile industry was located in 16 provinces/cities in the south representing 93 percent of the total number of projects with 98 percent of registered capital. In particular, Dong Nai, Long An, Binh Duong and Ho Chi Minh City make up the overwhelming share.

The situation is similar for the apparel industry. Up to 1997, foreign investment in the apparel industry was made in 18 provinces or cities; most projects (84 percent), with 96 percent of registered capital, were concentrated in the south. Ho Chi Minh City is the center of apparel-sector foreign investment, followed by the Dong Nai and Binh Duong provinces. Among locations that attract large amount of foreign investment in the apparel industry, Hanoi was ranked as number six with 12 percent of the total number of projects and 12 percent of invested capital in 1997.

Trends in Technology of Vietnam's Textile and Apparel Industry

The situation with equipment and technology of the T&A industry varies across sectors. The five distinct types of technologies in the T&A industry include fiber spinning, shuttle weaving, knitted weaving, dyeing and printing, and apparel assembling.

Given the shortage of foreign exchange and the availability of cheap labor the government of Vietnam's promotion effort has concentrated in the apparel sector. The average investment required to start a new apparel enterprise is approximately $500,000 to $1 million, as compared to the cost of a new textile enterprise which is at least $10 million.

Fiber Spinning

In the late 1980s, the T&A industry had 860,000 spindles and 2,000 spinning rotors without spindles belonging to 13 SOEs. The annual output at that time was 60,000 tons with an average Nm index of 40. Most of these spindles had been used for more than ten years by that time and they were in need of renewal. By the year 1996, the industry had 800,124 spindles and 3,520 rotors. Among those spindles, 90,600 were new (about 11.32 percent of total), 55,960 were replaced by second-hand spindles from west Europe (7.0 percent of total), and 107,000 spindles were upgraded (13.4 percent of total). The production capacity increased by 72,000 tons of fibers per year. The average Nm index was 61.

Shuttle Weaving

The industry had 10,500 weaving machines by 1996. The newly imported machines accounted for 15 percent of total imports. The share of machines that could be restored was 45 percent, whereas the remainder needed to be sold off. Central SOEs owned 7,973 units, and among those units the number of weaving machines was 978 or 12.26 percent. To that date, half of the total weaving machines in the textile industry were too old and unable to run. For example, in the north, approximately 5,000 units (made in China) were dated to the 1950s, 1960s, and early 1970s. In the south, some of the old textile equipment were imported from Japan, the United States, and Korea in the period 1960-1974.

Knitted Weaving

The technologies of the knitting industry are relatively more modern than other textile technologies. Most out-of-date machines that were imported before 1986 from China, Czechoslovakia, and East Germany have been liquidated or transferred to localities, and all machines in use now were imported after 1996. The equipment was imported mostly from Japan, Korea, Taiwan, and Germany. Thirty percent of those are new generation machines, with some being controlled by computer, and the rest are older and less advanced. Because of the low quality of cotton fiber, almost all enterprises have chosen production plans using Pe/Co fiber to produce simple consumer goods, such as mosquito nets and valise fabrics, but not to produce decorated cloth, carpet, cloth for construction, and the like.

Dyeing and Printing Sector

All dyeing, printing, and finishing equipment was imported from abroad and belongs to the SOEs. Approximately 35 percent of the dyeing and printing equipment in the industry was imported since 1986 (about 400 units). All of the equipment is of the A2 and A3 generations and is still operating well. Thirty percent of dyeing and printing equipment was imported in the period 1970-1985. This equipment is in need of repair for further use. The rest was imported in the period 1959-1969. This equipment should be scrapped gradually.

Apparel Sector

At the beginning, the industry used man-powered sewing machines, which were then gradually replaced by industrial sewing machines made in China, the former Soviet Union, West Germany, Hungary, and Japan. From 1991 up to now the industry has invested in technology renovation in order to expand production and improve the quality of products to meet requirements of international markets. Almost all sewing machines are moderns with high speed of 4,000 to 5,000 circles per minute. Some enterprises, such as Garment Company No 10 and the Viet Tien Garment Company, are equipped with sewing machines with some automatic functions.

The industry has also bought numerous specialized machines. Some enterprises have invested in synchronous production lines by using many specialized machines to produce one category of apparel such as shirts or jeans. Almost all apparel enterprises use steam-ironing systems.

Since 1991, technology in the apparel sector has been renovated. Production lines have been set up with medium and small scales, consisting of 25 or 26 sewing machines with 34 to 38 laborers. Consequently, apparel enterprises are now capable of handling production shifts in response to style changes within two days. Some enterprises have used new technology and computers in some production functions such as cutting. These changes enhance the competitiveness of apparel producers, most notably their ability to respond quickly to changing demand.

Finishing stages, such as ironing, pressing, and packaging, are considered to be of great importance, as they help increase the value added to the final product. Relatively few technology innovations have been made at this production stage to ensure high quality. As compared to production capacity, actual production in the textile sector is low; production of fabrics has reached 60 percent only. The reason is that the shift from a centralized economy to a market economy prevented many enterprises from catching up. Several large-scale enterprises equipped with outdated equipment produced fabrics of narrow width, low quality, and high cost, and were unable to sell their products in the new economy. These companies either had to cut back their production or close their factories for equipment renovation.

Labor productivity of Vietnam's T&A industry as measured by value added per worker was very low in the early 1990s in comparison with other countries. Productivity was particularly low as compared to Korea, Taiwan, and Singapore, but in recent years, Vietnam's ratio of value added per worker has caught up with China. The financial crisis had a significant negative impact on Asian countries in 1998, and as a consequence, labor productivity in these countries fell dramatically, whereas Vietnam and China were less affected and productivity of the T&A industry in these countries continued to increase.

Overall, one can argue that Vietnam's T&A industry is still in the early stage of development, and therefore it mainly exploits comparative advantage based on cheap labor. The share of labor cost in total value added of Vietnam's T&A industry is lower than in other countries. The lower ratio of labor share in total value added could be explained by the low relative price of labor over capital in Vietnam, which is much lower than in some other countries. This indicates the scarcity of capital in Vietnam as compared to other countries. Within Vietnam, share of labor in total value added of the textile industry is lower than that of the apparel industry, as the textile industry is more capital intensive than the apparel industry.

THE U.S.-VIETNAM TEXTILE AGREEMENT DEBATE

In February 1994, President Clinton took a major step toward normalizing relations between the United States and Vietnam when he lifted the 19-year-old trade embargo. Diplomatic relations with Vietnam resumed the following year. In 1998 President Clinton granted Vietnam a waiver of the Jackson-Vanik amendment's[2] freedom-of-emigration requirements, a step which opened the way for the Overseas Private Investment Corporation and the Export-Import Bank of the United States to support U.S. trade and investment in Vietnam.

On July 13, 2000, the United States and Vietnam signed a sweeping bilateral trade agreement (BTA), marking a historic moment in the normalization of economic relations.[3] The BTA, which entered into force on December 10, 2001, restored reciprocal Most Favored Nation (MFN) status and commits Vietnam to undertake a broad range of market-oriented reforms.[4] Vietnam's temporary MFN status reduces U.S. tariffs on Vietnamese goods from an average of 40 percent to about 3 percent.

In return for market access at reduced tariffs, Vietnam commits to adjust and implement numerous laws and policies related to opening its domestic market. Many of these commitments are linked to compliance with other international commitments that it has acceded to, or is negotiating to accede to, such as the WTO. In a number of cases (for example, intellectual property, investment, and customs), BTA compliance requires meeting WTO standards, which will accelerate Vietnam's WTO accession process.

The BTA should boost significantly bilateral trade and investment between the two countries, contributing to each country's mutual economic benefit and toward a further normalization of relations. Furthermore, the ratification of the BTA, as an important component of a broader set of policy changes being taken by Vietnam, reinforces Vietnam's efforts to integrate with the global economy in the manner that has served its East Asian neighbors so well.[5]

Discussion regarding a potential textile agreement with Vietnam began during the debate over the BTA, which contains no restrictions on textile and apparel imports from Vietnam. Some members of Congress urged the Bush administration to negotiate a separate bilateral textile agreement that would place quotas on imports of Vietnamese textile and apparel products, due to concerns that such imports would significantly affect the U.S. textile industry. Chapter VII, Article 3, of the BTA allows for the negotiation of an agreement on trade in "textiles and textile products."

The Agreement on Textiles and Clothing (ATC), negotiated in the Uruguay Round that established the World Trade Organization (WTO), replaced the MFA in 1995. The ATC was a transitional instrument designed to integrate textile and apparel trade into WTO rules governing other products by phasing out existing quotas over a ten-year transition period. The transition period, which allowed manufacturers in industrial countries to prepare for increased competition from developing countries, ended on January 1, 2005, when all import quotas on textile and apparel products ceased.

Vietnam is currently not a WTO member and, therefore, not a party to the ATC. This puts Vietnam at a significant disadvantage in the international textile and apparel trade in two ways. First, Vietnam does not benefit from the current phase out of existing import quotas. Second, since Vietnam is still not a WTO member as of 2005, its trade in textiles and apparel will be limited by whatever existing quotas it faces. WTO members, on the other hand, will then operate under quota-free trade in textiles and apparel.

In 2000, the U.S. textile and apparel industry employed 1.2 million people, 6.5 percent of total employment in manufacturing. This marked a 35 percent and 50 percent decline in employment in the textile and apparel industries, respectively, since 1980. This decrease in employment can largely be attributed to both productivity gains and increased importation of textile and apparel products. Over the same twenty-year period, U.S. production of textiles rose, while apparel production fell slightly.

The United States is currently the world's largest import market for textile and apparel products. In 2001, the United States imported more than $70 billion in apparel and textiles, of which $56 billion was apparel. During the same period, the United States exported more than $16.5 billion worth of apparel and textiles worldwide, with $6.5 billion in apparel and $10 billion in textiles. Vietnam's textile and apparel exports have risen substantially in recent years, surpassing $2 billion in 2001. Vietnam's largest markets for textile and apparel exports are Japan and the European Union, with exports of $617 million and $512 million, respectively, in 2001. Approximately half of Vietnam's 2001 exports went to the EU, Canada, Norway, and Turkey, countries with which Vietnam has completed bilateral textile and garment agreements. The other half of its exports went to its non-quota markets of Japan, Asia, and the United States.

The Vietnamese government and the textile industry have taken several measures to expand both production and U.S. sales. The government is granting an export subsidy of 7 percent to textile companies that export to the United States. VINATEX opened a representative office in New York, sent several producers to the World Source Exhibition, and is building four specialized industrial parks in Vietnam. In addition, the government plans to invest $100 million in the domestic cotton industry, with the goal of expanding production to meet 60 percent of local demand by 2010. Currently, Vietnam's domestic producers can only supply 10 percent of the cotton and 20 percent of the fabrics used in garment production (discussions with the management of VINATEX and officials of the Ministry of Foreign Trade, summer 2002). The present level of Vietnamese cotton production may benefit the United States, since raw cotton is one of its leading export items to Vietnam.

Prior to the BTA, Vietnam's textile and apparel exports to the U.S. market were negligible. In 2001, Vietnam ranked sixty-fourth among countries exporting textile and apparel products to the United States, with an estimated $50 million in products. Overall, the United States imported more than $70 billion in textiles and apparel last year, making Vietnam a small player in the U.S. market.

With lower MFN tariff rates under the BTA, Vietnamese exports of garment products to the United States are expected to increase rapidly. However, given the short amount of time that has passed since the BTA came into effect, it is not clear how significant or sustained the increase will be.

Some observers expect a dramatic surge in Vietnamese textile and apparel exports. The Vietnamese textile and garment industry would like to expand sales to the United States. The post-MFN experience of Cambodia and the People's Republic of China in the 1980s supports the view that one should expect a major surge in Vietnamese exports to the U.S. market. In 1996, prior to receiving MFN status, the United States imported $2.4 million in textiles and apparel from Cambodia. That amount rose to $98 million in 1997, $360 million in 1998, and was more than $950 million in 2000. (Import data taken from the Office of Textiles and Apparel, U.S. Department of Commerce.) Others assert that many Vietnamese textile companies are not ready to compete in the U.S. market, and, therefore, exports in the first year after the BTA will be lower than most expectations. As can be seen from our earlier discussion potential export expansion will be limited by factory and industry constraints, such as outdated technology, low output capacity, lack of capital for investment, and limited domestic fabrics and other inputs. Based on discussions with Vietnamese textile companies it is a safe bet that it will take time for many to understand the preferences of the U.S. market and to meet U.S. quality and social accountability standards. Also, some Vietnamese companies may be cautious in shifting production to target the U.S. market for fear of hurting current sales to their larger markets, such as Japan and the EU.

Initial data for 2002 show a substantial increase in textile and apparel imports from Vietnam, compared to the same period from last year. In the first quarter of 2002, the United States imported approximately $38 million in Vietnamese textile and apparel products, an almost 300 percent increase from last year's first quarter amount of $14 million. Several products in particular posted dramatic increases, such as men's and boys' man-made fiber coats and jackets, of which imports rose from $1,400 in the first quarter of 2001 to $1.3 million in the first quarter of 2002. U.S. imports of women's cotton blouses and shirts also increased significantly, from $13,000 to more than $2 million. Although this represents impressive growth, Vietnam still lags far behind China, whose textile and apparel exports to the United States in the first quarter of 2002 surpassed $1.5 billion. (Import data taken from the Office of Textiles and Apparel, U.S. Department of Commerce.)

The U.S. textile industry has called for a U.S.-Vietnam textile agreement to protect domestic producers against a potential surge of Vietnamese exports. It is their expectation that Vietnam, with its low labor costs, MFN status, and unrestrained access to the U.S. market, would be a threat to the domestic industry (*Inside U.S. Trade,* 2002). The U.S. textile industry's association, the American Textile Manufacturers Institute, along with representatives from four textile-producing states have all urged President Bush to "recognize that the U.S. textile industry, like the steel industry, is facing a crisis of survival that is not of its own making" (ATMI, 2002; IMRA, 2001).

Since Vietnam is not a WTO member, and it has just begun discussions with the United States regarding a possible textile agreement, it may be very vulnerable to U.S. pressure (Wiseman and Cox, 2002). The fact that Pakistan, arguably one of the United States' most critical allies in the war on terrorism, received significantly less support than its initial proposal does not bode well for Vietnam, since it may indicate the degree to which U.S. policymakers are willing to support the domestic textile industry in the face of international competition.

Furthermore, the United States may seek to conclude a textile agreement with Vietnam in the interest of equity, since it has textile arrangements in place with all other members of the Association of Southeast Asian Nations, except for Burma and Brunei.[6]

Labor rights proponents have also pressed for a textile agreement with Vietnam as a mechanism to promote improvements in Vietnam's labor conditions, possibly similar to the provisions under the 1999 U.S. textile agreement with Cambodia. At this point, it is unclear what type of labor provision, if any, would be acceptable to both countries ("USTR officials visit Vietnam," 2002).

From the existing data on Vietnam's textile industry it is questionable whether Vietnam can truly be considered a threat. Moreover, in order for Vietnam's production to be a true threat to U.S. domestic producers, it has to be shown that Vietnam's increased market share would come out of the market share of U.S. producers. The more likely scenario would be that increased imports from Vietnam would displace other developing-country producers.

Quota levels are typically based on historical performance. In the case of Cambodia, there was a period of over two years between the United States granting of MFN status and the signing of a bilateral textile agreement. The latter occurred after textile and apparel imports from Cambodia surpassed $350 million. In the case of Vietnam a move toward a bilateral agreement would be clearly premature. If an attempt were made to engineer such an agreement at this time, quota levels may be set too low or may be applied to the wrong categories.

The imposition of quotas would be inconsistent with the spirit and intent of the BTA. Potential investors eyeing a post-BTA Vietnam may choose not to risk being stranded in an industry that cannot compete well in the world market after 2005. Increased foreign investment in the Vietnam textile and apparel sector, on the other hand, may increase economic opportunities for U.S. textile machinery, construction, telecommunications, and financial companies, which could gain from that sector's expansion. U.S. producers of raw cotton, one of the United States' leading export items to Vietnam, may also benefit from expansion of the garment sector.

In August 2001, four U.S. trade associations—representing apparel retailers, importers, and manufacturers—sent a letter to President Bush urging him to reject additional protection for the textile and garment industry. Asserting that the industry was already highly protected, with more than "1,000 quotas" and relatively high duty rates on imports, they dismissed any comparisons with the U.S. steel industry (IMRA, 2001). In March 2001, the same trade associations urged U.S. Trade Representative Robert Zoellick to hold off on textile negotiations with Vietnam.

CONCLUDING REMARKS

With the impending removal of the quantitative regulations of international trade in textiles and apparel, one would expect that importing countries would no longer rely on quotas to regulate exports of these products. The transition of Vietnam to a market economy has been supported by the United States in large part by its bilateral agreement, which reduced U.S. tariffs to their MFN levels in exchange for legal and institutional reforms in Vietnam. Despite these positive measures, the prospect of a textile and apparel agreement still looms.

The existing Vietnamese textile and apparel industry is far from being a threat to U.S. domestic producers. What is clear, however, is that continued discussion of a bilateral agreement does nothing more than add unwarranted uncertainty to investor confidence in Vietnam. The latter is inconsistent with the aim and spirit of the U.S.-Vietnam BTA.

NOTES

1. The year 2000 witnessed a new trend in the development of the private sector in Vietnam including both formal and informal firms. The number of new establishments at the end of 1999 was about 30 percent of total existing private firms. This improvement is largely explained by the introduction and implementation of the Enterprise Law and the progress of administration reform.

2. The Jackson-Vanik amendment, which is contained in the Trade Act of 1974, Title IV, § 402, prohibits the president from normalizing trade relations with selected non-market economy (NME) countries if they do not meet certain requirements regarding freedom of emigration. A presidential waiver of the Jackson-Vanik requirements—or, alternatively, a presidential determination that the NME country complies with the freedom-of-emigration requirements—gives that country access to certain specific economic benefits, such as access to U.S. government financial facilities (export credits, export credit guarantees, and investment guarantees) and the ability to conclude a bilateral trade agreement with the United States.

3. The text of the agreement, along with background documents, a separate annex on services, and two separate letters on investment, can be found on the Web site of the United States Trade Representative at http://www.ustr.gov/regions/asia-pacific/regional.shtml.

4. Although presidential waivers of the Jackson-Vanik requirements had been issued for Vietnam since 1999, Vietnam did not receive MFN status until the bilateral trade agreement came into effect in December 2001. Under the Jackson-Vanik amendment, two conditions must be met for NME countries to have their most-favored-nation status restored. First, the president must either (1) issue a determination that the country complies with the freedom-of-emigration requirements of the Jackson-Vanik amendment or (2) waive those requirements. Second, the country must conclude a bilateral trade agreement with the United States that includes a reciprocal MFN clause.

5. The BTA includes requirements related to dispute settlement in six of its seven chapters, with all of these obligations due upon entry into force of the agreement. Strengthening of laws, regulations, and administrative procedures are called for in: Chapter I for commercial disputes (arbitration); Chapter II for enforcement of civil actions for intellectual property rights; Chapter III for administrative rulings affecting trade in services; Chapter IV for investment disputes; Chapter VI for judicial review of administrative rulings (the right to appeal); and Chapter VII for government-to-government disputes.

6. The ASEAN countries with which the United States has concluded textile arrangements are Cambodia, Indonesia, Laos, Malaysia, the Philippines, Singapore, and Thailand. These arrangements include bilateral textile agreements, visa arrangements concerning textiles and textile articles/products, and administrative arrangements regarding textiles. Although the United States currently has no formal textile agreement with Burma, it has placed import quotas on selected Burmese textile and apparel products.

REFERENCES

American Textile Manufacturers Institute (2002). ATMI urges Congress, administration to adopt more equitable trade policies. Press release, February 7. Available at www.atmi.org/Newsroom/releases/PR200204.asp.

International Mass Retail Association (2001). President Bush urged to reject additional textile protection. Press release, August 2. Available at www.irma.org/public/pages.index.cfm?pageid=280.

"USTR officials visit Vietnam to begin talks on textile accord." *Inside U.S. Trade,* February 22.

Wiseman, P. and Cox, J. (2002). "Competing interests tangle textile policy." *USA Today,* April 2. Available at http://www.usatoday.com/money/covers/2002-04-02-pakistani-textile.htm.

Chapter 15

Competition for Market Share: A Markov Analysis of U.S. Apparel Imports

Kathleen Rees

INTRODUCTION

Export production of apparel destined for key international markets, such as the U.S. market, has been an important strategy used by a number of developed and developing countries as they have attempted to establish and maintain a presence within the global economy. The United States possesses the world's largest single-country market for apparel. In 2001, U.S. consumers spent over $315 billion on apparel and footwear (American Textiles Manufacturers Institute, 2003). As shown in Table 15.1, the U.S. share of world apparel imports has increased significantly during the past two decades, despite efforts to constrain imports through imposition of relatively high tariff rates and quota constraints. In 2000, almost one-third of world exports were destined for the United States (World Trade Organization, 2002).

To protect the interests of domestic producers and to avoid disruption of developed countries' markets from textile and apparel imports originating in developing countries possessing significantly lower wages and other competitive advantages, a bilateral quota system was created under the auspices of the Multifiber Arrangement (MFA) and implemented in 1974. As indicated in Figure 15.1, despite attempts to constrain the volume of garments entering from developing country suppliers, U.S. imports of apparel have continually increased. Fol-

Globalization and East Asia: Opportunities and Challenges

doi:10.1300/5463_15

TABLE 15.1. Leading Import Markets for Apparel, 1980-2000

Importing Countries	$ Billions of Apparel Imports 2000	Share of World Imports 1980	1990	2000
United States	$66.39	16.4%	24.1%	31.6%
Japan	$19.17	3.6%	7.8%	9.4%
Germany	$19.31	19.7%	18.2%	9.2%
United Kingdom	$12.99	6.8%	6.2%	6.2%
France	$11.48	6.2%	7.5%	5.5%
Italy	$6.07	1.9%	2.3%	2.9%

Source: Adapted from World Trade Organization, 2001.

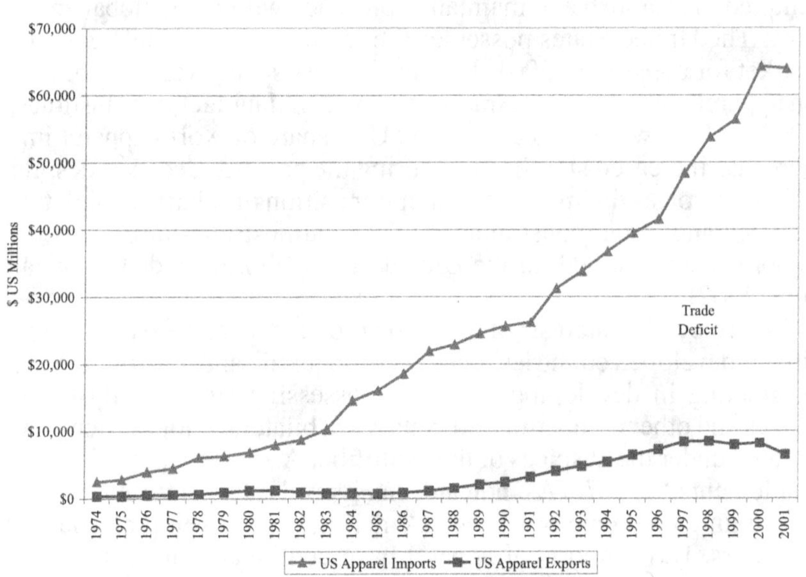

FIGURE 15.1. U.S. Trade in Apparel, 1974-2001 (*Source:* Adapted from American Textile Manufacturers Institute, 1993; 2002.)

lowing enactment of the Multifiber Arrangement, aggregate U.S. apparel imports have increased, on average, more than 12 percent annually (American Textile Manufacturers Institute, 1993, 2002). At the time the MFA quota system was originally implemented, the United States possessed just under a $2.12 billion trade deficit for apparel, with imports of approximately $2.52 billion and exports of approximately $400 million (American Textile Manufacturers Institute, 1993). By 2002, U.S. imports of apparel had risen to almost $59.67 billion, exports had increased to $5.64 billion, and the domestic trade deficit for apparel had reached an all-time high of nearly $54.03 billion (Office of Textiles and Apparel, 2003).

As levels of apparel imports have steadily increased, import penetration of the domestic market has been accompanied by concern regarding displacement of domestic production. According to estimates published by the American Textile Manufacturers Institute (1994, 1995), import penetration of the U.S. apparel market increased from 25.1 percent in 1974 to 66.8 percent in 1994. Subsequently, it has been proposed that as much as 90 percent of ready-to-wear garments currently available within the domestic market are imported (Ellis, 2002). Examination of apparel imports by select categories, however, suggests import penetration in the range of slightly less than 55 percent to more than 90 percent. As shown in Table 15.2, import penetration has been highest for categories requiring basic construction, such as cotton sleepwear and men's and boys' woven cotton shirts. Categories in which domestic manufacturers have maintained higher portions of domestic market share include women's and girls' manufactured fiber dresses and men's and boys' cotton knit shirts.

With the U.S. market remaining one of the most lucrative markets for foreign suppliers of apparel, access to this market has been actively sought by a number of developing and developed countries attempting to establish or maintain a global presence in textile and apparel trade. Historically, dominant suppliers of U.S. apparel imports have been located in Asia. As illustrated in Figure 15.2, significant competition has existed between world regions desiring shares of the U.S. market. Countries within East Asia (China, Hong Kong, Korea, and Taiwan) have been among the primary exporters of apparel to the United States, with China or Hong Kong traditionally providing the largest share. Until the 1990s, the "Asian tigers" supplied more than 50 percent of U.S. apparel imports. Following imple-

TABLE 15.2. U.S. Domestic Market Share for Select Apparel Categories, 1992-2001

Categories	1992	1995	1998	2001
Men's & Boys'				
338: Cotton shirts (knit)	74.52%	63.21%	46.84%	37.62%
340: Cotton shirts (not knit)	25.52%	16.61%	13.71%	10.46%
347: Cotton trousers, breeches, & shorts	58.83%	53.01%	42.13%	33.46%
443: Wool suits	58.18%	41.04%	32.59%	33.68%
634: Other MMF coats	44.52%	42.61%	27.54%	12.33%
647: MMF trousers, breeches, & shorts	66.42%	57.53%	35.93%	21.21%
Women's & Girls'				
339: Cotton shirts & blouses (knit)	33.00%	35.00%	27.83%	17.94%
341: Cotton shirts & blouses (not knit)	29.63%	31.58%	27.53%	25.62%
348: Cotton trousers, slacks, & shorts	43.32%	47.50%	37.59%	26.19%
636: MMF dresses	75.61%	67.36%	57.83%	45.84%
641: MMF shirts & blouses (not knit)	51.26%	54.08%	40.37%	32.44%
644: MMF suits	73.38%	54.86%	39.60%	21.72%
Aggregate				
345: Cotton sweaters	61.08%	63.30%	28.26%	14.99%
351: Cotton nightwear & pajamas	35.34%	19.93%	13.37%	8.79%
352: Cotton underwear	75.46%	55.52%	37.60%	28.86%
645/646 MMF sweaters	37.59%	36.37%	29.14%	29.65%
651: MMF nightwear & pajamas	68.47%	62.73%	42.96%	28.28%
652: MMF underwear	60.89%	50.90%	35.53%	29.65%

Source: Office of Textiles and Apparel, 1997; 2002b.

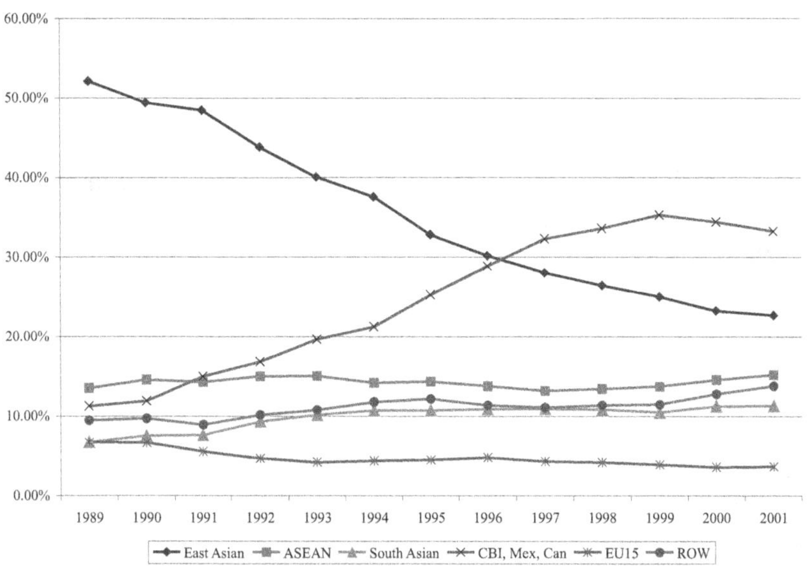

FIGURE 15.2. U.S. Apparel Market Share by World Region, 1989-2001 (*Source:* Office of Textiles and Apparel, 2002a.)

mentation of the North American Free Trade Agreement in 1994, however, Mexico emerged and overtook China as the largest foreign supplier of garments to the U.S. market. With preferential access granted apparel assembled within Caribbean Basin Initiative (CBI) countries through the 807 and 9802 programs, as well as further liberalization of trade in textiles and apparel provided under the Trade Act of 2000, the largest share of imported garments entering the U.S. market since 1997 has originated within the region comprised of the Caribbean Basin, Canada, and Mexico. During the past five years, this region has produced approximately one-third of U.S. apparel imports, while countries within East Asia have supplied about 25 percent. Collectively, countries comprising the Association of Southeast Asian Nations (ASEAN) have provided nearly 15 percent of U.S. ready-to-wear garment imports, while countries within South Asia have supplied just over 10 percent. In contrast, countries within the European Union (EU), being more highly developed and possessing far less competitive wage rates than developing countries engaged in export production, have supplied less than 5 percent of all apparel imports entering the U.S. market (Office of Textiles and Apparel, 2002a).

The present study was designed to examine movements in U.S. market shares among primary world regions supplying apparel to the U.S. market. It builds on seminal analysis of market penetration and shift in market shares by Dardis and Sul (1983) and subsequent research by Xiao and Rees (1999). Dardis and Sul's work was undertaken using import data prior to implementation of the MFA. Xiao and Rees' analysis included the post-MFA period, but only up to the mid-1990s. No study to date, therefore, has examined changes in market share following implementation of the North American Free Trade Agreement (NAFTA), enactment of the Trade Act of 2000, and the phase-out of the MFA instituted with establishment of the World Trade Organization in 1995. While it has been observed that changes in trade policy have resulted in movement of U.S. imports away from the "Big Four" Asian producers and toward the Caribbean Basin, Canada, and Mexico, potential exists—especially with full implementation of the phase-out of MFA quotas—for export production to shift, again, toward traditional Asian suppliers such as China. Little empirical analysis has been undertaken to examine contemporary change in market shares held by foreign suppliers of apparel to the U.S. market following implementation of the MFA quota phase-out, and the present study helps fill this void.

METHODOLOGY

A Markov probability model was used to examine change in market shares held by six world regions for eighteen categories of U.S. apparel imports. As indicated in Table 15.3, the six world regions included: East Asian countries; Southeast Asian countries; South Asian countries; European Union countries; Caribbean Basin countries, Canada, and Mexico; and rest of the world (ROW). Aggregation of countries into these regions was based on level of economic development and geographic considerations, as well as geopolitical linkages established within regions.

The 18 categories of apparel imports were based on major shippers categories and included six categories of men's and boys' apparel, six categories of women's and girls' apparel, and six aggregated categories. The men's and boys' categories included: (338)

TABLE 15.3. Major Apparel Import Supply Regions

Regions	Countries Within Each Region
East Asian	Hong Kong, China, Korea (South), Taiwan
Southeast Asian (ASEAN)	Brunei, Indonesia, Lao's, Malaysia, Burma, Philippines, Singapore, Thailand, Vietnam
South Asian	Bangladesh, Bhutan, India, Nepal, Pakistan, Sri Lanka
CBI, Canada, and Mexico	Anguilla, Antigua, Aruba, Bahamas, Barbados, Belize, British Virgin Islands, Costa Rica, Dominica, Dominican Republic, El Salvador, Grenada, Guatemala, Guyana, Haiti, Honduras, Jamaica, Montserrat, Netherlands Antilles, Nicaragua, Panama, Saint Kitts and Nevis, Saint Lucia, Saint Vincent and the Grenadines, Trinidad and Tobago, Canada, Mexico
European Union (EU15)	Austria, Belgium, Denmark, Finland, France, Germany, Greece, Ireland, Italy, Luxembourg, Netherlands, Portugal, Spain, Sweden, United Kingdom
Rest of world	All other countries

cotton (knit) shirts; (340) cotton (not knit) shirts; (347) cotton trousers, breeches, and shorts; (443) wool suits; (634) other manufactured fiber coats; and (647) manufactured fiber trousers, breeches, and shorts. The women's and girls' categories included: (339) cotton (knit) shirts and blouses; (341) cotton (not knit) shirts and blouses; (348) cotton trousers, slacks, and shorts; (636) manufactured fiber dresses; (641) manufactured fiber (not knit) shirts and blouses; and (644) manufactured fiber suits. The aggregate apparel categories included: (345) cotton sweaters; (351) cotton nightwear and pajamas; (352) cotton underwear; (645/646) manufactured fiber sweaters; (651) manufactured fiber nightwear and pajamas; and (652) manufactured fiber underwear.

Data used in the estimation process were percent market shares based on annual customs value ($US) of imports from each world region for each apparel category. Data were obtained from the Office of Textiles and Apparel (2002a) and included the time period 1989 through 2001. As suggested by Dardis and Sul (1983), market shares based on dollar value of imports, rather than volume of imports, were used to overcome potential problems with structural distortions presented by quota constraints imposed on apparel imports in specific categories entering the U.S. market from many developing countries. Although quotas have constrained changes in the volume of apparel imports, many countries have increased the quality and/or value of apparel produced for export, in order to maximize both quota utilization and market share (Dardis and Sul, 1983; Dickerson, 1999).

Markov Process

The Markov process has been used in a variety of research studies designed to examine changes in both market structure (Adelman, 1958; Collins and Preston, 1961; Hart and Prais, 1956; Judge and Swanson, 1962; Padberg, 1962) and market shares (Azzam et al., 1993; Dardis and Sul, 1983; Dent, 1967; Jarrett and Dent, 1966; Tesler, 1962; Xiao and Rees, 1999). In the present study, Markov analysis was employed to determine the probability of U.S. consumers, in aggregate, purchasing imported apparel of a given category originating from a given world region or shifting to another region of origin over time.

Alternative methods have been proposed to estimate transition probabilities from aggregated time series data. Least squares techniques (Tesler, 1963), probability-constrained quadratic programming, the sum of median absolute deviations (Kim and Schaible, 1988), and probability-constrained linear programming minimizing the sum of absolute deviations (Lee et al., 1970) can be used. In the present study, the parameters were estimated from percent market share time series data as described in Lee et al. (1970).

The transition matrix describing the probability of transitions from one world region to another is:

$$P = \begin{bmatrix} p_{11} & p_{12} & p_{13} & \cdots & p_{1j} \\ p_{21} & p_{22} & p_{23} & \cdots & p_{2j} \\ \vdots & & & & \\ p_{j1} & p_{j2} & p_{j3} & \cdots & p_{jj} \end{bmatrix} \tag{15.1}$$

and the p_{ik} are the transition probabilities such that $\sum_{k=1}^{j} p_{ik} = 1$. Percentages on the principle diagonals of the matrices indicate the portion of market shares retained by the regions. Gains in market shares are indicated within the vertical elements, whereas losses in market shares are given within the horizontal elements of the matrices.

FINDINGS

Examination of the transition probability matrices indicates that, across apparel categories, significant competition for U.S. market share existed between and among foreign supply regions. All regions were found to have experienced gains in some categories, while they incurred loss of market shares in other categories. During the time period covered by the study, the East Asian region was found to be most successful in maintaining market share across all categories. With exceptions in only several categories, this region retained between 80 and 95 percent of its market share each year. In contrast, the region comprised of the European Union countries and the South Asian region tended to experience the greatest difficulty maintaining market shares in many categories.

Men's and Boys' Apparel Categories

Transition probability matrices for the men's and boys' apparel categories are presented in Table 15.4. The East Asian region tended to gain significant levels of market share from the EU. This was especially notable in both the woven and knit cotton shirt categories, for which the East Asian region gained 56.37 and 43.13 percent net market share respectively from the EU, and the manufactured trousers category in which the East Asian region experienced a net gain of approximately 60 percent share from the EU. The East Asian region also gained very small portions of market share, on net, from the ASEAN region in the cotton (not knit) shirts category, as well as the cotton and manufactured fiber trousers categories.

The East Asian region also experienced competition for import share. This region lost nearly 17 percent market share in the cotton knit shirts category and approximately 3 percent in both the other manufactured fiber coats and wool suits categories to the ASEAN region. A sizable portion of market share was also relinquished to the ROW in the wool suits category. The East Asian region incurred addi-

TABLE 15.4. Transition Probability Matrices: Men's and Boys' Apparel Categories

Categories		East Asian	ASEAN	South Asian	CBI, Can, Mex	EU	ROW
Category 338 Cotton shirts (knit)	East Asian	.8154	.1668	.0000	.0000	.0178	.0000
	ASEAN	.0000	.6124	.1126	.0000	.0000	.2750
	South Asian	.0000	.0000	.6689	.3311	.0000	.0000
	CBI, Can, Mex	.0000	.0000	.0081	.8867	.0028	.1025
	EU	.4491	.0912	.0000	.0000	.4597	.0000
	ROW	.0000	.2664	.2763	.0000	.0275	.4298
Category 340 Cotton shirts (not knit)	East Asian	.7801	.1064	.0422	.0713	.0000	.0000
	ASEAN	.1730	.6653	.0000	.0000	.0000	.1617
	South Asian	.0000	.1852	.7548	.0000	.0600	.0000
	CBI, Can, Mex	.0000	.0000	.1948	.7444	.0225	.0383
	EU	.5637	.0000	.0000	.0000	.4363	.0000
	ROW	.0000	.0000	.0684	.2798	.0121	.6397
Category 347 Cotton trousers, breeches, & shorts	East Asian	.8534	.0509	.0000	.0854	.0103	.0000
	ASEAN	.0750	.5769	.1465	.0000	.0340	.1677
	South Asian	.0000	.0000	.1873	.3511	.0000	.4616
	CBI, Can, Mex	.0000	.0427	.0805	.8426	.0070	.0272
	EU	.0000	.9291	.0000	.0000	.0709	.0000
	ROW	.0000	.0000	.0183	.4863	.0000	.4954
Category 443 Wool suits	East Asian	.8320	.0328	.0000	.0000	.0000	.1352
	ASEAN	.0000	.4637	.0000	.0000	.0000	.5363
	South Asian	.0000	.0000	1.0000	.0000	.0000	.0000
	CBI, Can, Mex	.0000	.0113	.0008	.8901	.0000	.0980
	EU	.0141	.0000	.0000	.1448	.8155	.0256
	ROW	.0000	.0000	.0000	.0131	.4279	.5590
Category 634 Other MMF Coats	East Asian	.9557	.0295	.0000	.0000	.0002	.0146
	ASEAN	.0000	.5854	.1978	.0000	.0000	.2167
	South Asian	.0000	.0000	.6140	.1345	.0000	.2515
	CBI, Can, Mex	.0000	.0000	.1665	.8335	.0000	.0000
	EU	.0000	.5636	.0000	.0000	.4364	.0000
	ROW	.0136	.8438	.0000	.0019	.0777	.0630

Categories		East Asian	ASEAN	South Asian	CBI, Can, Mex	EU	ROW
Category 647 MMF trousers, breeches, & shorts	East Asian	.8555	.0554	.0859	.0000	.0033	.0000
	ASEAN	.0925	.6926	.0484	.1444	.0221	.0000
	South Asian	.0000	.0000	.0000	1.0000	.0000	.0000
	CBI, Can, Mex	.0000	.1121	.1246	.7379	.0000	.0255
	EU	.6042	.0000	.0000	.0000	.3958	.0000
	ROW	.0000	.0000	.1540	.0000	.0000	.8460

tional loss of market shares to the CBI, Canada, and Mexico in the cotton shirts (not knit) and cotton trousers categories.

The region comprised of the Caribbean Basin countries, Canada, and Mexico was successful in maintaining market share across the men's and boys' apparel categories. Over the time period covered by the analysis, this region retained approximately 75 to 90 percent market share within these categories. The region gained market share from South Asian suppliers in the cotton knit shirts category, as well as both the cotton and manufactured fiber trousers categories. The CBI, Canada, and Mexico also experienced net gains in market share from the ROW and East Asian regions in the cotton shirts (not knit) and cotton trousers categories. A gain of almost 15 percent market share in the wool suits category occurred at the expense of the EU region. Net losses of market share to the ROW region were incurred in the cotton knit shirts, wool suits, and manufactured fiber trousers categories. In addition, this region experienced a loss of nearly 20 percent in cotton (not knit) shirts to South Asian suppliers.

The ASEAN region tended to maintain approximately 45 to 70 percent market share in each of the men's and boys' categories. Net gains in market share were most notable in the cotton knit shirts, cotton trousers, and other manufactured fiber coats categories and tended to occur at the expense of the EU region. The ASEAN region also gained market share from East Asia in the cotton knit shirts, wool suits, and other manufactured fiber coats categories. In the cotton shirts (not knit) category, a significant portion of market share (18.52 percent) was gained from South Asian suppliers; however, losses of market share in this category were incurred, with shares shifting to the East Asian and ROW regions. The ASEAN countries also lost between 10 and 20 percent market share to the South Asian region in the cotton knit shirts, cotton trousers, and other manufactured fiber coats categories. Additional loss of shares to the ROW occurred in the cotton trousers category. A heavy loss of market share, over 50 percent, was experienced in the wool suits category, with the EU receiving this portion of market share.

The South Asian region tended to lose market share in most categories and was able to retain more than 50 percent market share in only three men's and boys' categories: cotton (knit) shirts, cotton (not knit) shirts, and other manufactured fiber coats. In these categories, South Asian suppliers experienced gains in market shares from the ASEAN, ROW, and CBI, Canada, and Mexico regions. The most significant losses of market share for the South Asian region occurred in the cotton and manufactured fiber trousers categories. Net loss in excess of 30 percent market share occurred to the CBI, Canada, and Mexico region in the cotton knit shirts, cotton trousers, and manufactured fiber trousers categories. Significant loss of shares to the ROW also occurred in the cotton trousers and other manufactured fiber coats categories. Analysis of the wool suits category revealed 100 percent retention of market share for the South Asian region. This is referred to as an absorbing matrix, and suggests that this region will totally consume market share from the other regions over a period of time. In this case, however, it is likely the result of the South Asian region maintaining a constant market share in this category over the time period included in the data set.

The EU region was most successful in maintaining market share in the wool suits category, for which it retained more than 80 percent of its market share. Net gain in share for this category occurred at the expense of imports from the ROW, while loss of market share primarily was experienced to the CBI, Canada, and Mexico region. In each of the other categories of men's and boys' apparel, the EU was able to maintain less than 50 percent market share. This region gained little market share from other regions and experienced heavy loss of market share to the East Asian region in both cotton shirts categories, relinquishing more than 40 to 50 percent share in these categories. In the manufactured fiber trousers category, the EU lost in excess of 60 percent share to the East Asian region. Market shares also were lost to the ASEAN region, with most notable net losses occurring in the cotton trousers category (more than 90 percent) and the other manufactured fiber coats category (more than 50 percent).

Women's and Girls' Apparel Categories

Transition probability matrices for the women's and girls' apparel categories are presented in Table 15.5. Within the six categories of women's and girls' apparel categories, the East Asian region, again, was dominant in retaining market share and gained market share from all other world regions in one category or another. East Asian suppliers experienced a net gain of market share from the EU in most categories. In the manufactured fiber dress category, for example, the East Asian region retained more than 89 percent market share and gained almost 78 percent of the EU's market share. East Asian countries gained additional market share at the expense of the South Asian region in the cotton knit shirts and blouses category, as well as the manufactured fiber (not knit) shirts and blouses category. This region further benefited from a net gain of market share from both the CBI, Canada, and Mexico and ASEAN regions in the cotton shirts and blouses (not knit) category, gaining approximately 15 percent and 10 percent, respectively, from these regions. Although highly successful in retaining market share in most categories of women's and girls' apparel, the East Asian region also experienced loss of market shares to each of the other world regions. Sizable losses occurred to the ROW in the cotton knit shirts and blouses category and to South Asian suppliers in the cotton (not knit) shirts and blouses category.

The CBI, Canada, and Mexico displayed significant ability to maintain market share for some categories of women's and girls' apparel, such as cotton knit shirts and blouses, manufactured fiber (not knit) shirts and blouses, and cotton slacks and trousers, while simultaneously lacking ability to retain market share in other categories, such as cotton (not knit) shirts and blouses. This region was able to maintain more than 92 percent of its market share in the cotton knit shirts and blouses category, receiving net gains of market share from the ASEAN and ROW regions. CBI, Canada, and Mexico also retained more than 90 percent market share in the manufactured fiber (not knit) shirts and blouses category, with net gains in excess of 30 percent market share from the EU and an additional gain of almost 10 percent from South Asia. A significant increase in market share also

TABLE 15.5. Transition Probability Matrices: Women's and Girls' Apparel Categories

Categories		East Asian	ASEAN	South Asian	CBI, Can, Mex	EU	ROW
Category 339 Cotton shirts & blouses (knit)	East Asian	.8390	.0000	.0158	.0000	.0150	.1302
	ASEAN	.0000	.7654	.0000	.1388	.0532	.0427
	South Asian	.1458	.0560	.1933	.0000	.0305	.5744
	CBI, Can, Mex	.0000	.0762	.0000	.9238	.0000	.0000
	EU	.1991	.1416	.0000	.0000	.5841	.0752
	ROW	.0000	.0000	.1776	.1020	.0000	.7204
Category 341 Cotton shirts & blouses (not knit)	East Asian	.6964	.0000	.2304	.0000	.0000	.0731
	ASEAN	.0000	.5691	.1159	.2812	.0338	.0000
	South Asian	.0000	.1075	.7957	.0012	.0000	.0955
	CBI, Can, Mex	.4273	.4522	.0000	.0000	.1205	.0000
	EU	.5191	.0000	.0000	.3826	.0983	.0000
	ROW	.7271	.0000	.0000	.0597	.0804	.1328
Category 348 Cotton trousers, slacks, & shorts	East Asian	.8224	.0879	.0726	.0053	.0117	.0000
	ASEAN	.0000	.1883	.0000	.0000	.0000	.8117
	South Asian	.0000	.0000	.0000	1.0000	.0000	.0000
	CBI, Can, Mex	.0000	.0771	.0324	.8905	.0000	.0000
	EU	.5383	.0000	.0000	.0000	.4617	.0000
	ROW	.0847	.1317	.1347	.0000	.0335	.6156
Category 636 MMF dresses	East Asian	.8907	.0871	.0222	.0000	.0000	.0000
	ASEAN	.0000	.6988	.1672	.0000	.1340	.0000
	South Asian	.0000	.0000	.6730	.1869	.0000	.1401
	CBI, Can, Mex	.0210	.0675	.0009	.8012	.0000	.1094
	EU	.7798	.0000	.0000	.0000	.2202	.0000
	ROW	.0000	.2608	.0000	.4228	.0000	.3164

Categories		East Asian	ASEAN	South Asian	CBI, Can, Mex	EU	ROW
Category 641 MMF shirts & blouses (not knit)	East Asian	.7424	.0000	.1853	.0000	.0179	.0544
	ASEAN	.0000	.6274	.3391	.0000	.0000	.0335
	South Asian	.4915	.2195	.1845	.1046	.0000	.0000
	CBI, Can, Mex	.0000	.0518	.0075	.9022	.0385	.0000
	EU	.0000	.0000	.0000	.3454	.4135	.2411
	ROW	.0000	.7542	.0235	.0000	.0000	.2223
Category 644 MMF suits	East Asian	.8658	.0675	.0169	.0000	.0000	.0498
	ASEAN	.1521	.8479	.0000	.0000	.0000	.0000
	South Asian	.0000	.3311	.5722	.0000	.0000	.0968
	CBI, Can, Mex	.1474	.0000	.0000	.5800	.1668	.1058
	EU	.3733	.0000	.0000	.0714	.5552	.0000
	ROW	.0000	.0000	.0000	.5282	.1911	.2808

was obtained from the South Asian region for the cotton slacks and trousers category, and gains occurred at the expense of the ROW in both the manufactured fiber suits and manufactured fiber dresses categories. This region experienced net losses of market share to East Asian and ASEAN suppliers in the cotton shirts and blouses (not knit) category, as well as the manufactured fiber dresses category. Additional net losses of market share were incurred to East Asia and the EU in the manufactured fiber suits category.

Among the women's and girls' categories, the ASEAN region was most able to retain market share in the manufactured fiber suits, manufactured fiber dresses, and cotton knit shirts and blouses categories, maintaining approximately 70 to 85 percent market shares in these categories. ASEAN suppliers experienced a gain of more than 30 percent share from the South Asian region in the manufactured fiber suits category, while gaining 26 percent share in manufactured fiber dresses from the ROW. The ASEAN region also experienced a net gain of market share from the CBI, Canada, and Mexico region in the cotton (not knit) shirts and blouses, cotton trousers and slacks, and manufactured fiber dresses categories. The most significant loss of market share for the ASEAN countries occurred in the cotton trousers and slacks category, in which they experienced a net loss of almost 70 percent to the ROW region. Smaller losses of market share occurred in the manufactured fiber dresses and suits categories. The ASEAN region lost more than 16 percent share to South Asia in the manufactured fiber dress category and almost 10 percent to East Asia in the manufactured fiber suits category.

The South Asian region was able to maintain between 50 and 80 percent market share in only three categories of women's and girls' apparel. This region was most successful in retaining market share (79.57 percent) in the cotton (not knit) shirts and blouses category. In this category, it gained more than 23 percent market share from the East Asian region. In the manufactured fiber dress category, South Asia maintained 67.30 percent share, gaining more than 15 percent market share from the ASEAN region and an additional smaller percentage from the East Asian region. Significant market share in this category, however, was simultaneously lost to both the CBI, Canada, and Mexico and ROW regions. The South Asian region was able to retain slightly more than half of its market share in the manufactured fiber suits category, gaining less than 2 percent of East Asia's share and losing more substantial market shares to ASEAN and ROW suppliers. South Asian countries also suffered significant loss of market share in the cotton knit shirts and blouses category, with lost shares primarily going to the ROW and East Asian regions.

As with the men's and boys' categories, the EU region had difficulty maintaining significant market share in the women's and girls' categories. This region was most successful in retaining market share in the cotton knit shirts and blouses and manufactured fiber suits categories, while losing more than 50 percent share in each of the other categories. Across categories, the EU tended to relinquish the largest portion of its market share to the East Asian region. Smaller net losses occurred to the CBI, Canada, and Mexico in the cotton shirts and blouses (not knit) category and to the ASEAN region in the cotton knit shirts and blouses category.

Aggregate Apparel Categories

Transition probability matrices for the six aggregate apparel categories are presented in Table 15.6. In these categories, the East Asian region, again, tended to be most successful in maintaining market share. Significant market share was gained from the CBI, Canada, and Mexico in both categories of sweaters. In the manufactured fiber sweaters category, this region acquired in excess of 75 percent market share from the ROW. East Asian suppliers also gained approximately 50 percent of the ASEAN region's share in the manufactured fiber sweater category and more than 30 percent of the ASEAN region's share in both the manufactured fiber underwear and the manufactured fiber nightwear categories. Producers in the East Asian region also acquired large portions of market share from the EU and ROW regions in the cotton underwear category. The East Asian region lost little market share in most of the aggregate apparel categories. The primary exceptions included losses of shares in the cotton and manufactured underwear categories, with notable portions of market shares going to the CBI, Canada, and Mexico.

In the aggregate apparel categories, the CBI, Canada, and Mexico region's primary success in retaining market share was in the two categories of underwear, for which more than 90 percent market share was maintained, as well as the manufactured fiber nightwear category, for which almost 80 percent share was maintained. In both categories of underwear, market share was gained from the East Asian region, and additional market share was obtained at the expense of the ROW in the cotton underwear category. Significant net gain in market share (approximately 65 percent) in the manufactured fiber nightwear category came from the South Asian region, accompanied by a smaller gain from the East Asian region. In all other categories, the CBI, Canada, and Mexico experienced difficulty in maintaining market share, with losses incurred to all other regions except South Asia. Substantial market shares were lost to the East Asian region in both categories of sweaters, and large portions of shares were transferred to the ASEAN and EU regions in the cotton sweater category. In addition, the CBI, Canada, and Mexico experienced net loss of market share in manufactured sweaters and cotton nightwear and pajamas to the ROW region.

TABLE 15.6. Transition Probability Matrices: Aggregate Apparel Categories

Categories		East Asian	ASEAN	South Asian	CBI, Can, Mex	EU	ROW
Category 345 Cotton sweaters	East Asian	.8702	.0268	.0000	.0878	.0151	.0000
	ASEAN	.0000	.8609	.0000	.0484	.0251	.0657
	South Asian	.0000	.0000	.6478	.0000	.0000	.3522
	CBI, Can, Mex	.3346	.3893	.0000	.0000	.2671	.0000
	EU	.0883	.1212	.0747	.0000	.7158	.0000
	ROW	.0000	.0000	.3071	.0000	.0000	.6929
Category 351 Cotton nightwear & pajamas	East Asian	.9111	.0000	.0680	.0000	.0209	.0000
	ASEAN	.0000	.8461	.1539	.0000	.0000	.0000
	South Asian	.0375	.0000	.3268	.0620	.0000	.5737
	CBI, Can, Mex	.0000	.0579	.0000	.3386	.0000	.6035
	EU	.0000	.0000	.5311	.0000	.4689	.0000
	ROW	.0000	.1299	.1600	.3974	.0039	.3087
Category 352 Cotton underwear	East Asian	.6926	.0109	.0656	.2074	.0106	.0128
	ASEAN	.0000	.5768	.2378	.0000	.0000	.1854
	South Asian	.0000	.0000	.1543	.0000	.0319	.8137
	CBI, Can, Mex	.0000	.0426	.0546	.9029	.0000	.0000
	EU	.7310	.0000	.0000	.0000	.2690	.0000
	ROW	.2167	.0000	.0000	.4607	.0103	.3122
Category 645/646 MMF sweaters	East Asian	.7395	.1632	.0279	.0298	.0186	.0210
	ASEAN	.7643	.1689	.0495	.0000	.0174	.0000
	South Asian	.0000	.8739	.0172	.0269	.0820	.0000
	CBI, Can, Mex	.4161	.0000	.0000	.2128	.0000	.3711
	EU	.0000	.0000	.1764	.4094	.4142	.0000
	ROW	.7909	.0000	.0000	.0781	.0000	.1310

Categories		East Asian	ASEAN	South Asian	CBI, Can, Mex	EU	ROW
Category 651 MMF nightwear & pajamas	East Asian	.8760	.0000	.0000	.0888	.0015	.0366
	ASEAN	.3095	.6465	.0440	.0000	.0000	.0000
	South Asian	.0000	.0000	.0000	.8233	.0000	.1767
	CBI, Can, Mex	.0000	.0172	.1767	.7933	.0025	.0102
	EU	.0000	.0000	.5047	.0000	.4953	.0000
	ROW	.0000	.9967	.0000	.0000	.0033	.0000
Category 652 MMF underwear	East Asian	.8294	.0222	.0104	.1378	.0000	.0000
	ASEAN	.3778	.6005	.0000	.0000	.0217	.0000
	South Asian	.0000	.0000	.8428	.0529	.0000	.1043
	CBI, Can, Mex	.0081	.0000	.0152	.9516	.0251	.0000
	EU	.0000	.2821	.0000	.0000	.3049	.4131
	ROW	.0000	.0936	.0000	.0000	.0000	.9064

The ASEAN region retained between 55 to 85 percent market share in most of the aggregate apparel categories. This region was most successful in maintaining shares in the cotton sweaters and cotton nightwear and pajamas categories. In the cotton sweater category, this region acquired, in net, more than 30 percent share from the CBI, Canada, and Mexico and less than 10 percent share from the EU. Primary gains in market shares in the cotton and manufactured fiber nightwear categories were from the ROW region. Substantial losses of market share were incurred to East Asian suppliers in manufactured fiber sweaters, manufactured fiber nightwear, and manufactured fiber underwear. Notable shares were lost to the South Asian region in the cotton nightwear and cotton underwear categories. In addition, the ASEAN region lost almost 20 percent market share to the ROW in the cotton underwear category.

The South Asian region, the EU, and the ROW experienced significant difficulty maintaining market share in most of the aggregate apparel categories. The South Asian and ROW regions primarily were able to retain market shares in the manufactured fiber underwear category, while the EU was able to maintain market share in the cotton sweater category. The South Asian region tended to lose market share to the ROW in most categories. The EU incurred net losses of market shares to a variety of regions. In both nightwear and pajamas categories, as well as the manufactured fiber sweaters category, this region lost shares to South Asian suppliers. Shares were lost to the East Asian region in the cotton underwear category and to the CBI, Canada, and Mexico in the manufactured fiber sweaters category. In the manufactured fiber underwear category, market shares were given up to both the ASEAN and the ROW regions.

CONCLUSIONS

The findings of this study verify that significant competition has existed between and among primary supply regions for shares within the U.S. apparel market. As expected, regions that have traditionally held the largest shares, including the "Asian tigers" and the region formed by the Caribbean Basin, Canada, and Mexico tended to be most successful in maintaining their market shares. Regions comprised of newer and less developed suppliers, such as the South Asian region, as well as the most highly developed region, the EU, tended to have greater difficulty gaining and retaining market shares across categories. A notable exception to this, however, existed in the men's and boys' wool suits category, in which the EU, possessing greater technical skills and ready access to higher quality inputs, was able to retain a significant portion of its market share each year.

Although significant competition was found to exist across categories, it was also noted that each world region was able to maintain market share in one or more specific categories. As mentioned previously, the EU region was able to maintain a larger portion of market share in the men's and boys' wool suits category than other categories of apparel included in the analysis. The CBI, Canada, and Mexico retained a large percentage of market share in the cotton and manufactured fiber underwear, cotton knit shirts and blouses, wool suits, manufactured fiber shirts and blouses (not knit), and women's and girls' cotton slacks and trousers categories. East Asian suppliers were able to maintain market shares in cotton and manufactured fiber nightwear and pajamas, men's and boys' manufactured fiber other coats, manufactured fiber dresses, and cotton sweaters categories. The ASEAN region was best able to retain market share in women's and girls' manufactured fiber suits, cotton sweaters, and cotton nightwear, whereas ROW suppliers maintained more than 90 percent market share in the manufactured fiber underwear category. This supports, in large part, conceptualization of the development of the textile and apparel industry in various countries and world regions relative to overall economic development as proposed by Toyne et al. (1984) and discussed by Dickerson (1999).

Aggregation of countries into world regions may have tempered competitiveness of individual countries contained within the various regions. In the East Asian region, for example, China, as the world's largest apparel exporter, has gained significant U.S. market share while other countries within in the region, such as Taiwan and Hong Kong, have lost market share in many categories in recent years. Results, in large part, supported expectations that as quotas on key apparel categories were phased out in 2005 and trade in textiles and apparel returned to normal World Trade Organization rules, traditional supply regions such as East Asia would gain additional market share at the expense of less competitive suppliers. Under the quota system, the volume of textile and apparel exports was severely limited for countries within some regions (especially those within the East Asian region), while relative newcomers, such as Cambodia and Vietnam entered the U.S. market with only minimal quota constraints imposed. A number of countries, including Bangladesh and the Philippines, relied heavily on quota allocations for uncontested market share.

The impact of China's ability to vastly increase exports to the U.S. market once quota restraints were lifted on the most sensitive apparel categories has been of great interest. Given the ability of the East Asian region to maintain a significant portion of its market share while under quota constraints and dramatic increases in the volume of goods exported by China alone in categories for which quotas were released in January 2002 and January 2005, this region appears to possess the capacity to overwhelm other regions, such as the South Asian and ASEAN regions, as well as to reclaim market share lost to countries in the Western Hemisphere following implementation of NAFTA and the Trade Act of 2000. To forestall this eventuality and thereby protect interests of both domestic and less competitive foreign suppliers, the United States has acted upon agreements included in legislation granting China permanent normal trade relations as part of U.S. support for China's accession to the World Trade Organization. While reimposition of temporary quota constraints per these provisions may provide some measure of short-term relief for less competitive suppliers, many countries that relied on quota allocations for uncontested U.S. market share will continue to find it difficult to compete for market share during the post-quota period.

The threat of China becoming the supplier of choice for the U.S. market may be exacerbated by increased ability of Chinese producers to provide more fashion-forward goods of local design, as well as U.S. buyers' desires to decrease the number of suppliers through concentrated matrix buying and greater focus on repeat purchasing from established vendors (Biederman, 2002; Malone, 2002). Producers within the Caribbean Basin, Canada, and Mexico may be able to remain competitive based on geographic proximity to the U.S. market, ability to provide full package service, and capabilities related to supplying goods with abbreviated lead times. This would be a special benefit for supplying midseason reorders and replenishment stock for basic apparel items (Lee, 2002). For producers in other regions, the primary means of maintaining market share may likely involve strategies related to development of special capabilities in niche markets. Findings of this study illustrate the level of competition that exists within the apparel industry. The magnitude of competition for U.S. market share will remain high, with only the most creative, efficient, and capable suppliers maintaining a global presence.

REFERENCES

Adelman, I.C. (1958). A stochastic analysis of the size distribution of firms. *American Statistical Association Journal, 53,* 893-904.

American Textile Manufacturers Institute (1993; 1994; 1995; 2002; 2003). *Textile Highlights: The Quarterly Economic Review of the Textile Industry.* Washington, DC: ATMI.

Azzam, A., Azzam, S., and Guest, T. (1993). A probability model of aggregate meat consumption in the U.S.A. *Journal of Consumer Studies, 17,* 355-365.

Biederman, D. (2002). Weaving logistics: With apparel quotas set to fall, textile shippers are looking at new patterns in global supply chains. *World Cargo, 92*(9), 46-51.

Collins, N.R. and Preston, L. (1961). The structure of food processing industries, 1935-1955. *Journal of Industrial Economics, 9,* 265-279.

Dardis, R. and Sul, J. (1983). Competition in the U.S. apparel import market. *Home Economics Research Journal, 12*(2), 237-248.

Dent, W.T. (1967). Application of Markov analysis to international wool flows. *Review of Economics and Statistics, 49,* 613-616.

Dickerson, K.G. (1999). *Textiles and apparel in the global economy,* Third Edition. Upper Saddle River, NJ: Merrill.

Ellis, K. (2002). 55 years of breaking barriers. *Women's Wear Daily,* May 21, 16.

Hart, P.E. and Prais, S.J. (1956). The analysis of business concentration: A statistical approach. *Journal of the American Statistical Society, 119,* 150-175.

Jarrett, F.G. and Dent, W. (1966). Fiber substitution—A Markov process analysis. *Australian Economic Papers, 5,* 107-130.

Judge, G.G. and Swanson, E.R. (1962). Markov chains: Basic concepts and suggested uses in agricultural economics. *Australian Journal of Agricultural Economics, 6,* 49-61.

Kim, C.S. and Schaible, G. (1988). Estimation of transition probabilities using median absolute deviations. *Journal of Agricultural Economics Research, 40*(4), 12-19.

Lee, G. (2002). Panelists: Keep your eyes open. *Women's Wear Daily,* October 15, S15.

Lee, T.C., Judge, G.G., and Zellner, A. (1970). *Estimating the parameters of the Markov probability model from aggregate time series data.* Amsterdam: North Holland Publishing Company.

Malone, S. (2002). On the road to 2002: Who loses to China? *Women's Wear Daily,* November 26, 2, 10.

Office of Textiles and Apparel (1997). *U.S. Imports, Production, Markets, Import Production Ratios, and Domestic Market Shares for Textile and Apparel Product Categories.* CD ROM. OTA.

Office of Textiles and Apparel (2002a). *U.S. general imports in U.S. Dollars, data for Category 1,* September. Available at http://otexa.ita.doc.gov/scripts/tqads1 .exe/catpage.

Office of Textiles and Apparel (2002b). *U.S. Imports, Production, Markets, Import Production Ratios, and Domestic Market Shares for Textile and Apparel Product Categories.* CD ROM. OTA.

Office of Textiles and Apparel (2003). *Textile and Apparel Trade Balance Report.* CD-ROM. OTA.

Padberg, D.I. (1962). The use of Markov processes in measuring changes in market structure. *Journal of Farm Economics, 44,* 189-199.

Tesler, L.G. (1962). Advertising and cigarettes. *Journal of Political Economy, 70,* 471-499.

Tesler, L.G. (1963). Least-squares estimates of transition probabilities. In Christ, C.F. et. al. (Eds.), *Measurement in economics: Studies in mathematical economics and econometrics in memory of Yehuda Grunfeld.* Stanford, CA: Stanford University Press, 270-292.

Toyne, B., Arpan, J., Barnett, A., Ricks, D., and Shimp, T. (1984). *The global textile industry.* London: George Allen & Unwin.

World Trade Organization. (2001). *Leading exporters and importers of clothing, 2000.* September 21. Available at http://www.wto.org/english/res_e/statis_e/its2001_e/section4/iv80.xls.

Xiao, Y. and Rees, K. (1999). Analysis of U.S. apparel imports [Abstract]. In Owens, N.J. (Ed.), *Proceedings of the Annual Meeting of the International Textile and Apparel Association.* Monument, CO: ITAA.

Chapter 16

Globalization and Future Research Interests on East Asia

M. Raquib Zaman

INTRODUCTION

The achievement of the East Asian countries in transforming their economies to the status of "newly industrialized countries" in a relatively short period of time has drawn significant admiration and attention from researchers and development experts all over the world. Some even termed it "the Asian Miracle." Volumes have been produced on various aspects of the East Asian experience, and more will be forthcoming. Predicting the future is always a risky business, and it is more so when we are dealing with human behavior and its likely impact on economic development. Yet an attempt will be made here to foresee the future!

CONTINUATION OF THE PAST AND CURRENT TREND

For some time to come, researchers will try to produce discourses on the linkages between particular socioeconomic policies and economic development for individual countries as well as for the region as a whole. With the availability of time series, and/or large cross-sectional data, those who are quantitatively inclined, will try to present "models" that prove or disprove the hypotheses they fancy to create.

Globalization and East Asia: Opportunities and Challenges

doi:10.1300/5463_16

None of the existing theories and models of growth quite fit the East Asian pattern, and this will provide incentive to create new ones.

The financial market's collapse, which is frequently referred to as the Asian Financial Crises of 1997-1998, will generate a few more treatises, such as "Rethinking the East Asian Miracle" (Stiglitz and Yusuf, 2001). Such works may be on the experience of individual countries or on the region. Some of these studies may dwell on the evils of:

1. lack of transparency and accountability in the public as well as private sectors;
2. high levels of corruption in various walks of life;
3. faulty policy recommendations by the IMF and the World Bank;
4. ineffective and/or defective fiscal and monetary policies, and the like.

Reform of banking and financial markets will continue to be important topics for further analysis. Determination of the adequacy of bank capital and enforcement of regulations related to bank lending are of primary interest to researchers and policy makers. Measures to control speculative capital inflows and outflows will get further attention. Finance professors, practitioners, and doctoral students will continue their efforts in deciphering the relationship between risks and returns under different strategies of investment management, market capitalization, and regulations. Again, those who are fond of quantitative analyses will have a field day, as the markets open to the public by making more information readily available.

Globalization and its impact on East Asia and the world at large will become a major field of study in the coming years. This is specially so because a consensus is developing among scientists, governments, and business that globalization is indeed a serious problem and it threatens the entire eco system with dire consequences. Studies will come out with suggestions for modified production strategies by manufacturing firms as well as by farms in the agricultural sectors. There is a likelihood that some researchers will try to identify enterprises and consumers who endanger the earth's atmosphere willfully, with suggestions to combat their practices.

FUTURE DIRECTION OF RESEARCH

The increased debate on globalization has spawned issues of sustainable economic development. Sustainability has become a cause to be promoted by environmentalists, intellectuals, concerned citizens, entrepreneurs, and even by some large corporations. Studies showing techniques of measuring performance that promote sustainable development are being sought by the business community. The investing public's reliance on the "bottom line" to judge performance will give way to new standards of measurement of success. The World Bank has begun to use a new measure, "adjusted net savings" as a percentage of GDP, to gauge performance of economies in terms of sustainability. The performance of business entities needs to be judged not by net income, but by some measure of benefits over social, economic, and environmental costs. A number of studies are expected to come out on the sustainability of East Asian economic development.

In light of the continued enlargement of the European Union interest will emerge to explore the possibility of an East Asian Union (EAU). True, China and the Koreas may not like to deal with Japan the crimes due to committed during World War II, but economic benefits may bring them together in the near future. Studies are likely to be made on the benefits and pitfalls of an EAU.

With rising income and lowering poverty, the countries of East Asia are likely to experience an increase in consumer spending on appliances and automobiles. This will increase per capita consumption of energy. Alternative sources of energy, cheaper than oil, must be found to make it possible to sustain development. A number of studies on this subject are likely to be made in the future.

There will be some increase in interest in studying the management style of the enterprises that are part of a business network. This is of particular interest to the regulators who are seeking ways to trim the power of network bosses. Researchers would like to know how they contributed to the financial markets' collapse in 1997-1998.

The continued lackluster performance of the Japanese economy has raised issues about the effectiveness of fiscal and monetary policies of advanced economies in combating stagnation and even recession. Studies on the subject would be of immense interest to the third largest economy of the world, Germany, among others.

The impact of aging populations and scarcity of labor in the advanced economies, such as Japan, may draw the attention of some researchers. Japan has been developing new technologies and tools to assist the elderly in maintaining health and mobility, and how this is going to assist other advanced countries facing similar problems in the near future is going to be of immense interest. Whether this technological development will propel Japan to new heights of economic growth remains to be seen.

Perhaps it is prudent to end this discourse with the usual disclaimer of an economist, ceteris paribus, i.e., with other things remaining the same, the future direction of research and publications will be what has been outlined here.

REFERENCE

Stiglitz, J.E. and Yusuf, S. (Eds.) (2001). *Rethinking the East Asian Miracle.* New York: Oxford University Press.

Index

Page numbers followed by the letter "f" indicate figures; those followed by the letter "t" indicate tables.

Globalization and East Asia: Opportunities and Challenges

doi:10.1300/5463_17

www.ingramcontent.com/pod-product-compliance
Lightning Source LLC
Chambersburg PA
CBHW070600270326
41926CB00013B/2369

* 9 7 8 0 7 8 9 0 2 7 4 4 3 *